Contents

CONTENTS

PART II
The Social Affliction of Racism

PART III
Divining a Nation's Salvation

And We Are Not Saved

And We Are Not Saved

The Elusive Quest for Racial Justice

DERRICK BELL

Basic Books, Inc., Publishers

NEW YORK

Library of Congress Cataloging-in-Publication Data

Bell, Derrick A.
    And we are not saved.

    Bibliographical notes: p. 259.
    Includes index.
    1. Afro-Americans—Civil rights.   2. Racism—United
States.   3. Afro-Americans—Legal status, laws, etc.
4. United States—Race relations.   I. Title.
E185.615.B39   1987   305.8'96073'073   87–47512
ISBN   0–465–00328–1

To Ada Elisabeth Bell, my mother;

to Jewel Hairston Bell, my wife;

and to all our Genevas

The harvest is past, the summer is ended, and we are not saved.

—JEREMIAH 8:20

Preface

THE HEROINE of my book, Geneva Crenshaw, and her Chronicles owe their being to America's most prestigious legal periodical, the *Harvard Law Review*, and its annual practice of inviting a legal scholar to write the foreword to the Supreme Court issue. The roll of past foreword authors is impressive, and, to put it mildly, I did not expect to join the list. When the editorial board of volume 99 selected me to write its foreword in 1985, I doubted whether they would take kindly to a radical departure from the doctrinal analysis of the Supreme Court's work, an analysis that previous authors have undertaken with great competence. And yet I wanted to examine from a new perspective—beyond even the most exacting exegesis of case decisions—the civil rights movement since 1954 and the *Brown* school decision: that is, to explain or justify what has happened, or not happened, and how black people (or some of us) feel about it.

The civil rights movement is, after all, much more than the totality of the judicial decisions, the antidiscrimination laws, and the changes in racial relationships reflected in those legal milestones. The movement is a spiritual manifestation of the continuing faith of a people who have never truly gained their rights in a nation committed by its basic law to the freedom of all. For my foreword, then, I sought a method of expression adequate to the phenomenon of rights gained, then lost, then gained again—a phenomenon that continues to surprise even though the cyclical experience of blacks in this country predates the Constitution by more than one hundred years.

As the deadline for the article hovered imminent, there came to my rescue Geneva Crenshaw and her tales, challenging the accepted view of how blacks gain, or might gain, from civil rights laws and policies. Thereafter the writing, while not easy, became a labor of enormous fulfillment. And to my great relief, the *Harvard Law Review* editors accepted my unorthodox approach and contributed their energy, skill, and enthusiasm to the editing process. Carol Steiker, the *Review*'s president for volume 99, Elena Kagan, supervising editor, William Forbush, executive editor, and several staff members became collaborators in the challenge to express jurisprudential matters of significant importance in a language and format more usual in literature than in law.

Encouragement and sound advice for both the article and this book came from a host of friends, family, teaching colleagues, and students. My long-time friend, Teachers College of Columbia University Professor Diane Ravitch, disagreed with some aspects of my thesis but enthusiastically recommended the work to her publisher, Martin Kessler, president and editorial director of Basic Books. Mr. Kessler graciously offered to serve as general editor and, having helped shape the book's structure, assigned copyediting responsibility to Phoebe Hoss, whose fiction-writing skills, careful eye, and infinite patience reduced the gap between my thoughts and their expression. Linda Carbone handled the production chores efficiently and quickly. My thanks to family members, and the many friends, colleagues, and students, especially the members of my Fall 1986 seminar, "Civil Rights at the Crossroads," all of whom reviewed chapters and offered suggestions. I want to thank particularly Sharon Carter, Dr. Jane DeGidio, Paul Dimond, Lani Guinier, Elena Kagan, Elaine McGrath, Stephanie Moore, Audrey Selden, Carol Steiker, Gloria Valencia-Weber, and professors Regina Austin, Denise Carty-Bennia, Linda Greene, Joel F. Handler, Randall Kennedy, Henry W. McGee, Jr., Arthur S. Miller, Daniel J. Monti, Cass Sunstein, and Patricia Williams. Ken Diamond and Elizabeth Wilkerson at Stanford and Rodney Akers and Areva Bell at Harvard provided research assistance, and Marian Holys at Stanford and Debra Ayles at Harvard handled secretarial chores. The Harvard Law School Summer Research Project granted financial support.

And We Are Not Saved

Introduction

JEREMIAH's lament that "we are not saved" echoes down through the ages and gives appropriate voice to present concerns of those who, flushed with the enthusiasm generated by the Supreme Court's 1954 holding that segregated public schools are unconstitutional, pledged publicly that the progeny of America's slaves would at last be "Free by 1963," the centennial of the Emancipation Proclamation. That pledge became the motto for the National Association for the Advancement of Colored People's 1959 convention in New York City, where were gathered, in jubilant euphoria, veterans of racial bias and society's hostility who believed that they had finally, and permanently, achieved the reform of the laws that had been for a century vehicles for the oppression of black men, women, and children. Not even the most skeptical at that convention could have foreseen that, less than three decades later, that achievement would be so eroded as to bring us once again into fateful and frightful coincidence with Jeremiah's lament.

With the realization that the salvation of racial equality has eluded us again, questions arise from the ashes of our expectations: How have we failed—and why? What does this failure mean—for black people and for whites? Where do we go from here? Should we redirect the quest for racial justice? A response to those questions—more accurately, a series of responses—is the purpose of this book. Rather than offering definitive answers, I hope, as law teacher rather than social seer, mainly to provoke discussion that will provide new insights and prompt more effective strategies.

3

I recognize that most of what can be said about racial issues in this country has been said, and likely more than once. Over and over, we have considered all the problems, tried many of the solutions, and concluded—reluctantly or with relief—that, while full racial equality may some day be achieved, it will not be in our time. Developments in the civil rights field have been dutifully reported and analyzed by the media. And scholars have not been silent. Library shelves creak under the weight of serious studies on racial issues. Surely, one might think, the literature would not suffer, and might even benefit, from a period of repose.

For better or worse, though, race is not like other public problems. Throughout America's history, racial issues have been high among, if not central to, the country's most important concerns. Often—as when the Constitution was written, during the Civil War and Reconstruction, and throughout the decades of the civil rights movement since the Supreme Court's *Brown* decision in 1954—racial issues have riveted attention. At no time has race slipped far down the list of the most crucial matters facing both the nation's top policy makers and its most humble citizens. Consider the predictable self-congratulation as we celebrate the two hundredth anniversary of the Constitution's signing in 1787, its ratification in 1789, and the adoption of the Bill of Rights in 1790. During the conferences and commemorations, few will wish to risk discord by reminding us of what has not been accomplished. On the agenda of unfinished business, America's continuing commitment to white domination looms especially large for those citizens of color whose lives are little less circumscribed than were those of their slave forebears.

Racism is more than a pejorative hurled in powerless frustration at an omnipotent evil. As Professor Charles Lawrence more precisely puts it:

Racism in America is much more complex than either the conscious conspiracy of a power elite or the simple delusion of a few ignorant bigots. It is a part of our common historical experience and, therefore, a part of our culture. It arises from the assumptions we have learned to make about the world, ourselves, and others as well as from the patterns of our fundamental social activities.[1]

Even in the face of this enormous obstacle, the commitment of those who seek racial justice remains strong. Tangible progress has been made, and the pull of unfinished business is sufficient to strengthen and spur determination. But the task of equal-justice advocates has not become easier simply because neither slavery's chains, nor the lyncher's rope, nor humiliating Jim Crow signs are any longer the main means of holding black people in a subordinate status. Today, while all manner of civil rights laws and precedents are in place, the protection they provide is diluted by lax enforcement, by the establishment of difficult-to-meet standards of proof, and, worst of all, by the increasing irrelevance of antidiscrimination laws to race-related disadvantages, now as likely to be a result as much of social class as of color.

How are we to assess the unstable status of a struggle that all but the most perversely pessimistic predicted would end in triumph many years ago? Even those most deeply involved in this struggle are at a loss for a rational explanation of how the promise of racial equality escaped a fulfillment that thirty years ago appeared assured. Indeed, logical explanation fails before the patterns of contemporary racial discrimination so close in intent to, if different in form from, those practiced in earlier times. Rationales based on political concerns and economic realities do not alone explain the increasing viability of concepts of white superiority that long ago should have been consigned to the obsolete. The discrepancy between the nation's deeply held beliefs and its daily behavior add a continuing confusion to racial inequities that undermine effective action. Thus, we take refuge in the improbable and seek relief in increasingly empty repetitions of tarnished ideals.

In order to appraise the contradictions and inconsistencies that pervade the all too real world of racial oppression, I have chosen in this book the tools not only of reason but of unreason, of fantasy. The historian Robert Darnton reminds us that fairy tales in their early versions did not always have happy endings but, rather, usually reflected, through the folktales on which many were based, the harsh life of eighteenth-century peasants. Darn-ton reports that many classic fairy tales "undercut the notion that virtue will be rewarded or that life can be conducted according to any principle other than basic mistrust."[2] The historic subordina-tion of American blacks is not unlike that of eighteenth-century French peasants.[3] The role and fate of civil rights measures can be compared to those of the brides in the French fairy tale *Bluebeard's Castle*, in which Bluebeard woos and brings to his castle a series of brides in the hope that each will free him from the burden of his past crimes. But the brides are rebellious rather than redemp-tive, and each is condemned either to death or to a dark chamber. Thus, first after the Civil War and again in 1954, America pro-duced symbols of redemption in the form of civil rights measures seemingly intended to rectify past racial cruelties and expunge the dark stain of slavery. But, after a brief period of hope, compliance with these measures has impeded other goals and, like Blue-beard's brides, they have been abandoned, leaving the blacks' so-cial subordination firmly entrenched.

In resorting to the realm of fairy tale—and its modern counter-part, science fiction—I have devised ten metaphorical tales, or Chronicles, one of which opens each of the chapters in this book. These Chronicles, as my friend Professor Linda Greene reminds me, follow as well an ancient tradition in using fantasy and dia-logue to uncover enduring truths.[4] As illustration, she cites the works of Plato[5] as well as law school professors who maintain that Socratic dialogue effectively illuminates essential principles.[6] A well-known example of the genre is Professor Lon Fuller's *The Case of the Speluncian Explorer.*[7] In law practice, too, as more than one teacher has observed, a "lawyer's primary task is translating human stories into legal stories and retranslating legal story end-ings into solutions to human problems."[8] (On the other hand, as the public knows too well, legal jargon often distorts beyond rec-ognition legal stories claimed to be factual.)

My expectations for the Chronicles are ambitious precisely be-cause, as Professor Kim Crenshaw has put it, "allegory offers a method of discourse that allows us to critique legal norms in an ironically contextualized way. Through the allegory, we can discuss legal doctrine in a way that does not replicate the abstractions of legal discourse. It provides therefore a more rich, engaging, and suggestive way of reaching the truth."[9] Thus, the Chronicles employ stories that are not true to explore situations that are real enough but, in their many and contradictory dimensions, defy understanding.

The book is divided into three parts. Part I deals with the intricacies of the barriers to racial equality established in law by the society at the very beginning of this nation's history. For the identifiable factors determining today's racial policy—jurisprudential, economic, political, even psychological—are neither novel nor new. They were active at the start of the colonial era; and by the time the present government was conceived in 1787, they were full-blown with consequences far beyond the bondsmen who were the objects of the policies.

Following the prologue to part I, in which the narrator introduces himself and recounts the story of the extraordinary visitation of my heroine, Geneva Crenshaw, chapter 1 opens with the Chronicle of the Constitutional Contradiction. In this Chronicle, I take the liberty of tampering with time and history to examine the original contradiction in the Constitution of the United States—a contradiction that is at the heart of the blacks' present-day difficulty of gaining legal redress. Thus, I dramatize the concerns that likely led even those Framers opposed to slavery to sanction its recognition in a Constitution whose Preamble pledges to "secure the Blessings of Liberty to ourselves and our Posterity." At the conclusion of this Chronicle, Geneva and the narrator further discuss the implications of this original contradiction for contemporary conditions. This pattern of Chronicle and discussion is followed by subsequent chapters, where the one serves as the springboard for the other in which Geneva and the narrator express their strong, and usually conflicting, views.

Thus, in chapter 2, the Chronicle of the Celestial Curia, with its otherworldly setting, raises pragmatic questions about whether law and litigation can achieve meaningful reform for the victims of racial and economic inequality. Geneva and the narrator compare the dichotomy between civil rights lawyers' unshaken belief in and reliance on the courts and the serious questions posed by legal scholars regarding the role of the Supreme Court in racial reform. Voting-rights cases illustrate these points in preparation for the voting rights measure examined in the next Chronicle. In this second Chronicle as well, Geneva begins to explain the origin of her Chronicles and their role in her quest for racial justice.

Chapter 3 examines, through the Chronicle of the Ultimate Voting Rights Act, the limitations on the voting rights of blacks and asks whether an ideal "ultimate" voting rights act would not only survive constitutional challenge but be effective as well.

Any examination of the civil rights era that began with the Supreme Court's 1954 *Brown* decision must inquire into the ensuing and widespread strife carried on in the courtrooms and in the streets. Thus, chapter 4 and the Chronicle of the Sacrificed Black Schoolchildren center on the real beneficiaries of the *Brown* school decision. Geneva and the narrator speculate about policies that might have more effectively improved the quality of education provided for black children, but were never much tried because of the civil rights community's commitment to achieving school desegregation through racial balance.

The Chronicle of the Black Reparations Foundation, in chapter 5, raises the question whether the cost of a black reparations program is the main basis for white society's opposition to improving the economic status of blacks. This question leads to a discussion about the elevation of "reverse discrimination" from an opposition slogan to a judicially recognized limit on the remediation of racial justice.

In chapter 6, affirmative action, a contemporary policy intended to compensate for the damaging effects of past racial discrimination, is examined in the Chronicle of the DeVine Gift. The frequent complaint that "we can't find qualified blacks" may be proof that the affirmative-action policy is serving its real, though unacknowledged, goal: excluding all but a token number of minorities from opportunities that previously were available only to whites. Exploring this notion in the context of whites' desire to maintain what Professor Manning Marable calls "cultural hegemony,"[10] Geneva and the narrator discuss the relative ineffectiveness of employment-discrimination law, and consider as well the civil rights community's acceptance of benign housing quotas.

Many who labor to make real Dr. Martin Luther King's idealistic vision for this country firmly believe that if all Americans faced a common crisis or extraordinary peril, the need to work together for survival would eliminate racial prejudice—a belief tested, both humanly and legally, in chapter 7's Chronicle of the Amber Cloud. Geneva and the narrator review current policies, such as civil service tests, that perform some useful social function, and conclude that such utility serves to insulate the policy from consti-tutional challenge even when in operation it seriously disadvan-tages blacks.

In part II, I move from analyzing civil rights campaigns in-tended to gain recognition of black rights, to the human difficul-ties within the black community arising from the blacks' long in-voluntary status as secondary members of society. The internal stresses resulting from living as "strangers in a strange land" (as Harriet Tubman put it) can, paradoxically, be worsened as a result of civil rights gains. In the prologue to this part, I explore the com-plex relationship between Geneva and the narrator and, by exten-sion, the ambivalence of close male-female relationships based on respect and friendship rather than on romance and sex. Here the narrator comes up once again against the psychologically dis-abling fact that contemporary black men are, like their slave fore-bears, unable to guarantee their women and families protection against the society's racism and the violence founded in that rac-ism. This disability, among many others, provides a cogent argu-ment for advocates of black emigration, a subject also touched on in this interlude.

The differences in sex-role expectations between black men and black women are the subject of the narrator's own Chronicle of the Twenty-Seventh-Year Syndrome in chapter 8. This chapter focuses on how black male sexism as well as white racism has damaged the black community, and on how the tardily recog-nized right to interracial sex and marriage has affected black male-female relationships.

Self-help, perhaps the most frequently prescribed cure for the malaise of black poverty and disadvantage, is the concern of chapter 9 and the Chronicle of the Slave Scrolls. Here are reviewed several legal approaches that might offer constitutional protection for a black community competing successfully with whites and no longer begging for either bread or rights.

Part III brings us to Geneva's ultimate strategy, based on the Chronicle of the Black Crime Cure, and to her eloquent appeal for new ways of seeing and using old civil rights strategies in a situation where a positive outcome, while not assured, can still be hoped for.

In my plan for this book, I have been guided by the observation of Justice Oliver Wendell Holmes, Jr., that law is more than logic: it is experience. And long experience teaches that legal outcomes are not determined by advocacy alone. Nor, alas, will the justice of one's cause suffice to ensure justice. Constitutional protections, and the judicial interpretations built on them, have real importance but, all too often, work out in practice in unanticipated, and destructive, ways. Moreover, both practice and law are affected by a major, though seldom acknowledged, factor: the self-interest of segments of the dominant society. For what both elite policy-making whites and working-class whites perceive as their self-interest can be very different—a difference that can have destructive implications for all black people even as they applaud the latest recognition of their civil rights by the highest court in the land.

PART I

The Legal Hurdles to Racial Justice

Prologue to Part I

UNTIL NOW, I had thought that law faculty meetings were the most frustrating gatherings known to the Western world. But I had forgotten that special futility I always experience at civil rights conferences where seemingly every participant espouses with fervent and unflinching faith a different strategy for our racial deliverance.

And it was happening again. After two days of intense wrangling, it seemed clear that—barring a miracle—what promised to be a memorable gathering of the country's best-known black leaders, would end—as had so many others—with much said and precious little accomplished. My sense of futility was heightened as I remembered how the invitation to this "Black Bicentennial Convention," impressively engraved on high-quality paper, had lifted my spirits, wearied after a particularly unhappy session with my faculty colleagues. In accepting, I felt confident that the civil rights gathering would respond more positively to my suggestions than had my mainly white faculty colleagues whose backgrounds and outlooks on racial matters differed drastically from my own.

Foolishly perhaps, I had recommended at a recent faculty meeting that the law school commemorate the Constitution's two-hundredth anniversary by hosting a national conference devoted to the role of race in constitutional law development. After listening quietly as I explained my proposal, the faculty members—without discussion or formal rejection—simply smothered my idea under the weight of their enthusiasm for other less controversial and, as one committee member put it, more "patriotic" proposals.

AND WE ARE NOT SAVED

At a younger age, I would have reacted dramatically, filling the room with angry accusations and then departing in a rage. Experience had taught that such displays are always good for the ego and can, on occasion, actually shock my white colleagues into taking me seriously. But, during this time when civil rights has lost its urgency, my departure not only would have been quietly applauded by members whom my suggestion had irritated, but, worse, might intensify a search—already rumored to be under way—for the appointment of another black from among those academicians who are definable less by their disparate ideologies than by their perverse willingness to denigrate their race in ways that many whites believe true but dare not publicly assert.

Hardly new are contemporary assertions that black deficiencies, and not white racism, are the root cause of our lowly status. In the post-Reconstruction era of the 1870s, the nation, weary of racial issues, prematurely proclaimed the former slaves free and able to rise or fail on their own efforts. Experts from fields as diverse as religion and social science gained prominence by proclaiming that the inherent inferiority of black people made further efforts on their behalf futile, even dangerous.[1] Today, as policy makers again seek to abandon civil rights enforcement, certain experts assert that the plight of blacks is the fault of blacks or of the social programs on which the poor rely.[2] When such claims are expounded by blacks, they obtain a deceptive authenticity.[3]

Such blacks, knowingly or not, dispense a product that fills the present national need for outrageous anti-black comment. Many whites welcome it. The black neoconservatives, as some of these black critics describe themselves, gain wide recognition for their views; while the angry denials and demands for equal time by dissenting blacks are ignored just as my law faculty had, from its position of power, ignored my proposal.

I sat. By occupying the faculty's "minority seat," I was at least not letting a black neoconservative use it as another forum in which to spout the white-racist rhetoric that obtains a spurious legitimacy because it emanates from a black mouth. It will be a measure that we have arrived in this society, I thought to myself, when whites give positive statements by blacks about other blacks the same weight whites now reserve for our disparagements of one another. In the meantime, we must deem ourselves advantaged when blacks in public positions are willing, in their unelected representation of black people, to apply the physician's cardinal rule: "Do no harm."

Now, I was sitting again, both bored with the repetitious statements, and angry with the self-righteous rigidity with which each civil rights speaker championed one cause while disparaging all others. And because participants had been transported to the conference site, I was unable simply to leave, my usual remedy for unproductive discussions. In fact, I was not even sure where we had been meeting for two long days, with one more to go. Sadly, I was sure that the sessions, while interesting, had not fulfilled the high expectations set during the exciting trip to the conference site.

At dawn on the day of the Convention, the delegates who represented every point on the civil rights spectrum, had met—as our invitations directed—on Harlem's Lenox Avenue at the Schomburg Center for Research in Black Culture, known better as the Schomburg Library and famous for its contributions to black scholarship. Rather than remaining at the library, as I had expected, chartered buses took us away to a remote area at Kennedy Airport, where we boarded a 747. We all had questions about the unusual arrangements, but the host committee members, all well-known faces, assured us that all was proceeding according to plan.

The flight was more than three hours long, but the time passed quickly as each of us greeted old friends, made new acquaintances, and discussed various racial issues. All veterans in one way or another of civil rights campaigns, we shared war stories and reported on current activities and interests. My apprehension, allayed by the welcome opportunity of fellowship with individuals with whom I had worked, returned when we began our landing in fog so thick it seemed more than a match for even the most sophisticated radar and on-board computers. After a period of circling, though, the big plane touched down smoothly.

I breathed more easily as we taxied to a landing area where, through the fog, we could see three other large planes and a long line of buses, all bearing Convention delegates from other parts of the country. If anything, the fog seemed to thicken as the buses rolled away from the landing area and headed down a tree-lined road on which as far as I could see there were no other vehicles. Perhaps the others did not notice for our hosts were distributing handsome conference folders that contained the meeting agendas, position papers, and draft resolutions.

The Convention building loomed out of the fog, which seemed to be lifting. The structure's architecture, all glass and wood, was modern but mysterious, evoking a mood that was sober, austere, serious—and far more impressive than the cold concrete monstrosities that, though called convention centers, host every activity from rock concerts to horse shows. In contrast, this was a conference center more than worthy of the name. There were elegantly equipped meeting rooms of all sizes, offices, a library, as well as impressive dining facilities. The main auditorium, the Great Hall, was designed to reflect the architecture and atmosphere of both church and courtroom. It was both the focal point and an almost sacred nucleus of the conference complex.

For the first day, the presentations were interesting and the discussions following them lively. We genuinely felt that our decisions would be important; that, in ways we could not explain, history was being made and we were a part of it. The delegates, mainly lawyers, represented every segment of the black community from elite academics to grassroots spokespeople from poverty-stricken black areas, both urban and rural. Most of the delegates were black, but some whites, long identified with black causes, were also present. At first, potentially divisive differences in political beliefs were muted as delegates worked for consensus and understanding. Spirits were high, but delegates were sobered by the continuing reminders of how much more had to be accomplished despite the gains made during the past decades. Sobering as well was the predicament of the black poor which was without precedent in our people's bleak past.

In this unique setting, the presentation of the major policy alternatives was familiar to regular attendees at civil rights meetings stretching back to the post–Civil War era. There was much urging, particularly by representatives of the mainline civil rights organizations, that we not neglect the unfinished integration agenda. Despite admitted setbacks and disappointments, advocates viewed racial integration as the only answer to discrimination. Their uniform response to critics was that "integration had not worked because it had not really been tried."

In stark contrast, delegates representing many smaller groups voiced strong separatist motifs. Then a series of "third stream" strategies were advanced as more flexible and realistic alternatives to either all-out integration or black nationalism. Advocates for the various positions generally emphasized the ability of their strategies to provide support and protection to blacks in a nation where racial hostility was again on the rise.

By the second day, the harmony the Convention hosts had worked hard to maintain began to break down in the clash of disparate views. I had heard all these arguments before. I longed for the conciliating presence of Geneva Crenshaw, the civil rights attorney who—except for a mysterious encounter some weeks before—I had not heard from for twenty years. My quick decision to rearrange my schedule so that I could accept the Convention's invitation was prompted by the likelihood of her presence; but now I was beginning to fear that the proceedings had degenerated beyond the point of saving by even her persuasive advocacy.

It did not help that I understood our basic problem all too well. Each of us, veterans of the racial struggle, have willingly risked life and career and, in so doing, have escaped the fate of most blacks whose lives are narrowly walled in by racism. By our actions, we have already gained a large measure of personal independence and overcome society's built-in racial impediments. That is, we have achieved the essence of freedom, the ideal on which our society is based. We value the hard-won ability to work through problems, to implement approaches that we find right, and to hell with anyone, white or black, who disagrees or urges a different course.

We came here because we want the same thing for other blacks, and, viewing ourselves as the leaders or at least representatives of other blacks, we willingly join civil rights organizations and attend conferences like this one. But, unconsciously, at some point our personal independence comes into conflict with the requirements of a consensus that could give a large group strong and meaningful direction. In the end, while we seek and sincerely want consensus, the need to sacrifice the hard-gained independence of personal action proves too high a price to pay. Not recognizing either inner conflict or its unconscious resolution, each of us has a personal investment in our strategy. Thus is agreement rendered impossible and conflict inevitable.

The last hours of debate before the final day's plenary sessions dragged as delegates maneuvered to get their proposals on the agenda. In self-defense, I allowed my mind to wander back in time to the early 1960s, when I first met and began working with Geneva Crenshaw as we both represented clients with civil rights cases across the South. She had come to New York right out of law school to join the NAACP Legal Defense Fund's legal staff. Despite her youth, she was soon a highly respected civil rights advocate, well known for her willingness to go South to represent blacks in rural settings where living conditions were poor and personal risk was considerable.

Strikingly tall, well over six feet, Geneva, as I soon learned, was able to display an impressive intelligence honed by hard work. She would have confounded the findings that caused the sociologist E. Franklin Frazier to characterize our middle class as "Black Bourgeoisie."[4] Apparently oblivious of her stunning looks, highlighted by a smooth, ebony complexion, she was proud of her color and her race at a time when middle-class "Negroes" (as we then insisted on being called) were ambivalent about both. Even in that pre–"black is beautiful" period, she insisted on using the term *black* because it was more direct, if less accurate, than *Afro-American*.

Geneva would have applauded Mary Hamilton, a black woman who took her case to the Supreme Court to gain, in 1964, judicial confirmation for her insistence that she be addressed in a state court as "Miss Hamilton" rather than as "Mary."[5] But Geneva did not like to spend time discussing, much less litigating about, what black people are called. What she deemed "image projects" irritated her as a sad waste of limited resources. "Titles follow status," she would say. "Those that precede it are gratuitous when they're not intended insults." These views and others like them tended to defy the accepted civil rights orthodoxy, but Geneva had, in the 1960s, espoused them with a skill and commitment not easily ignored.

I appreciate her prescience now, but must confess that in those days I was more impressed with her courage. Watching her articulate her views at staff meetings, and later working with her in Southern courtrooms, I saw her as the embodiment of the great nineteenth-century abolitionists Harriet Tubman and Sojourner Truth, even resembling photographs I'd seen of those stern black women who both fought and spoke for their cause. "I've seen those pictures," Geneva responded when I once, unchivalrously, remarked on the resemblance. "And were I given to vanity, I would hardly find the resemblance complimentary. But those women had an inner vision that enabled them to defy the limits on their lives imposed by the world around them. I try to be a good lawyer, but my devotion, too, is to an inner vision that makes me feel close to old Harriet and Sojourner—so your thinking I resemble them is not only a compliment, it is an honor."

Inner vision or not, Geneva was an excellent advocate—as more than one Southern white attorney who refused to shake her hand learned at some expense to his case and his psyche. But much as she loved litigation, Geneva decided finally that she should teach. The fateful trip to Mississippi was to have been her last before leaving the NAACP to join the Howard Law School faculty. It was fortunate that Geneva wanted to teach at Howard because in the mid-1960s, despite her academic record and litigation success that more than justified predictions of a brilliant teaching career, her opportunities were, for the most part, limited to black law schools.[6]

Of course, in those days, there were few women law teachers, black or white. Geneva's colleagues, though, confidently predicted that she would follow in the footsteps of the Howard faculty members, including William Hastie and Charles Houston, and of Howard alumni, including Thurgood Marshall and Robert L. Carter, all of whom were her mentors.[7] Geneva's intelligence and accomplishments made her a definitive example of W. E. B. DuBois's expectations for those blacks he designated the "Talented Tenth," the exceptional individuals who would save the race. It was the great black thinker's hope in 1903 that, by "developing the Best of this race . . . they may guide the Mass away from the contamination and death of the Worst, in their own and other races."[8] And yet the working-class people Geneva represented, and among whom she lived, thought of her as she did herself: an ordinary person, or "drylongso."[9]

Her concern about the common folks motivated that last trip to the South. Approximately one thousand volunteers, mainly college students, had been recruited by the Council of Federated Organizations (COFO), representing several civil rights organizations, and organized into the Mississippi Summer Project to register black voters.[10] Geneva was concerned that both the volunteers and those they hoped to help would face harassment by state officials and private vigilantes. She was right.

Neither her legal talents nor her promise as a black leader and legal scholar saved Geneva the evening she was driving to a voter-registration meeting in the Delta during what came to be known as the violent summer of 1964. She never made it. Her car, forced off the rural country road, turned over and rolled down an embankment. A student riding with her reported that the pick-up truck that hit them while traveling at high speed paused only long enough to see that no one emerged from the demolished car. Then it sped away, the sound of gleeful laughter echoing, with the engine's roar, across the hot summer night.

Given Geneva's reputation, the attempt to kill her would have provoked a national furor in some other year; but during the summer of 1964, there were one thousand arrests, thirty-five shooting incidents, thirty buildings bombed, thirty-five churches burned, eighty people beaten, and at least six murders during the period of the summer campaign. The most infamous of these were the deaths in Philadelphia, Mississippi, of civil rights workers Michael H. Schwerner and Andrew Goodman, whites, and James E. Chaney, a black, all three murdered by local whites. Lemuel A. Penn, a black Washington, D.C., school administrator, was shot and killed as he drove through Georgia, returning from Army Reserve duty at Fort Benning.[11]

Geneva's attackers were never found, and state officials denied any racial motivation to the collision—a ludicrous suggestion accepted by those who wanted to believe the pick-up truck owner's claim that the vehicle had been stolen earlier that day by "two negras." The media, confused by the conflicting stories, lost interest and turned their attention to the numerous attacks on civil rights workers where the racial hostility behind the attacks was not in doubt. Geneva's physical injuries eventually healed; but for more than twenty years, her mind wandered in realms where medical science could not follow. Those who knew her were shocked by the attack, outraged that no arrests were made, and saddened by the discouraging reports on her continuing poor health. After Geneva failed to recover, we who were her friends spoke of her in those terms of unqualified respect and affection usually reserved for the dead; and gradually in my preoccupation with my own life, I permitted myself to forget her.

"Brother! Brother! Wake up! They have adjourned for the day, and the hosts want the delegates to pick up additional reading material for tomorrow's sessions." Thanking the delegate who had roused me from my reverie, I noticed with some embarrassment that the Great Hall was almost empty. Quickly I headed for the main doors where the reading packets were being distributed. Deciding to pass up the post-meeting reception, I obtained my materials and retired to my room. It had been a long day filled with frustration and disappointment.

Then came the shock. I opened my reading packet and found it contained only a single book, handsomely bound and with a title that brought me out of my chair: "The Civil Rights Chronicles as related by Geneva Crenshaw and reviewed with a friend." I scanned the pages, my hands shaking so much that it was difficult to read. But there was no mistaking the contents, which I had experienced firsthand. I sat down, took several deep breaths, wiped the cold perspiration from my face, and tried to remember how the discussions with Geneva, now recorded word for word in this book, had been arranged.

I recalled the evening a month earlier when I was both surprised and more than a little guilty to find a message from her on my computer which, through a national electronic mail service, allows me a speedy means of communication with friends and associates—a revolution in modern technology that had occurred in the decades since I had last seen Geneva. After so many years, her words, in her elegantly formal style, were appearing on my computer screen:

Dearest friend, I have folded my wings for a little while and returned to this world. I have learned all that I can from reading about our people's condition. It appears that my worst fears have been realized: We have made progress in everything yet nothing has changed. Our people's faith has altered the law of the land, yet their lives are deprived and stunted.

Like the Crusaders of old, we sought the Holy Grail of "equal opportunity" and, having gained it in court decisions and civil rights statutes, find it transformed from the long-sought guarantee of racial equality into one more device that the society can use to perpetuate the racial status quo. Our cause is righteous, but have we prevailed?

This, though, is no time to bewail our fate. I have always respected your views and now need your help. For the moment, you must not share word of my return. I have no time for reunions, for I have come back with a purpose. My mind is filled with allegorical visions that, taking me out of our topsyturvy world and into a strange and a more rational existence, have revealed to me new truths about the dilemma of blacks in this country. To be made real, to be potent, these visions—or Chronicles, as I call them—must be interpreted. I have chosen you to help me in this vital task.

The message went on to give me directions for finding her in a cottage in Virginia, not far apparently from Thomas Jefferson's Monticello, and ended: "Please come! Please come soon!"

I could not refuse. It took but a short while to clear my schedule and pack, and then, that evening, I said goodbye to my wife in the airport and flew eastward across the country. I took with me only a briefcase filled with writings that might further our discussions, an overnight case (I could spare no more than two days), and my trusty tape recorder, which I'm never without in these electronic days.

I landed at dawn and, in a rented car, headed for Geneva's cottage which, even with her precise directions, I had some difficulty finding on those winding country roads. But finally I was driving up to an old-fashioned cottage, somewhat in need of paint. The door was open, and Geneva was standing there, waiting, and then coming down the steps. It was like old times, as though the intervening years of my life as a law professor and her illness had never been, and we were about to sit down to thrash out one of the many civil rights cases we'd worked on in the 1960s.

We hugged each other, and then Geneva took me inside, into a large sitting room which, in striking contrast to the cottage's exterior, she had transformed into a library complete with books packing the shelves lining the walls, books stacked in every free space on the floor, and a legal databank terminal—but no telephone. It seemed an ideal place for serious research and writing.

Geneva sat me down in a big armchair and handed me a cup of a green herbal tea that seemed as strong (and tasted as bitter) as black coffee. As she poured her own cup, I took a long look at her. Her long ordeal had not left her unchanged. She was much thinner than I remembered; her once-black hair was gray though still in the Afro style she had always affected, even before it became popular during the black pride period of the late 1960s and 1970s. Her hair served to halo her face with its high cheekbones and eyes that seemed strangely fixed on me.

"Have I changed so much?" she asked abruptly, letting me know I was staring.

"I've likely changed more than you—and for the worse."

Geneva laughed. Her voice had not changed. It still had all the warmth and richness of tone characteristic of black women's voices and reminded me of the long-running debate among classical music lovers over whether that distinctive voice quality can be discerned even in black women opera singers.[12]

For an hour, Geneva and I chatted about mundane matters, and gossiped about working associates from the old days who now occupied positions of prestige impossible to even contemplate back in the early 1960s. After reciting an impressive list of judges, law teachers, law partners in prestigious firms, and high government officials, I noted the discrepancy between the grim situation of working-class blacks and our own success, which we have achieved by representing them.

Then I reminded Geneva of my fantasy shared with her long ago in which I imagined myself going back in time to counsel the Founding Fathers about two centuries of development in American constitutional law. "How," I had asked her, "should I begin so major a teaching task?"

Geneva's response had been as quick as her keen wit. "First," she had said gently, "you would have to explain to the Framers how you, a black, had gotten free of your chains and gained the audacity to teach white men anything." Rather than join me in laughing about her quip, she immediately became serious and sad. Though surprised, I wanted to pursue my idea.

"Suppose," I suggested, "we could recruit a battalion of the best black lawyers from the era of *Brown* v. *Board of Education* (1954)[13]—Thurgood Marshall, Robert L. Carter, Constance Baker Motley, Robert Ming, William Hastie, Spottswood Robinson, and Charles Houston—and send them as a delegation back through time to reason with the Framers before they decided to incorporate slavery into the Constitution. Surely that impressive body would influence decisions made by those who knew blacks only as slaves?"

"What you suggest," said Geneva when I paused, "is precisely what I myself have done."

At my look of incredulity, she smiled. "Yes, friend, I have, in one of the Chronicles I spoke of in my message to you, been enabled by extraordinary forces to address the Framers of the Constitution just as they were about to sign it. Of course, you don't believe me—but now that you're here, I hope you will let my Chronicles speak for themselves, and then you and I can discuss them together."

I suppose I must have been looking dazed, for she came over to me and, touching my arm, said, "Are you ready?"

"Yes, yes," I answered, and had just presence of mind to set my tape recorder going. Geneva watched me with a quizzical smile; then, leaning back in her old-fashioned rocking chair, she closed her eyes and began to speak.

Chapter 1

The Real Status of Blacks Today

The Chronicle of the Constitutional Contradiction

AT THE END of a journey back millions of light-years, I found myself standing quietly at the podium at the Constitutional Convention of 1787. It was late afternoon, and hot in that late summer way that makes it pleasant to stroll down a shaded country lane, but mighty oppressive in a large, crowded meeting room, particularly one where the doors are closed and locked to ensure secrecy.

The three dozen or so convention delegates looked tired. They had doubtless been meeting all day and now, clustered in small groups, were caucusing with their state delegations. So intense were their discussions that the few men who looked my way did not seem to see me. They knew this was a closed meeting, and thus could not readily take in the appearance, on what had just been an empty platform, of a tall stranger—a stranger who was not only a woman but also, all too clearly, black.

Though I knew I was protected by extraordinary forces, my hands were wet with nervous perspiration. Then I remembered why I was there. Taking a deep breath, I picked up the gavel and quickly struck the desktop twice, hard.

"Gentlemen," I said, "my name is Geneva Crenshaw, and I appear here to you as a representative of the late twentieth century to test whether the decisions you are making today might be altered if you were to know their future disastrous effect on the nation's people, both white and black."

For perhaps ten seconds, there was a shocked silence. Then the chamber exploded with shouts, exclamations, oaths. I fear the delegates' expressions of stunned surprise did no honor to their distinguished images. A warm welcome would have been too much to expect, but their shock at my sudden presence turned into an angry commotion unrelieved by even a modicum of curiosity.

The delegates to the Constitutional Convention were, in the main, young and vigorous.[1] When I remained standing, unmoved by their strong language and dire threats, several particularly robust delegates charged toward the platform, determined to carry out the shouted orders: "Eject the Negro woman at once!"

Suddenly the hall was filled with the sound of martial music, blasting trumpets, and a deafening roll of snare drums. At the same time—as the delegates were almost upon me—a cylinder composed of thin vertical bars of red, white, and blue light descended swiftly and silently from the high ceiling, nicely encapsulating the podium and me.

The self-appointed ejection party neither slowed nor swerved, a courageous act they soon regretted. As each man reached and tried to pass through the transparent light shield, there was a loud hiss, quite like the sound that electrified bug zappers make on a warm summer evening. While not lethal, the shock each attacker received was sufficiently strong to knock him to the floor, stunned and shaking.

The injured delegates all seemed to recover quickly, except one who had tried to pierce the light shield with his sword. The weapon instantly glowed red hot and burned his hand. At that point, several delegates tried to rush out of the room either to escape or to seek help—but neither doors nor windows would open.

"Gentlemen," I repeated, but no one heard me in the turmoil of shouted orders, cries of outrage, and efforts to sound the alarm to those outside. Scanning the room, I saw a swarthy delegate cock his long pistol, aim carefully, and fire directly at me. But the ball hit the shield, ricocheted back into the room, and shattered an inkwell, splattering my intended assassin with red ink.

At that, one of the delegates, raising his hand, roared, "Silence!" and then turned to me. "Woman! Who are you and by what authority do you interrupt this gathering?"

27

"Gentlemen," I began, "delegates"—then paused and, with a slight smile, added, "fellow citizens, I—like some of you—am a Virginian, my forefathers having labored on the land holdings of your fellow patriot, the Honorable Thomas Jefferson. I have come to urge that, in your great work here, you not restrict the sweep of Mr. Jefferson's self-evident truths that all men are equal and endowed by the Creator with inalienable rights, including 'Life, Liberty and the pursuit of Happiness.' " It was, I thought, a clever touch to invoke the name of Thomas Jefferson who, then serving as American minister to France, was not a member of the Virginia delegation.[2] But my remark could not overcome the offense of my presence.

"How dare you insert yourself in these deliberations?" a delegate demanded.

"I dare," I said, "because slavery is an evil that Jefferson, himself a slave owner and unconvinced that Africans are equal to whites, nevertheless found involved 'a perpetual exercise of the most boisterous passions, the most unremitting despotism on the one part, and degrading submissions on the other.' Slavery, Jefferson has written, brutalizes slave owner as well as slave and, worst of all, tends to undermine the 'only firm basis' of liberty, the conviction in the minds of the people that liberty is 'the gift of God.'[3]

"Gentlemen, it was also Thomas Jefferson who, considering the evil of slavery, wrote: 'I tremble for my country when I reflect that God is just; that his justice cannot sleep forever.' "[4]

There was a hush in the group. No one wanted to admit it, but the ambivalence on the slavery issue expressed by Jefferson obviously had meaning for at least some of those in the hall. It seemed the right moment to prove both that I was a visitor from the future and that Jefferson's troubled concern for his country had not been misplaced. In quick, broad strokes, I told them of the country's rapid growth, of how slavery had expanded rather than withered of its own accord, and finally of how its continued presence bred first suspicion and then enmity between those in the South who continued to rely on a plantation economy and those Northerners committed to industrial development using white wage workers. The entry into the Union of each new state, I explained, further dramatized the disparity between North and South. Inevitably, the differences led to armed conflict—a civil war that, for all its bloody costs, did not settle those differences, and they remain divisive even as we celebrate our two-hundredth anniversary as one nation.

"The stark truth is that the racial grief that persists today," I ended, "originated in the slavery institutionalized in the document you are drafting. Is this, gentlemen, an achievement for which you wish to be remembered?"

Oblivious to my plea, a delegate tried what he likely considered a sympathetic approach. "Geneva, be reasonable. Go and leave us to our work. We have heard the petitions of Africans and of abolitionists speaking in their behalf. Some here are sympathetic to these pleas for freedom. Others are not. But we have debated this issue at length, and after three months of difficult negotiations, compromises have been reached, decisions made, language drafted and approved. The matter is settled. Neither you nor whatever powers have sent you here can undo what is done."

I was not to be put off so easily. "Sirs," I said, "I have come to tell you that the matter of slavery will not be settled by your compromises. And even when it is ended by armed conflict and domestic turmoil far more devastating than that you hope to avoid here, the potential evil of giving priority to property over human rights will remain. Can you not address the contradiction in your words and deeds?"

"There is no contradiction," replied another delegate. "Gouverneur Morris of Pennsylvania, the Convention's most outspoken opponent of slavery, has admitted that 'life and liberty were generally said to be of more value, than property, . . . [but] an accurate view of the matter would nevertheless prove that property was the main object of Society.' "[5]

"A contradiction," another delegate added, "would occur were we to follow the course you urge. We are not unaware of the moral issues raised by slavery, but we have no response to the delegate from South Carolina, General Charles Cotesworth Pinckney, who has admonished us that 'property in slaves should not be exposed to danger under a Govt. instituted for the protection of property.' "[6]

"Of what value is a government that does not secure its citizens in their persons and their property?" inquired another delegate. "Government, as Mr. Pierce Butler from South Carolina has maintained here, 'was instituted principally for the protection of property and was itself . . . supported by property.' Property, he reminded us, was 'the great object of government; the great cause of war; the great means of carrying it on.'[7] And the whole South Carolina delegation joined him in making clear that 'the security the Southern states want is that their negroes may not be taken from them.' "[8]

"Your deliberations here have been secret," I replied. "And yet history has revealed what you here would hide. The Southern delegates have demanded the slavery compromises as their absolute precondition to forming a new government."

"And why should it not be so?" a delegate in the rear called out. "I do not represent the Southern point of view, and yet their rigidity on the slavery issue is wholly natural, stemming as it does from the commitment of their economy to labor-intensive agriculture. We are not surprised by the determined bargaining of the Georgia and South Carolina delegations, nor distressed that our Southern colleagues, in seeking the protection they have gained, seem untroubled by doubts about the policy and morality of slavery and the slave trade."

"Then," I countered, "you are not troubled by the knowledge that this document will be defended by your Southern colleagues in the South Carolina ratification debates, by admissions that 'Negroes were our wealth, our only resource'?"[9]

"Why, in God's name," the delegate responded, "should we be troubled by the truth, candidly stated? They have said no less in these chambers. General Charles Cotesworth Pinckney has flatly stated that 'South Carolina and Georgia cannot do without slaves.' And his cousin and fellow planter, Charles Pinckney, has added, 'The blacks are the laborers, the peasants of the Southern states.' "[10]

At this, an elderly delegate arose and rapped his cane on his chair for attention. "Woman, we would have you gone from this place. But if a record be made, that record should show that the economic benefits of slavery do not accrue only to the South.

Plantation states provide a market for Northern factories, and the New England shipping industry and merchants participate in the slave trade. Northern states, moreover, utilize slaves in the fields, as domestics, and even as soldiers to defend against Indian raids."[11]

I shook my head. "Here you are then! Representatives from large and small states, slave states and those that have abolished slavery, all of you are protecting your property interests at the cost of your principles."

There was no response. The transparent shield protected my person, served as a language translator smoothing the differences in English usage, and provided a tranquilizing effect as it shimmered softly in the hot and humid room. Evidently, even this powerful mechanism could not bring the delegates to reassess their views on the slavery issue.

I asked, "Are you not concerned with the basic contradiction in your position: that you, who have gathered here in Philadelphia from each state in the confederacy, in fact represent and constitute major property holders? Do you not mind that your slogans of liberty and individual rights are basically guarantees that neither a strong government nor the masses will be able to interfere with your property rights and those of your class? This contradiction between what you espouse and what you here protect will be held against you by future citizens of this nation."[12]

"Unless we continue on our present course," a delegate called out, "there will be no nation whose origins can be criticized. These sessions were called because the country is teetering between anarchy and bankruptcy. The nation cannot meet its debts. And only a year ago, thousands of poor farmers in Massachusetts and elsewhere took up arms against the government."

"Indeed," I said, "I am aware of Shay's Rebellion, led by Daniel Shay, a former officer who served with distinction in the war against England. According to historians of my time, the inability of Congress to respond to Massachusetts's appeal for help provided 'the final argument to sway many Americans in favor of a stronger federal government.'[13] I understand the nature of the crisis that brings you here, but the compromises you make on the slavery issue are———"

31

"Young woman!" interrupted one of the older delegates. "Young woman, you say you understand. But I tell you that it is 'nearly impossible for anybody who has not been on the spot to conceive (from any description) what the delicacy and danger of our situation . . . [has] been. I am President of this Convention, drafted to the task against my wishes. I am here and I am ready to embrace any tolerable compromise that . . . [is] competent to save us from impending ruin.' "[14]

While so far I had recognized none of the delegates, the identity of this man—seated off by himself, and one of the few who had remained quiet through the bedlam that broke out after my arrival—was unmistakable.

"Thank you, General Washington," I responded. "I know that you, though a slave owner, are opposed to slavery. And yet you have said little during these meetings—to prevent, one may assume, your great prestige from unduly influencing debate. Future historians will say of your silence that you recognize that for you to throw the weight of your opinion against slavery might so hearten the opponents of the system, while discouraging its proponents, as to destroy all hope of compromise. This would prevent the formation of the Union, and the Union, for you, is essential."[15]

"I will not respond to these presumptions," said General Washington, "but I will tell you now what I will say to others at a later time. There are in the new form some things, I will readily acknowledge, that never did, and I am persuaded never will, obtain my cordial approbation; but I did then conceive, and do now most firmly believe, that in the aggregate it is the best constitution, that can be obtained at this epoch, and that this, or a dissolution, awaits our choice, and is the only alternative."[16]

"Do you recognize," I asked, "that in order to gain unity among yourselves, your slavery compromises sacrifice freedom for the Africans who live amongst you and work for you? Such sacrifices of the rights of one group of human beings will, unless arrested here, become a difficult-to-break pattern in the nation's politics."[17]

"Did you not listen to the general?" This man, I decided, must be James Madison. As the delegates calmed down, he had returned to a prominent seat in the front of the room directly in front of the podium. It was from this vantage point that he took notes of the proceedings which, when finally released in 1840, became the best record of the Convention.[18]

"I expect," Madison went on, "that many will question why I have agreed to the Constitution. And, like General Washington, I will answer: 'because I thought it safe to the liberties of the people, and the best that could be obtained from the jarring interests of States, and the miscellaneous opinions of Politicians; and because experience has proved that the real danger to America & to liberty lies in the defect of *energy & stability* in the present establishments of the United States.' "[19]

"Do not think," added a delegate from Massachusetts, "that this Convention has come easily to its conclusions on the matter that concerns you. Gouverneur Morris from Pennsylvania has said to us in the strongest terms: 'Domestic slavery is the most prominent feature in the aristocratic countenance of the proposed Constitution.'[20] He warned again and again that 'the people of Pennsylvania will never agree to a representation of Negroes.'[21]

"Many of us shared Mr. Morris's concern about basing apportionment on slaves as insisted by the Southern delegates. I recall with great sympathy his questions:

> Upon what principle is it that the slaves shall be computed in the representation? Are they men? Then make them citizens & let them vote? Are they property? Why then is no other property included? . . .
>
> The admission of slaves into the Representation when fairly explained comes to this: that the inhabitant of Georgia and S.C. who goes to the Coast of Africa, and in defiance of the most sacred laws of humanity tears away his fellow creatures from their dearest connections & damns them to the most cruel bondages, shall have more votes in a Govt. instituted for protection of the rights of mankind, then the Citizen of Pa or N. Jersey who views with a laudable horror, so nefarious a practice.[22]

"I tell you, woman, this Convention was not unmoved at these words of Mr. Morris's only a few weeks ago."

"Even so," I said, "the Convention has acquiesced when representatives of the Southern states adamantly insisted that the proposed new government not interfere with their property in slaves. And is it not so that, beyond a few speeches, the representatives of the Northern states have been, at best, ambivalent on the issue?"

"And why not?" interjected another delegate. "Slavery has provided the wealth that made independence possible. The profits from slavery funded the Revolution. It cannot be denied. At the time of the Revolution, the goods for which the United States demanded freedom were produced in very large measure by slave labor. Desperately needing assistance from other countries, we purchased this aid from France with tobacco produced mainly by slave labor.[23] The nation's economic well-being depended on the institution, and its preservation is essential if the Constitution we are drafting is to be more than a useless document. At least, that is how we view the crisis we face."

To pierce the delegates' adamant front, I called on the oratorical talents that have, in the twentieth century, won me both praise and courtroom battles: "The real crisis you face should not be resolved by your recognition of slavery, an evil whose immorality will pollute the nation as it now stains your document. Despite your resort to euphemisms like *persons* to keep out of the Constitution such words as *slave* and *slavery*, you cannot evade the consequences of the ten different provisions you have placed in the Constitution for the purpose of protecting property in slaves.*

---

* The historian William Wiecek has listed the following direct and indirect accommodations to slavery contained in the Constitution:

1. Article I, Section 2: representatives in the House were apportioned among the states on the basis of population, computed by counting all free persons and three-fifths of the slaves (the "federal number," or "three-fifths," clause);
2. Article I, Section 2, and Article I, Section 9: two clauses requiring, redundantly, that direct taxes (including capitations) be apportioned among the states on the foregoing basis, the purpose being to prevent Congress from laying a head tax on slaves to encourage their emancipation;
3. Article I, Section 9: Congress was prohibited from abolishing the international slave trade to the United States before 1808;
4. Article IV, Section 2: the states were prohibited from emancipating fugitive slaves, who were to be returned on demand of the master;
5. Article I, Section 8: Congress empowered to provide for calling up the states' militias to suppress insurrections, including slave uprisings;
6. Article IV, Section 4: the federal government was obliged to protect the states against domestic violence, including slave insurrections;
7. Article V: the provisions of Article I, Section 9, clauses 1 and 4 (pertaining to the slave trade and direct taxes) were made unamendable;

"Woman!" a delegate shouted from the rear of the room. "Explain to us how you, a black, have gotten free of your chains and gained the audacity to come here and teach white men anything."

I smiled, recognizing the eternal question. "Audacity," I replied, "is an antidote to your arrogance. Be assured: my knowledge, despite my race, is far greater than yours."

"But if my race and audacity offend you, then listen to your contemporaries who have opposed slavery in most moving terms. With all due respect, there are few in this company whose insight exceeds that of Abigail Adams who wrote her husband, John, during the Revolutionary War: 'I wish most sincerely there was not a slave in the province; it always appeared a most iniquitous scheme to me to fight ourselves for what we are daily robbing and plundering from those who have as good a right to freedom as we have.'[25] Mrs. Adams's wish is, as you know, shared by many influential Americans who denounce slavery as a corrupting and morally unjustifiable practice.[26]

"Gentlemen," I continued, "how can you disagree with the view of the Maryland delegate Luther Martin that the slave trade and 'three-fifths' compromises 'ought to be considered as a solemn mockery of, and insult to that God whose protection we had then implored, and . . . who views with equal eye the poor African slave and his American master'? I can tell you that Mr. Martin will not only abandon these deliberations and refuse to sign the Constitution but also oppose its ratification in Maryland. And further, he will, in his opposition, expose the deal of the committee on which he served, under which New England states agreed to give the slave trade a twenty-year immunity from federal restrictions in exchange for Southern votes to eliminate restrictions on navigation acts. What is more, he will write that, to the rest of the world, it must appear 'absurd and disgraceful to the last degree, that we should *except* from the exercise of that power [to regulate commerce], the *only branch of commerce* which is *unjustifiable in its nature*, and *contrary* to the rights of *mankind*.' "[27]

"Again, woman," a Northern delegate assured me, "we have

---

8. Article I, Section 9, and Article I, Section 10: these two clauses prohibited the federal government and the states from taxing exports, one purpose being to prevent them from taxing slavery indirectly by taxing the exported product of slave labor.[24]

heard and considered all those who oppose slavery. Despite the remonstrations of the abolitionists—of whom few, I must add, believe Negroes to be the equal of white men, and even fewer would want the blacks to remain in this land were slavery abandoned—we have acted as we believe the situation demands."

"I cannot believe," I said, "that even a sincere belief in the superiority of the white race should suffice to condone so blatant a contradiction of your hallowed ideals."

"It should be apparent by now," said the delegate who had shot at me, but had now recovered his composure and shed his ink-stained coat, "that we do not care what you think. Furthermore, if your people actually had the sensitivities of real human beings, you would realize that you are not wanted here and would have the decency to leave."

"I will not leave!" I said steadily, and waited while the delegates conferred.

Finally, a delegate responded to my challenge. "You have, by now, heard enough to realize that we have not lightly reached the compromises on slavery you so deplore. Perhaps we, with the responsibility of forming a radically new government in perilous times, see more clearly than is possible for you in hindsight that the unavoidable cost of our labors will be the need to accept and live with what you call a contradiction."

The delegate had gotten to his feet, and was walking slowly toward me as he spoke. "This contradiction is not lost on us. Surely we know, even though we are at pains not to mention it, that we have sacrificed the rights of some in the belief that this involuntary forfeiture is necessary to secure the rights for others in a society espousing, as its basic principle, the liberty of all."

He was standing directly in front of the shield now, ignoring its gentle hum, disregarding its known danger. "It grieves me," he continued, "that your presence here confirms my worst fears about the harm done to your people because the Constitution, while claiming to speak in an unequivocal voice, in fact promises freedom to whites and condemns blacks to slavery. But what alternative do we have? Unless we here frame a constitution that can first gain our signatures and then win ratification by the states, we shall soon have no nation. For better or worse, slavery has been the backbone of our economy, the source of much of our wealth. It was condoned in the colonies and recognized in the Articles of Confederation. The majority of the delegates to this convention own slaves and must have that right protected if they and their states are to be included in the new government."

He paused and then asked, more out of frustration than defiance, "What better compromise on this issue can you offer than that which has been fashioned over so many hours of heated debate?"

The room was silent. The delegate, his statement made, his question presented, turned and walked slowly back to his seat. A few from his state touched his hand as he passed. Then all eyes turned to me.

I thanked the delegate for his question and then said, "The processes by which Northern states are even now abolishing slavery are known to you all.[28] What is lacking here is not legislative skill but the courage to recognize the evil of holding blacks in slavery—an evil that would be quickly and universally condemned were the subjects of bondage members of the Caucasian race. You fear that unless the slavery of blacks is recognized and given protection, the nation will not survive. And my message is that the compromises you are making here mean that the nation's survival will always be in doubt. For now in my own day, after two hundred years and despite bloody wars and the earnest efforts of committed people, the racial contradiction you sanction in this document remains and threatens to tear this country apart."

"Mr. Chairman," said a delegate near the podium whose accent indicated that he was from the deep South, "this discussion grows tiresome and I resent to my very soul the presence in our midst of this offspring of slaves. If she accurately predicts the future fate of her race in this country, then our protection of slave property, which we deem essential for our survival, is easier to justify than in some later time when, as she implies, negroes remain subjugated even without the threats we face."

"Hear! Hear!" shouted a few delegates. "Bravo, Colonel!"

"It's all hypocrisy!" the Colonel shouted, his arms flailing the air, "sheer hypocrisy! Our Northern colleagues bemoan slavery while profiting from it as much as we in the South, meanwhile avoiding its costs and dangers. And our friends from Virginia, where slavery began, urge the end of importation—not out of humanitarian motivations, as their speeches suggest, but because they have sufficient slaves, and expect the value of their property will increase if further imports are barred.

"Mr. George Mason, of the Virginia delegation, in his speech opposing the continued importation of slaves expressed fear that, if not barred, the people of Western lands, already crying for slaves, could get them through South Carolina and Georgia. He moans that: 'Slavery discourages arts & manufactures. The poor despise labor when performed by slaves. They prevent the immigration of Whites, who really enrich & strengthen a Country. They produce the most pernicious effect on manners.' Furthermore, according to Mr. Mason, 'every master of slaves is born a petty tyrant. They bring the judgment of heaven on a Country . . . [and] by an inevitable chain of causes & effects providence punishes national sins, by national calamities.'[29]

"This, Mr. Chairman, is nothing but hypocrisy or, worse, ignorance of history. We speak easily today of liberty, but the rise of liberty and equality in this country has been accompanied by the rise of slavery.[30] The negress who has seized our podium by diabolical force charges that we hold blacks slaves because we view them as inferior. Inferior in every way they surely are, but they were not slaves when Virginia was a new colony 150 years ago. Or, at least, their status was hardly worse than the luckless white indentured servants brought here from debtors' prisons and the poverty-ridden streets of England. Neither slave nor servant lived very long in that harsh, fever-ridden clime."

The Colonel, so close to the podium, steadfastly refused to speak to me or even to acknowledge my presence.

"In the beginning," he went on, "life was harsh, but the coming of tobacco to Virginia in 1617 turned a struggling colony into a place where great wealth could be made relatively quickly. To cultivate the labor-intense crop, large numbers of mainly white, male servants, indentured to their masters for a period of years, were imported. Blacks, too, were brought to the colony, both as slaves and as servants. They generally worked, ate, and slept with the white servants.

"As the years passed, more and more servants lived to gain their freedom, despite the practice of extending terms for any offense, large or small. They soon became a growing, poverty-stricken class, some of whom resigned themselves to working for wages; others preferred a meager living on dangerous frontier land or a hand-to-mouth existence, roaming from one county to another, renting a bit of land here, squatting on some there, dodging the tax collector, drinking, quarreling, stealing hogs, and enticing servants to run away with them."

"It is not extraordinary to suggest that the planters and those who governed Virginia were caught in a dilemma—a dilemma more like the contradiction we are accused of building into the Constitution than may at first meet the eye. They needed workers to maintain production in their fields, but young men were soon rebellious, without either land of their own or women, who were not seen as fit to work the fields. Moreover, the young workers were armed and had to be armed to repel attacks from Indians by land and from privateers and petty-thieving pirates by sea.

"The worst fears of Virginia's leaders were realized when, in 1676, a group of these former servants returned from a fruitless expedition against the Indians to attack their rulers in what was called Bacon's Rebellion. Governor William Berkeley bemoaned his lot in terms that defined the problem: 'How miserable that man is that Governes a People wher six parts of seaven at least are Poore Endebted Discontented and Armed.'[31]

"The solution came naturally and without decision. The planters purchased more slaves and imported fewer English servants. Slaves were more expensive initially, but their terms did not end, and their owners gained the benefits of the slaves' offspring. Africans, easily identified by color, could not hope to run away without being caught. The fear of pain and death could be and was substituted for the extension of terms as an incentive to force the slaves to work. They were not armed and could be held in chains.

"The fear of slave revolts increased as reliance on slavery grew and racial antipathy became more apparent. But this danger, while real, was less than that from restive and armed freedmen. Slaves did not have rising expectations, and no one told them they had rights. They had lost their freedom. Moreover, a woman could be made to work and have children every two years, thereby adding to the income of her master. Thus, many more women than indentured servants were imported.

"A free society divided between large landholders and small was much less riven by antagonisms than one divided between landholders and landless, masterless men. With the freedmen's expectations, sobriety, and status restored, he was no longer a man to be feared. That fact, together with the presence of a growing mass of alien slaves, tended to draw the white settlers closer together and to reduce the importance of the class difference between yeoman farmer and large plantation owner.

"Racial fears tended to lessen the economic and political differences between rich and poor whites. And as royal officials and tax collectors became more oppressive, both groups joined forces in protesting the import taxes on tobacco which provided income for the high and the low. The rich began to look to their less wealthy neighbors for political support against the English government and in local elections.

"Wealthy whites, of course, retained all their former prerogatives, but the creation of a black subclass enabled poor whites to identify with and support the policies of the upper class. With the safe economic advantage provided by their slaves, large landowners were willing to grant poor whites a larger role in the political process."

"So, Colonel," I interrupted, "you are saying that slavery for blacks not only provided wealth for rich whites but, paradoxically, led also to greater freedom for poor whites. One of our twentieth-century historians, Edmund Morgan, has explained this paradox of slave owners espousing freedom and liberty:

Aristocrats could more safely preach equality in a slave society than in a free one. Slaves did not become leveling mobs, because their owners would see to it that they had no chance to. The apostrophes to equality were not addressed to them. And because Virginia's labor force was composed mainly of slaves, who had been isolated by race and removed from the political equation, the remaining free laborers and tenant farmers were too few in number to constitute a serious threat to the superiority of the men who assured them of their equality.[32]

"In effect," I concluded, "what I call a contradiction here was deemed a solution then. Slavery enabled the rich to keep their lands, arrested discontent and repression of other Englishmen, strengthened their rights and nourished their attachment to liberty. But the solution, as Professor Morgan said, 'put an end to the process of turning Africans into Englishmen. The rights of Englishmen were preserved by destroying the rights of Africans.' "[33]

"Do you charge that our belief in individual liberty is feigned?" demanded a Virginian, outraged.

"It was Professor Morgan's point," I replied, "not that 'a belief in republican equality had to rest on slavery, but only that in Virginia (and probably in other southern colonies) it did. The most ardent American republicans were Virginians, and their ardor was not unrelated to their power over the men and women they held in bondage.' " [34]

And now, for the first time, the Colonel looked at me, amazed. "My thoughts on this slavery matter have confounded my mind for many years, and yet you summarize them in a few paragraphs. I must, after all, thank you." He walked back to his seat in a daze, neither commended nor condemned by his colleagues. Most, indeed, were deep in thought—but for a few delegates I noticed trying desperately to signal to passersby in the street. But I could not attend to them: my time, I knew, must be growing short.

"The Colonel," I began again, "has performed a valuable service. He has delineated the advantages of slavery as an institution in this country. And your lengthy debates here are but prelude to the struggles that will follow your incorporation of this moral evil into the nation's basic law."

"Woman! We implore you to allow us to continue our work. While we may be inconsistent about the Negro problem, we are convinced that this is the only way open to us. You asked that we let your people go. We cannot do that and still preserve the potential of this nation for good—a potential that requires us to recognize here and now what later generations may condemn as evil.

And as we talk I wonder—are the problems of race in your time equally paradoxical?"

I longed to continue the debate, but never got the chance. Apparently someone outside had finally understood the delegates' signals for help, and had summoned the local militia. Hearing some commotion beyond the window, I turned to see a small cannon being rolled up, pointing straight at me. Then, in quick succession, the cannoneer lighted the fuse; the delegates dived under their desks; the cannon fired; and, with an ear-splitting roar, the cannonball broke against the light shield and splintered, leaving me and the shield intact.

I knew then my mission was over, and I returned to the twentieth century.

GENEVA had related the Chronicle of the Constitutional Contradiction as though she were living it again—and, indeed, I felt, as she talked, as though I, too, were in that hot and humid hall arguing along with her. Now she sat back in her chair and looked toward me in anticipation. She was waiting for me to say something, but what? Clearly she didn't consider her Chronicles mere flights of high fantasy. She would never have asked me to cross the country simply to listen to her recount a series of dreams. She had always been pragmatic—a realist in an idealist world, she had said back in the early 1960s while trying to explain why she could not accept the idea that the evil of racial discrimination would be swept away in a sea of legal precedents generated by the Supreme Court's decision in the 1954 school-desegregation case of *Brown* v. *Board of Education*.[35]

And, just as during the 1960s when we traveled across the South as co-counsel in dozens of civil rights cases, I resisted the unblinking pragmatism that was a part of Geneva's strength and the source of our constant arguments. But she was obviously still

42

waiting for me to express an opinion about the Chronicle.

"The story was very real for me," I told her honestly enough. "Knowing the difficulty I have trying to get bicentennial committees on which I serve even to acknowledge how the Constitution handled the slavery issue, I can understand your frustration with the Framers themselves, but——"

"But, had you been there, you might have succeeded where I failed?"

"I'm not sure I could have done better, Geneva. Your presence shocked them, and any black person seeking acceptance as a peer in that group would have been a shock, but a black woman——" I struggled without success for some suitable analogy. "I kept waiting for you to dazzle them with a devastating analysis of the increasing tension between slave and nonslave states, its threat to the Union, the Civil War, and the amendments that, in granting blacks full citizenship rights, altered the dimensions but not the essence of the racial contradiction."

"I wanted to, but I sensed that they did not want to know a future that lay outside their imagination. Their rhetoric spoke to the ages, but their attention was focused on events close at hand. I guess contemporary policy making is not much different."

"Perhaps," I agreed, and then ventured unwisely, "but if you had provided more information about the future, you might have better demonstrated your superior knowledge and your entitlement to be heard."

"*When* did you last win an argument with a white man by proving you were smarter than he was?" And certain she knew the answer to that question, she continued, "I hope you have not missed the real point of the Chronicle. It was not a debate. The Chronicle's message is that no one could have prevented the Framers from drafting a constitution including provisions protecting property in slaves. If they believed, as they had every reason to do, that the country's survival required the economic advantage provided by the slave system, than it was essential that slavery be recognized, rationalized, and protected in the country's basic law. It is as simple as that."

"And not so simple, to judge by the Colonel's revelations," I suggested. "As a result of your aggressive advocacy, you forced him and the rest of the Convention to think through motivations for the slavery compromises that went beyond the Southern delegates' refusal to compromise on this issue."

"The Colonel's reaction surprised me," Geneva admitted, "but his insight into the political as well as the economic importance of slavery simply added more compelling reasons for recognizing and providing protection for slavery in the Constitution."

"The implications for current civil rights work are a bit too close for comfort."

"Exactly right." Geneva leaned forward in her chair to give emphasis to her words. "Even in that extraordinary setting, what struck me as I fought for their attention was how familiar it all was. You know, friend, we civil rights lawyers spend our lives confronting whites in power with the obvious racial bias in their laws or policies, and while, as you know, the litany of their possible exculpatory responses is as long as life, they all boil down to: 'That's the way the world is. We did not make the rules, we simply play by them, and you really have no alternative but to do the same. Please don't take it personally.' The Colonel's speech revealed components of those rules far more complex than ignorant prejudice."

I smiled at her vehemence. "No one will be surprised to learn that you've not become a racial romantic during your long absence."

"Maybe not, but I am surprised that after all these years you continue to believe in this nation's Fourth of July fantasy which most people pack away on July fifth with the unused fireworks."

"We've all got to have faith."

"Faith is not foolishness, my friend," Geneva countered, serious now. "And, as we are reminded in Scripture, 'Faith, if it hath not works, is dead, being alone.' "[36]

"We in civil rights have worked hard," I said. "Why are you so ready to criticize those who try to end the evil of racism rather than those who perpetrate it?"

"Because," she said flatly, ignoring my irritation, "you seem so complacent even though you have lived to see your faith betrayed, your hard work undone. Through it all, you pretend that all is well or that 'real freedom' is almost here. The reports and statistics I have been reading about the current state of most black Americans make that character of belief seem closer to cowardice than to courage."

Before I could respond to the charge, Geneva continued on a less challenging tack. "Of course, I understand that, with the removal of formal segregation barriers, it is a rare area of endeavor where at least a few blacks have not made notable achievements—a progress in which civil rights workers can take pride. But all but the most optimistic among you must concede that the once swiftly moving march toward racial equality through law reform has slowed to a walk, leaving millions of black Americans no better off that they were before the civil rights movement."

Geneva handed me a sheaf of news clippings and reports along with a summary of each which she had copied out in long hand. "Though you know this material, I am sure," she said, frowning, "you can imagine how, after the many years I had been unaware of what was happening, it hit me to learn—as these data indicate—how little had in fact happened."

The reports were all too familiar. One study showed that "blacks in every income strata, from the poorest to the most affluent, lost ground and had less disposable income in 1984 than in 1980, after adjusting for inflation." In sharp contrast, the top 60 percent of the white population experienced income gains; and, worst of all, the study found "a consistent pattern of widening income inequality between blacks and whites since 1980."[37]

The National Urban League in its annual report, *The State of Black America*, charted the decline in the economic fortunes of many black people. In his overview written for the 1985 report, the Urban League president John E. Jacob found that, in virtually every area of life that counts, black people made strong progress in the 1960s, peaked in the 1970s, and have been sliding back ever since. In 1975, he reported, black unemployment was 14.1 percent, about double that of white unemployment (7.6 percent). At the end of 1984, black unemployment was 16 percent; white, 6.5 percent. Constituting some 10 percent of the labor force, blacks account for 20 percent of the jobless. Then in his 1986 overview, Jacob noted that "the median black family had about

45

56 cents to spend for every one dollar white families had to spend, which was two cents less than they had in 1980, and almost six cents less than they had in 1970."[38]

The long-term impact of joblessness and underemployment on the economic well-being of black households was traced with depressing figures in a Bureau of the Census report. Based on a sampling of 20,000 families, the study revealed that white families, whose median income is almost twice that of black families, have accumulated assets almost twelve times as high. Figures varied by age, income, and marital status; but while the median net worth of all families was $32,667, the overall black median was $3,397, compared with assets for the median white family of $39,135.[39]

"I would think," Geneva remarked, "that few civil rights proponents can feel much satisfaction about the progress of some blacks when the statistics on the woeful state of so many loom large even as they, month by month, grow worse."[40]

"You're right. We all acknowledge the devastating impact of these statistics on the black family. Focusing on female-headed households, a recent summary by a group of black academics pointed to statistics showing that 48 percent of black families with related children under eighteen are headed by women, and that half of all black children under eighteen live in female-headed households. The 1979 median income for black female-headed households was only $6,610 compared with close to $20,000 for all families.[41]

"We must, of course, keep in mind," I cautioned, "that, despite the disparate statistics on virtually every measure of black/white comparison, not all blacks are adrift on the sea of poverty. In the deluge of statistics concerning the plight of the black family, we must not lose sight of the fact that over half of them (53 percent) are intact, married-couple families. Such families represent the most economically viable family unit, boasting a median income in 1983 of $26,686 when both husband and wife were in the labor force. Unfortunately, the married-couple family as a percentage of all black families has declined over the last two decades from 68 percent in 1960 to 53 percent in 1983."[42]

"Isn't the major issue here," Geneva asked, "the disappearance of black men, whose absence has led to the tremendous growth in black-female-headed families and the accompanying rise in poverty among black families?"

"It would seem obvious," I replied, continuing to skim through the reports. "One paper here suggests the 'economic status of black, adult men is the other, largely unnoticed, side of the troubling increase in single-parent black families.'[43] The report focuses on your word *disappearance*, Geneva. Unemployment is only one cause of black male absence. As of 1982, there were 8.8 million black men from the ages of sixteen to sixty-four. Only 54 percent of them were working, compared with 78 percent of white males. The balance of these black men were unemployed (13.1 percent), not in the labor force (20 percent), in prison (2.1 percent), and unaccounted for (10.5 percent). These percentages are not only much higher than those for white males but are higher for black males than in 1960 when, according to the report, 'nearly three-quarters of all black men included in Census data were working; today, only 55 percent are working.'[44]

"But, beyond overt racial discrimination, these grim figures are influenced by a great many factors, including the automation of many jobs at low-skill levels and the loss of so-called smokestack industries where great numbers of blacks used to be employed. The severe cutback in social service programs has also worsened unemployment statistics for black workers, though whites have been hurt by all these factors as well."

"There is, I gather," Geneva broke in, "a widening income gap between the top and bottom of U.S. society. In fact, some of the most distressing data relate to income distribution of American families. In 1983, the wealthiest two-fifths of all U.S. families earned 67.1 percent of the total national income, while the poorest two-fifths earned only 15.8 percent, and the poorest fifth—where nearly one-half of all black families fell—earned only 4.7 percent of the national income."[45]

"What percentage of blacks are in the top fifth?" I asked, looking for some positive note.

"Only 7 percent of all black families are in this group. Worse yet, the top fifth of American families earned 42.7 percent of the income, or nine times as much as the bottom fifth—hardly a basis for your perverse optimism since 9.9 million blacks, nearly 36 percent of our population, are living in poverty. This is the highest black poverty rate since the Census Bureau began collecting data on black poverty in 1968."[46]

"Let me anticipate you, Geneva," I suggested. "Yes, these statistics reflect many ruined lives for whom the oft-heralded legal gains have been fatally tardy. Professor William J. Wilson, one of the most perceptive of contemporary observers, reports: 'The pattern of racial oppression in the past created the huge black underclass, as the accumulation of disadvantages were passed on from generation to generation, and the technological and economic revolution of advanced industrial society combined to insure it a permanent status.' "[47]

"My conclusion may be premature," Geneva interjected, "but my reading indicates that because the Supreme Court is unable or unwilling to recognize and remedy the real losses resulting from long-held, race-based subordinated status, the relief the Court has been willing to grant, while welcome, proves of less value than expected and exacts the exorbitant price of dividing the black community along economic lines."

"Precisely one of the points Professor Wilson makes as he compares the ever-worsening situation for unskilled black workers with the increased opportunities for educated blacks with skills. In fact, Wilson has upset some civil rights advocates by noting that 'affirmative action programs are not designed to deal with the problem of the disproportionate concentration of blacks in the low-wage labor market. Their major impact has been in the higher-paying jobs of the expanding service-producing industries in both the corporate and government sectors.' Furthermore, Wilson shares your concern, Geneva, about the 'deepening economic schism . . . developing in the black community, with the black poor falling further and further behind middle- and upper-income blacks.' "[48]

"So," said Geneva, "to sum up this discussion before moving on to my second Chronicle, there seems little doubt that the abandonment of overtly discriminatory policies has lowered racial barriers for some talented and skilled blacks seeking access to opportunity and advancement. Even their upward movement is, however, pointed to by much of the society as the final proof that racism is dead—a too hasty pronouncement which dilutes the achievement of those who have moved ahead and denies even society's sympathy to those less fortunate blacks whose opportunities and life fortunes are less promising today than they were twenty-five years ago.

"Despite your optimism, you seem ready to agree that the future for a great many black people is bleak. The necessary question that I hope we can decide during our discussions is whether this result—this economic-political disadvantage set in motion by the Framers—is beyond any known power to halt or even alter. Or, whether different strategies might make the annual observances of the *Brown* decision celebrations of great expectations realized rather than increasingly sorrowful commemorations of what might have been. And finally, whether, as I tried to suggest to the Framers, the real problem of race in America is the unresolved contradiction embedded in the Constitution and never openly examined, owing to the self-interested attachment of some citizens of this nation to certain myths—myths that I hope my Chronicles will allow us to examine in detail."

"Your summary, Geneva, is a good place to start, but my optimism about the future doesn't mean that I'm not as disturbed as you are about the current condition of black people in this country. It is all too true that much of our effort in the courts and in getting civil rights laws through Congress fell far short of eliminating our subordinate status in this society."

Geneva looked suspicious. "I sense a thinly veiled *but* in your statement."

"Not really. I am troubled, though, by the challenge you faced in your first Chronicle, and continue to wonder whether there wasn't some way to get the Framers to acknowledge that their compromises on slavery could only have dire human consequences."

For far from the last time that day, Geneva was exasperated. "And what makes you think that the Constitution's Framers who saw us as slaves, and used that lowly status to convince themselves that we were an inferior race, would have been more likely to recognize our humanity than are the country's contemporary leaders who, having every reason to know that we are not inferior, seem determined to maintain racial dominance even if that aim destroys us and the country?"

"Yes, white policy makers' racial motivations seem hardly to have changed at all over these two centuries—but, Geneva, before you go on to your next Chronicle, tell me, what was the main lesson you derived from your debate with the Framers?"

She answered at once. "That they would not, or could not, take seriously themselves or their ideals." Noticing my puzzled look, she tried to explain. "The men who drafted the Constitution, however gifted or remembered as great, were politicians, not so different from the politicians of our own time and, like them, had to resolve by compromise conflicting interests in order to preserve both their fortunes and their new nation. What they saw as the requirements of that nation prevented them from substantiating their rhetoric about freedom and rights with constitutional provisions—and thus they infringed on the rights and freedom not only of the slaves, who then were one-fifth of the population, but, ultimately, of all American citizens."

"If this situation is part of the nation's basic law, how are we to reach the whites in power today and gain redress?"

"That's a hard question," said Geneva, standing, "and one even the Celestial Curia has had trouble answering. Indeed, that's why they sent me here."

"The Celestial what?"

"Curia," she said calmly, heading for the kitchen, "a sort of supreme court with more than the usual judicial power. You'll understand in the next Chronicle—the one with which my visions began. But before I start on it, let me put on some more tea."

Chapter 2

The Benefits to Whites of Civil Rights Litigation

The Chronicle of the Celestial Curia

I ARRIVED after what seemed a long but very swift journey and was ushered into a great hall, like that of an ancient temple. The walls of highly polished rosewood were pierced from floor to ceiling at regular intervals by narrow windows. A double row of intricately carved columns supported the high ceiling, on which were painted frescoes of scenes depicting humans engaged in heroic struggles. The only light came through the windows, whose stained glass cast shadows of rose, indigo, gold, and green over the expectant faces of the throngs of men and women assembled there. Those faces, I later learned, belonged to social-reform activists from all over the world. Until I recalled that people of color populate most of the earth, I wondered why there were so few Caucasians present.

Everyone was dressed in plain black robes and spoke a formal language that I was able to understand but not identify. Suddenly, just as I was about to ask why we were there, there was a fanfare from an unseen organ, and a burst of spontaneous applause from the gathering.

"All rise for the Celestial Curia," the audience said in unison as they stood. Their applause now became rhythmic, as they provided accompaniment to a hymnlike chorale they were singing. The music was as infectious as its rhythms were intricate. To my great satisfaction, I was able to join in their singing though I had never before heard either the melody or the lyrics.

I glanced toward the massive doors behind us, seemingly the only entrance to the hall, but they remained closed. Somehow, in that instant, two of three ornately carved, thronelike chairs arrayed on a dias at the front of the hall were occupied by black women dressed in robes of some rich and gleaming fabric like lamé.

When the audience—with some reluctance—brought our song to a close, the Curia Sisters welcomed us, speaking in harmonic unison, and immediately launched into a concerned discussion about the delay in a much-needed transformation of an industrial nation's social structure that, as presently organized, espouses liberty for the individual but prospers through the systematic exploitation of the lower classes, particularly those who are not white. The women of the Curia seemed to agree in their criticism of suffering and injustices being visited by the system on the exploited groups, and were appalled by the uncaring stance of the upper classes who justify their superior status by reason of their ability, merit, and skill, and ignore the role of economic class, contacts, and luck.

"How can it be," the Curia asked, "that the exploited working-class whites—lulled by a surfeit of sports, sex, and patriotic fervor—readily acquiesce in so oppressive a system? And who would expect that this white majority could find solace in the knowledge that they are of the same race as the upper-class elite who hold most of the money and power and control the police and the military forces?

"Reform is also impeded," the Curia added, "because leaders of the benighted colored peoples shun economic and political transformation, and strive instead for pseudo-liberal social-welfare programs wholly incapable of really improving the lot of the lower classes. Accepting the majority's prattle about a society of equality under the law, minority activists limit themselves to the predictably inadequate remedies available within the existing socio-economic status quo. They know, or should know, that in a society where money is fundamental, equality that does not include economic equality is not equality at all."

America was obviously the country in question. It became just as obvious that, while united in describing the country's failings, the Curia Sisters were far from agreeing on what, if any, events would bring about the long-overdue social reform that would conform the nation's policies with its often-proclaimed ideals of equality and justice for all. The Curia member seated on the left urged disruptive protest and strident resistance to the multiple injustices suffered by the people of color. The tone of her declamations was fierce and fearsome. Her sister to the right, while deploring these racial wrongs, clearly despaired of their correction. She advocated a massive exodus by the nation's colored peoples and a new beginning in some more receptive land.

Suddenly, calling me by name, the Curia summoned me to stand before them. Addressing me, they again spoke in unison: "Great power does not always bring great wisdom. You hail from this country. Your commitment to ending its injustices is known by all. We want your counsel regarding a bold plan we call the 'Conservative Crusader' which will displace the rhetoric of complaint with firm action. Even now, the plan is being transmitted to your mind and heart. Share the plan's details with those assembled here, and tell us your honest views."

As I started to protest that I did not know of any such plan, it suddenly unfurled in my mind, and I understood it clearly. The Curia's means of communication was no more shocking than the diabolical scheme they had devised.

Surely, the audience of advocates would join in my objections to this devious design. Whatever their response, I seemed to have no choice. With unmistakable firmness, the Curia urged me to begin:

Come now. Detail for all our plan today
To place the poor where now the rich hold sway.

53

I took a deep breath, and the words came almost without my volition. "The Conservative Crusader will gain appointment to the land's Highest Court, and there will wage a ceaseless campaign against the liberal orientation of its decisions. In particular, the Crusader will oppose protections that shield the poor from the worst abuses of the system. This vigorous and militantly conservative crusade will be designed to convince the upper classes and their representatives that their selfish interests can best be protected by an even greater than usual lack of concern for the plight of the working classes and the poor. Most important of all, the Crusader will further policies designed to make clear to even the most ignorant of lower-class whites that their enemy is not the blacks but those responsible for economic and social policies that maintain both poor whites and poor blacks near the bottom of our society.

"While the political stance will be conservative, the intent will be to incite radical reform by the only means possible: hardening the hearts of the upper classes against those whom they exploit, and eliminating the present social programs, which even now manage only to stave off starvation while keeping the masses too weak to recognize their true status."

The audience, far from appalled, greeted my recitation of the Conservative Crusade plan with applause—enthusiasm that the Curia shared: "The disinherited will surely be stirred by this stimulus toward revolt or reasoned Emigration." Then the Curia member on the left rose and sang a solo in a voice like that of the great gospel singer Mahalia Jackson:

> The exploited poor will not be made whole
> By liberal souls of good intent
> Ringing changes on the golden rule.
>
> Separate but equal is not the way.
> Integration is not the way.
> And begging for rights will not suffice—
> For those who would be free
> Must free themselves.

In response, the audience sang, "Oh, Curia, when will they come to know?"—a line that became a new background beat to a series of statements and responses in harmony, just as the congregations responded to the preacher in black churches when I was a child. First, the Curia Sisters would chant the beginning of a question, which the audience would then complete:

"When will they come to know ——"

"That equality cannot be obtained merely by enacting civil rights laws or winning cases in the courts?"

"When will they come to know——"

"That equality will not come through an array of social programs which serve to provide minimum relief for the needy while providing the upper classes with stability, regularity, and the poor's acceptance of the status quo?"

"When will they come to know——"

"That while protecting upper-class privilege, liberal social programs too often offer the poor food without nutrition, welfare without well-being, job training without employment opportunities, and minimal legal services without real expectations of justice?"

"When will they come to know——"

"That true reform movements are motivated by adversity not by the beneficence of do-gooders who themselves are profiting from the misfortunes of those they claim they wish to help up— but not up too far?"

The music had now reached a crescendo of emotion, and I could not help but join in. Then, after several choruses in which both Curia and audience spoke together, the Curia Sister on the left stood and, in a deep contralto, sang:

> A revolution, with neither sword nor shield,
> And wrested through law alone,
> Is no Revolution. It is mirage:
> A changing of guards under
> Orders from unchanged rulers.

In response, the soaring soprano of the Curia Sister on the right floated out over our voices in a song that was new though it seemed to arise out of the one we were singing:

> Our Revolution must be an Emigration
> From causes lost and dreams long dead.
> Unchained from the old, we can sing a new song
> In a strange land any place but here.

When the singing ended, the Celestial Curia seemed ready to move on to the many other problems before them. They beckoned me to come forward and whispered an invitation to remain for some time to consider their plan. I accepted and for a happy period enjoyed that feeling of belonging that American blacks often sense while visiting a Third World country, but seldom feel at home.

T HAT'S ALL?" I asked when, after a few minutes of silence, it was clear that Geneva was waiting for me to say something.

"For the moment," she replied, and I thought to myself how clearly she recalled the details of her so-called Chronicles, not like most people recounting a dream. "For the moment," she went on, "I would like your thoughts on what you have just heard."

"Well, it sounded very much as though the Celestial Curia was trying to recruit you to join and exceed even the most conservative members of our Supreme Court. In fact, certain legal commentators would, on hearing your Chronicle, launch an even more careful review of Chief Justice William Rehnquist's ideological motivations than those already undertaken.[1] I rather doubt, though, that he will concede, or his biographers find, more than a lifetime of conservative experience to explain his judicial outlook. Indeed, there is reason to believe he would find your Chronicle rather humorous."[2]

"I hope," Geneva responded, without smiling, "that you found more than humor in the story."

"I did! I did! Much in the Chronicle is thought-provoking, though perhaps unrealistic."

"Well, think about it," she suggested, rising, "while I brew more tea."

When she returned, Geneva spoke with an air of anxiety foreign to her usually cool and commanding demeanor. "Before I recounted my Chronicle of the Celestial Curia," she reminded me, "we were discussing the ineffectiveness of civil rights litigation. Clearly, the Celestial Curia are convinced that social justice will gain a perverse impetus through the adverse decisions handed down by a conservative and uncaring Supreme Court. Do you agree?"

"Well, Geneva," I said, trying to relieve her nervousness, "it's your Chronicle, what do you think?"

"I asked you," Geneva said sternly, "to come here to help me interpret the Chronicles and not practice your Socratic classroom techniques on me." While Geneva's appearance may have changed during her long illness, the quick temper I well remembered had survived the years intact. The difference now was that I had adopted Geneva's less praiseworthy characteristics as well as her more estimable ones, and I was unwilling to submit to her browbeating. I said as much, adding, "I know you didn't ask me to cross the country simply to reminisce about the old days or engage in bickering. Why not tell me what's all the urgency?"

Geneva raised her hand slightly in a gesture of concession. "I apologize, friend, but I earnestly need your help. Your interpretations of the Chronicles are very important, though for now I can't explain more. Please trust me."

It was hard to imagine Geneva pleading for anything. Back at the Legal Defense Fund offices, the joke was that, even when she went to court, she made "demands" rather than "pleaded" for relief. But she was clearly pleading with me now, and after so many years of illness, it seemed both humane and politic to comply with her request.

"While they did not identify the country," I began, "it appears the Curia's concern is America, and that they, like many blacks, have lost hope in racial reform through the existing democratic mechanisms, particularly the courts. The Curia have concluded that only a major disruption in the society, precipitated by some form of revolt by a coalition of minorities and working-class whites, will bring substance to the nation's long-held myth of equality.

"I agree that a conservative Supreme Court hostile to existing rights and protection would certainly bring hardship to people whose lives are now desperate, but whether this would lead to some form of revolt or simply more passive despair is another question. And, Geneva, it's not an either/or question.

"For example, Frances Fox Piven and Richard Cloward would agree with the Celestial Curia 'that the poor gain more through mass defiance and disruptive protests than by organizing for electoral politics and other more acceptable reform policies.' But Piven and Cloward, two of the most thoughtful commentators on social-reform issues, caution that it is hard to get the poor involved in protests, particularly those involving serious risk of arrest or retaliatory violence. The poor usually remain acquiescent in the hardships of their lives, conforming 'to the institutional arrangements which enmesh them, which regulate the rewards and penalties of daily life, and which appear the only possible remedy.'[3]

"In any event," I concluded, "while the Celestial Curia have impressive powers at their command, they seem to lack real understanding of America's race problem and the limited role courts can play in its solution. Let me discuss a few areas in which your Curia miss the point.

"First, the duty of the Supreme Court as well as of others who exercise power in a democratic government is, as Justice Felix Frankfurter has said, 'not to reflect inflamed public feeling but to help form its understanding.'[4] In that role, however, the Court can seldom stray far from prevailing public moods, particularly on racial issues. Race has always been a politically sensitive subject in this country. And as the Court learned from its attempt in the *Dred Scott* case (1857)[5] to 'solve' the slavery issue by both invalidating a Congressional compromise between slave-holding and free states, and finding that blacks could not be citizens under the Constitution, the Court's reputation can be harmed more easily than enhanced. So, while members of the Court may hold wildly varying views on how to decide particular racial issues, they seem unified in the task of harmonizing those decisions with their determination to preserve and protect the Court as an institution."[6]

"If that is so," Geneva inquired, "why do civil rights people place such great faith in the courts?"

"I think that the judicial role as reformer rather than regulator may be overemphasized by representatives of relatively powerless groups who, lacking either economic or political power, feel they must rely on the courts for both the correction of injustices and their elevation to equal status in the society."

"And they maintain this stance," Geneva asked in exasperation, "even when the history of civil rights law teaches that reliance on courts for so heavy a responsibility will lead to disappointment?"

"Well," I hedged, "a growing number of civil rights advocates have been forced by the trend of judicial decisions to abandon their 'we can do anything' approach to the courts so prevalent in the heady years after *Brown*. Even so, it's difficult for any civil rights lawyer, past or present, to be objective about the worth of litigation in bringing about racial reform. Because legislatures and executives were so unresponsive, we and the organizations we represented came to rely on the courts as a matter of necessity; and for a very long time, criticism of our strategies was neither welcome nor well received."

"Yes," and Geneva sighed, "I guess I can remember how I felt when I was racing around the South like some light-black knight trying to save the poor defenseless cullid folk from segregationist dragons. Nobody could tell me I was not performing a wonderful work."

"Exactly. I can almost guarantee that the Curia's suggestion that Justice Rehnquist is secretly pursuing egalitarian ends with conservative means would be accepted by him with better grace than some civil rights proponents would accept the Curia's implication that their litigation efforts do more harm than good.

"You know, Geneva, there was a time when criticism of the Supreme Court which went beyond disagreement with individual decisions was deemed serious heresy by civil rights groups. It happened after your accident, but I must tell you that differences of precisely this character led to the resignation of the NAACP's legal staff back in the late 1960s."[7]

"What happened?" asked Geneva.

"A young NAACP staff attorney, Lewis M. Steel, published without prior approval a criticism of the Supreme Court's decisions during the fifteen years when Chief Justice Earl Warren presided over the Court. In his article, Steel argued that the Court's decisions were primarily intended to meet the needs of the white community rather than those of blacks. For example, in criticizing the Court's vague mandate requiring the elimination of segregated schools with 'all deliberate speed,'[8] Steel wrote—and I have his article here so I can quote it exactly:

> Never in the history of the Supreme Court had the implementation of a constitutional right been so delayed or the creation of it put in such vague terms. The Court thereby made clear that it was a white court which would protect the interests of white America in the maintenance of stable institutions.
>
> In essence, the Court considered the potential damage to white Americans resulting from the diminution of privilege as more critical than continued damage to the underprivileged. . . . Worse still, it gave the primary responsibility for achieving educational equality to those who had established the segregated institutions.[9]

"Coming as it did during the height of the civil rights movement, this was too much for the NAACP. As it happened, the organization's national board had a meeting scheduled on the day after the article appeared. The matter was discussed and Steel was summarily fired.[10] General Counsel Robert Carter and the rest of the legal staff resigned when the board adamantly refused to offer Steel a hearing.[11] Some months later, the NAACP published a brochure, 'The Issues in the Lewis M. Steel Case,' explaining that Steel was fired not because he criticized the Court for not moving fast enough or not doing enough, but because he charged that the organization's court victories 'have been merely symbolic and not substantive.' 'It was thus,' the essay concluded, 'a reflection upon the NAACP and a rejection of its many victories in civil rights cases in the courts, including the United States Supreme Court.' "[12]

"That was regrettable," Geneva acknowledged, "but it was also a long time ago. Surely the civil rights community must now understand and accept the limits on the Court's role in bringing about racial reform."

"They do to a certain extent, but I think there is a continued faith in the courts that is jarred by criticism. Several liberal scholars, on the other hand, might agree with the Curia's assessment. For example, Professor Arthur S. Miller's articles have reached conclusions quite like those that cost Lewis Steel his job. In Professor Miller's view, 'the Supreme Court before Warren was mainly concerned with the protection of the established property interests; under Warren, the High Bench, by moving to protect many of the poor and disadvantaged, also helped those highest in the social pecking order.'[13]

"Professor Miller might agree with the diagnosis offered by the Celestial Curia, though he would probably disagree with their prescription for a cure. He, like Lewis Steel, maintains that the civil rights decisions of the Warren Court were profoundly conservative and protected the economic and political status quo by responding to the pleas for justice by blacks and other severely disadvantaged groups just enough to siphon off discontent, thereby limiting the chances that the existing social order would pay more than minimal costs for the reforms achieved."

"A strange dichotomy," Geneva mused. "Civil rights people argue strenuously that the relief they seek will help the nation prevail in war or other crisis, but later forget and almost resent the implication that their hard-earned victory was likely brought about by outside events or strongly influenced by the perception that relief for blacks would serve interests of identifiable classes of whites."

I agreed. "I often cite the NAACP and government briefs in the *Brown* case, both of which maintain that abandonment of state-supported segregation would be a crucial asset as we compete with Communist countries for the hearts and minds of Third World people just emerging from long years of colonialism.[14] As far as I'm concerned, the Court's decision in the *Brown* case cannot be understood without considering the decision's value to whites in policy-making positions who are able to recognize the economic and political benefits at home and abroad that would follow abandonment of state-mandated racial segregation.

"Other civil rights advocates have seen the tie between our rights and the nation's foreign policy posture. As far back as 1945, NAACP lawyers William Hastie, Thurgood Marshall, and Leon Ransom argued that it would be unconscionable to allow segregation in interstate travel facilities after the end of a world war in which all of the people of the United States were joined 'in a death struggle against the apostles of racism.'[15]

"Our lawyers, though, tend to view such arguments as enhancements of rights based on the Constitution. They are reluctant to believe that vindication of even the most basic rights for blacks actually requires a perceived benefit to whites. And that's why Dr. DuBois didn't endear himself to civil rights advocates when, years after the *Brown* decision, he observed that 'no such decision would have been possible without the world pressure of communism,' which he felt rendered it 'simply impossible for the United States to continue to lead a "Free World" with race segregation kept legal over a third of its territory.'"[16]

Geneva had heard enough to interrupt and make sure she understood my point. "Would civil rights lawyers today not agree in any respect with the Curia's plan?" she asked.

"They would certainly concede that the disruption that might follow a loss of faith in the law is one way (though a dangerous one) to bring about change. It is, after all, how this country gained its independence. And when blacks rise up in some form of direct action, civil rights lawyers support those efforts—as was shown during the sit-in protests of the 1960s.[17] But lawyers representing a long-subordinated group of relatively powerless black people, in a country supposedly committed to justice under law, would not seem to be following an unreasonable course in continuing their reliance on the courts that have given them many important victories over the years.[18]

"Now I know you want to move on with the discussion, but a last story should explain just how disillusioned some of us have become. A few years ago, our best-known legal advocate, Justice Thurgood Marshall, returned to his alma mater, Howard University, to speak at some special occasion. Eschewing the usual homilies of hope, he spoke frankly and bitterly of what he and his fellow civil rights lawyers had failed to achieve:

> Today we have reached the point where people say, "We've come a long way." But so have other people come a long way. . . . Has the gap gotten smaller? It's getting bigger. . . . People say we are better off today. Better than what?
> I am amazed at people who say that, "the poorest Negro kid in the South is better off than the kid in South Africa." So what! We are not in South Africa. We are here. [People tell me] "You ought to go around the country and show yourself to Negroes; and give them inspiration." For what? Negro kids are not fools. They know when you tell them there is a possibility that someday you'll have a chance to be the o-n-l-y Negro on the Supreme Court, those odds aren't too good."[19]

"It seems to me," Geneva remarked, "that all you have said adds to rather than detracts from the Curia's view that further progress will come through tactics other than litigation."

"No, I do not go that far, but as a law teacher I've had the luxury denied most civil rights activists to examine the legal precedents, and there is no doubt in my mind that reforms resulting from civil rights litigation invariably promote the interests of the white majority."

"The classic example of that truth," suggested Geneva, "is the Fourteenth Amendment. Although it was enacted to give blacks the rights of citizens, for most of its early history it was utilized, as Professor Boris Bittker put it so well, to nurture 'railroads, utility companies, banks, employers of child labor, chain stores, money lenders, aliens, and a host of other groups and institutions . . . , leaving so little room for the Negro that he seemed to be the fourteenth amendment's forgotten man.' "[20]

"It is a truth," I conceded, "that most people would rather not remember, but the Fourteenth Amendment's due-process protection of 'liberty of contract' rights has proven of far greater value to corporations—to cite only one example—than to black people.

"While not going as far as those of us who claim the society benefits more from our victories than black people do, Paul Freund observed years ago that 'the frontiers of the law have been pushed back by the civil rights movement in many sectors that are far broader than the interests of the movement itself.'[21] Professor Freund cited the impact of several decisions: *New York Times* v. *Sullivan* (1964), which held that the defamation of a public official is not actionable unless the statement is published maliciously, with knowledge of its falsity, or with reckless disregard of its truth or untruth;[22] *NAACP* v. *Button* (1963), proclaiming that group representation of potential litigants in desegregation cases is constitutionally protected speech and association, not subject to attack by state bar rules;[23] and *Shelley* v. *Kraemer* (1948), finding unlawful 'state action' in the judicial enforcement of privately made, racially restrictive land covenants."[24]

"Well," Geneva said, "though not a law teacher, even I know that Professor Freund might have extended his list to include other civil rights precedents, including *Dixon* v. *Alabama State Board of Education* (1961), establishing a constitutional right of due process for students facing summary disciplinary action at state colleges.[25] In that case, the Court reversed the summary expulsion of black college students who had protested segregated public facilities. Then in the voting area, we cannot forget *Smith* v. *Allwright* (1944), one of the long series of civil rights challenges to the white primary.[26] This litigation made clear the need for oversight by the federal judiciary in the election process to ensure constitutional rights for blacks and whites alike."[27]

"Speaking of federal oversight," I observed, "all criminal defendants have gained from the century-long effort blacks have made to eliminate racial discrimination from the jury box."[28]

"That is true," Geneva admitted, "but the effort to make the right to a nonbiased jury more than silly symbolism will not be won as long as prosecutors can use their peremptory challenges to rid juries of prospective black jurors—a practice at least acquiesced in by the Court until quite recently."[29]

"Wait!" I said. "We shouldn't omit *NAACP* v. *Alabama* (1958), in which the Court responded to Alabama's effort to intimidate NAACP members and found that the state cannot use its power to control domestic corporations to interfere with First Amendment rights to 'engage in association for the advancement of beliefs and ideas . . .';[30] and, of course, *Gomillion* v. *Lightfoot* (1960), where for the first time the Court found it appropriate to apply constitutional standards to the apportionment of districts for elections.[31]

"Actually, that subject is worthy of a lengthier discussion, but let me mention first Professor Robert Cover's conclusion that 'although the Court had never treated them as race cases, there can be little doubt that decisions . . . made in *Moore* v. *Dempsey* [1923],[32] overturning the mob-dominated conviction of a black man on due process grounds; *Powell* v. *Alabama* [1932],[33] where the Court for the first time found a limited right to counsel essential to due process in capital cases; and *Brown* v. *Mississippi* [1936],[34] reversing as violative of the due process clause a state conviction based on a confession resulting from "physical brutality," all made new criminal procedure law in part because the notorious facts of each case exemplified the national scandal of racist southern justice.' "[35]

"Getting back to *Gomillion* v. *Lightfoot*, the *Tuskegee* voting case," said Geneva, "I seem to recall that it was one of NAACP general counsel Robert L. Carter's greatest Court victories. Since it is close to the definitive illustration of what we are talking about, I would hope that a review of what we civil rights lawyers did there, and how the precedent has been used subsequently, should bring you around to the Curia's view on the value of trying to obtain favorable race decisions in the courts."

"Geneva," I said, more testily than I had intended, "I see no reason to support the Curia's crazy plan just because I agree that *Gomillion* has become, as you predicted years ago, an excellent example of a civil rights case that helped increase substantially judicial involvement in electoral politics. Keep in mind, though, that the state's effort to frustrate black voters, by changing the town's boundaries from a square to what the Court found to be a 'strangely irregular twenty-eight-sided figure,'[36] was sufficiently shocking to gain relief from even the most conservative court.

"And don't forget that Justice Frankfurter tried his best to limit the *Gomillion* case to its extraordinary facts, carefully basing relief on a finding that the Alabama gerrymander had violated the Fifteenth Amendment rights of blacks to vote. His continuing opposition to judicial intervention in reapportionment cases did not change.[37] And he later dissented from the Court's change of view on the issue in *Baker* v. *Carr* (1962),[38] the case that set the stage for the 'one person, one vote' cases that made suffrage a fundamental right and recognized that the right could be denied both by unequally apportioned districts or by a 'debasement or dilution of the weight of a citizen's vote.'[39]

"Of course, in *Baker*," I admitted, "the Court majority did not actually rely on *Gomillion*, but Justice Tom Clark in concurring found 'the apportionment picture in Tennessee is a topsy-turvical of gigantic proportions'—and, moreover, that the majority of the people of Tennessee had no 'practical opportunities for exerting their political weight at the polls' to correct the existing 'invidious discrimination.'[40]

"In subsequent cases, the Court found similarly indefensible gerrymandering in other states.[41] Reapportionment suits from virtually every state led to the major precedent in *Reynolds* v. *Sims* (1964), where Chief Justice Earl Warren wrote that, despite 'political thickets' and 'mathematical quagmires,' the Court was required by 'our oath and our office' to hear cases in which constitutionally protected rights were denied."[42]

"I have not been able to catch up on all the reapportionment decisions," Geneva said, "but while the value of judicial oversight has been great, I gather that it has been as thorny an experience as the Court feared. With the computer becoming an increasingly useful tool, the courts are now being asked to determine the validity of district lines that are no less gerrymandered because they hardly deviate from pure equality."[43]

"Yes, Justice Frankfurter's warning that apportionment cases are a 'political thicket' the judiciary should avoid has returned to harass if not to haunt the current Court. And you won't be surprised to learn that, to complete the circle of protection provided blacks against racial gerrymanders in the *Gomillion* case, the Court has now agreed that purely political gerrymandering can be challenged in courts as violative of equal protection."[44]

"That is all well and good," Geneva observed, "but, while the Court is fine-tuning standards in the political gerrymandering cases, blacks whose litigation efforts in the voting field sparked the reapportionment revolution are still trying to beat back both simpleminded and sophisticated schemes designed either to keep them from voting or to dilute the impact of their vote below the minimum needed to elect anyone who will advocate their interests and be responsive to their needs."

"The two sets of cases have followed divergent paths as to proof," I explained. "In the reapportionment cases, the Court decided that the Constitution prohibited any substantial variation from equality among districts in drawing district lines—without regard to legislative intent or motivation."[45]

"Big deal!" Geneva scoffed. "The Court militantly insists on almost mathematical equality in weighing the validity of apportionment plans, while ignoring the fact that much of this legislative districting, supposedly undertaken to meet the 'one person, one vote' standard, is actually used to dilute black voting power by carving up the neighborhoods of racial minorities and placing them in majority white election districts."[46]

"A few cases," I responded in the Court's defense, "did suggest that the right of suffrage would prohibit at-large or multimember voting schemes; that is, those plans where all voters in a legislative district are able to vote for each candidate seeking office in that district, where—'designedly or otherwise'—such districts operate 'to minimize or cancel out the voting strength of racial or political elements of the voting population.' "[47] Unfortunately, as the voting rights case law developed, the Court concluded that, in attacking at-large district schemes that diluted black votes—the technique that had supplanted the white primary as the favorite means of discriminating against black voters[48]—civil rights litigants must prove that the legislature adopted or maintained at-large or multimember districts with the intention of diluting the value of minority votes."[49]

"One would think," Geneva suggested, "that if a state could deny the right of suffrage either by reapportioning a district or by establishing at-large districts, both dilution schemes should be subject to the same effect-oriented standard of proof."

"Think about it, Geneva! There is a distinction. The Court found that unequally apportioned electoral districts were in complete conflict with a meaningful right to vote. Requiring legislatures to draw district boundaries that aim for mathematical equality of voters was deemed a benefit to all and a harm to none. But at-large and multimember districts, while sometimes serving as vehicles of discrimination, can also serve legitimate functions. And single-member districts, the alternative to the at-large approach, are not a perfect remedy. Such districts are susceptible to gerrymandering. Lines drawn to favor some blacks, for example, can lead to charges of discrimination by other blacks[50] or by other ethnic groups."[51]

Geneva was unimpressed. "I see the distinction, but I also know that all too often the legitimate potential of at-large plans serves as a convenient shield for discriminatory intent. If plaintiffs have the burden of proving that intent, the task can be almost impossible."

"Not quite impossible. The Court has ruled for plaintiffs in a few cases.[52] But, yes, the task is very difficult."

"Does the Voting Rights Act help at all?" Geneva asked.

"One would have hoped so, but a plurality of the Court held, in *City of Mobile* v. *Bolden* (1980),[53] that proof of discriminatory intent was required to invalidate at-large election plans, whether the suit was brought under the Fourteenth and Fifteenth amendments or under the Voting Rights Act. Congress finally interceded and enacted amendments to the Voting Rights Act in 1982[54] to restore the pre-*Bolden* effects tests for proving discriminatory intent.[55] Even though the Justice Department argued that the amendments require proof of purposeful intent,[56] the Supreme Court upheld the new provisions."[57]

"And while the interpretation battles go on and on," said Geneva impatiently, "black voters face discrimination hurdles while trying to exercise the most basic right in the Constitution. The hard-to-meet intent requirements serve to insulate black vote–dilution schemes that would be struck down under the 'one person, one vote' rubric were they challenged in reapportionment suits."

"True," I conceded, "but the 1982 amendments have encouraged civil rights lawyers to continue their voting rights litigation, and the Court has remained responsive to voting complaints."[58]

"Well, friend, I am impressed with your review of the cases in the voting rights area, but the overall results of all this activity seem mainly to have sparked more opposition to the meaningful participation of black people in the election process. To my mind," she added, with more than a touch of acid in her voice, "the voting rights cases prove to a shocking degree that litigation—while perhaps a guaranteed employment program for lawyers—is a never-ending detour for blacks, at least for those seeking protection of their own rights as opposed to their lawyers seeking new and more exciting cases."

"That's a low blow!" I protested. "Why do black women transfer to their men hostility that should be hurled at the real culprit—society's racism? Moreover, I didn't come here to have my evaluation of the cases measured by some otherworldly standard of yours!"

"Now wait a minute," Geneva admonished, her own voice rising. "In the first place, you are not my man, and I resent your generalizations about black women. And, in the second place, I am upset not with your review of the precedents but with your sense that you have to defend them or at least defend civil rights lawyers' continued reliance on a freedom train that has run out of steam."

"I'm discussing, not defending."

"Wrong! You are defending, and I hear you also admitting that civil rights litigation, although no longer a primary weapon, is necessary 'busy work,' occupying those who feel that 'something should be done' even if it is not particularly helpful and may be a harmful delusion. Why cannot you simply concede that my conclusion is the correct one?"

"Sure, Geneva, litigation may be a leaky boat whose engine has run out of gas—to change metaphorical vehicles—but one can still paddle through treacherous waters. It's prudent to be aware of all of the boat's defects, making adjustments for them, even trying to fix a few of them as time permits. But it is not prudent to abandon the boat, particularly if you can't swim to shore."

"And what do you do, Mr. Prudent Man, when you look ahead and see that your leaky boat is heading toward the falls?"

"I stay with that boat, Geneva, unless and until a better option presents itself. Swimming is not an option for the nonswimmer. And talk of revolution makes for bravura rhetoric but is no more realistic or, I think, necessary for black Americans today than it was back in the 1930s when the NAACP's executive secretary James Weldon Johnson rejected it in favor of a strategy of 'creative disorder.'[59] A pragmatist, Johnson viewed violence in self-defense as an obligation, but urged blacks to eschew violence not on any moral or pacific grounds but because it would be futile. Now, Geneva, tell me what has changed since the 1930s that leads you to a different conclusion from Johnson's when he said: 'We would be justified in taking up arms or anything we could lay hands on and fighting for the common rights we are entitled to and denied, if we had a chance to win. But I know and we all know there is not a chance.' "[60]

"That," Geneva said, "is exactly my point. There has been less change than either of us would like because there has been too little creative protest, and too much focus on changing laws that are the products of racism, not its cause. I do not like the idea of blood being shed any more than Mr. Johnson did, or than you do, or do most black people for that matter. But does the alternative to litigation have to be violent revolution?"

"Several movements in this country have achieved major change by direct, nonviolent activity. And, Geneva, as I said before, lawyers have played important roles in direct-action campaigns. It was strong legal defense efforts that limited the risk of protestors being sentenced to long prison terms under laws that violated constitutional rights."

"Fine, but the question remains. How long do you expect our people will be dependent on the leaky boat of litigation? Surely, it keeps us afloat, but its deficiencies are obvious even to you. How long should we be kept, by continued reliance on litigation, from attacking the real causes of our subordinate status?"

"A typically militant statement, Geneva, but until you come up with a more effective technique, I guess I'll stay with litigation—along with, I might add, most other civil rights lawyers I know."

"Well," she said after a long moment's silence, "now that we have gotten that out of our systems, let me make sure I understand your position on the voting rights cases. As a starting point, I assume you agree with the statement that 'as a constitutional rule, the principle of one person, one vote actually is derived from cases decided under the fifteenth amendment, the explicit purpose of which is to protect against the abridgement of racial minorities' voting rights.'"[61]

I nodded.

"Then would you also agree with the statement that 'any evidentiary standard in racial vote dilution cases demanding a greater quantum of proof than that required to challenge population malapportionment works an intolerable inversion of constitutional and historical priorities'?"[62]

"I do also agree with that statement, Geneva, but I've never said the courts are always fair, or legal principles are always construed in our favor. But there's a world of difference between admitting that litigation is hard, uncertain, and frustrating, and concluding, as you do, that it's an impossible approach. The Court today has difficulty handling civil rights cases in which allegations of discrimination are not accompanied by proof of actual intent.

71

The Court has a real fear that, if blacks could successfully challenge the validity of government policies by simply proving that they burdened or were less fair to blacks than to whites, then— through the use of such a disparate-impact test—'they would raise serious questions about, and perhaps invalidate, a whole range of tax, welfare, public service, regulatory, and licensing statutes.'[63]

"Our challenge, Geneva, as lawyers and legal scholars is to move the Court beyond its current reluctance to redress racial harm in the absence of discriminatory intent—a difficult task, I admit, particularly because intuitively I feel that proof standards like intent and motivation are used by courts to conceal other concerns."

Geneva was on her feet, her arms raised high in mock supplication for heavenly strength. "It's not just a matter of feeling, friend. It's history! From the very beginning of this nation, blacks have been the exploited, the excluded, and often the exterminated in this society. For most of that time, racial policies were blatant, vicious, and horribly damaging, leaving most of us in a subordinate status when compared with all but the lowest whites. And now that the Court has, as a result of our ceaseless petitions, been forced to find that overt discrimination is unconstitutional, we are for all intents and purposes still maintained in a subordinate state by the so-called neutral policies of a still-racist society because— for God's sake—we are not white! Though I have been out of things during much of two decades, I can see the hypocrisy here. Why can't you?"

"It's not a matter of seeing," I said, trying to remain calm, "but of doing something about it. Civil rights lawyers do not have the power of your Celestial Curia. We're simply trying to do what we can in the courts and in the country to make white people understand that blacks continue to face discrimination based on their race, despite the legal advances of the last few decades. You and I know that this country's people of color—blacks, Hispanics, Asians, Native Americans—have given more and received less than whites and yet, for the most part, have, as Harlem's Congressman-preacher Adam Clayton Powell used to admonish us, 'kept the faith.' We want nothing more than our rightful share of opportunities long available to whites."

"An old sermon," Geneva interrupted, "and it seems always to fall on deaf ears. It is simply too comforting for many white people to ignore the facts, to hearken to their fears, and say with real belief that blacks are demanding privileges they have not earned to remedy injustices they have not suffered. And under the steady reiteration of the marvels of 'freedom' and 'equality,' whites not only become anesthetized to the injustices blacks suffer, but also are rendered incapable of comprehending the fact that, as the historian David Brion Davis put it, 'Americans bought their independence with slave labor' and then have systematically denied blacks both freedom and equality."[64]

"Well, while you'll find more understanding in today's society than you got from the Framers, the real history of slavery is certainly not on the nation's educational agenda."

"In other words, less has changed in racial attitudes than meets the eye?"

"No, Geneva. Much has changed. But a great many whites view black claims for justice in the voting area as elsewhere as unjustified bellyaching, and secretly harbor a deep-seated belief that the real cause of the blacks' plight is the inferiority of the black race."

"You spoke a moment ago of the Celestial Curia's power. Tell me, friend, if you had such superhuman power, what would you do to gain for blacks a fair shake in the electoral process?"

"To be honest, the devices used to prevent blacks from voting are effective because many black people are so low on the socio-economic scale that they see no value in voting. Whites are still the majority in most electoral districts and have the economic power in virtually every area. This is a majoritarian system, and, as you well described, whites tend to oppose those policies that blacks support."

"*You* describe the problem well," Geneva remarked, "but I ask for your solution."

"I'm not sure I see a solution other than to keep on chipping away at the dilution and other anti-black-vote schemes as they surface, to work on getting blacks to register and vote, and to hope that our efforts will move the next generation beyond our own."

Geneva shook her head sadly. "Must we transform the world to save ourselves? You confuse our freedom campaign with a religious crusade in which you are the proverbial Job of the civil rights movement. You suffer and seek relief in the suffering itself. I don't mean that as a criticism, but your suffering, while real, is on a very different and less harsh level than that endured by the black masses whose numbers are rapidly increasing. I doubt that many of them would subscribe to your stoicism."

"Maybe," I said, "I should ask you the question you posed for me. Short of waving a wand and eliminating racism, how would you exercise the power, for example, to obtain a law that would provide blacks with meaningful voting rights—rights not simply to walk into a booth and vote without harassment, but to get blacks and others supporting their interests into elective offices, from the bottom to the top?"

Geneva smiled. "You must be reading my mind. You've just given a pretty good description of my next Chronicle: the Chronicle of the Ultimate Voting Rights Act. Are you ready?"

"I am ready for at least a good story."

Chapter 3

The Racial Limitation
on Black Voting Power

The Chronicle of the Ultimate Voting Rights Act

THE Senator's black Mark VII Lincoln, coming too fast, failed to negotiate the curve and careened, out of control, onto the narrow two-lane bridge, hit the raised median divider, bounced across the opposite lane, and crashed through the bridge's steel railing without slowing down. The motor roared as the car plunged into the water. A spectacular splash and the car quickly sank from sight.

In one of those coincidences that confound fiction, a local news team was stationed above the bridge to film the Senator's triumphant return from a statewide speaking tour. The most powerful politician in this Southern state's history, and by all accounts the most racist, the Senator was a key sponsor of a controversial bill intended to reapportion the state's legislative districts. The redistricting scheme, while meeting legal standards, would make it virtually impossible for blacks to gain election to the state legislature or any statewide office. In fact, at the time of his auto accident, the Senator was rushing back to the state capital where he was to address the legislature on the eve of their vote on his measure.

Just as the Senator's car sank, the television cameras turned from the widening circles in the otherwise lazy river to the bridge's edge, to the break in the railing made by the Senator's car, to—surprisingly—the figure of a tall black woman. As the cameras focused on her, she raised her arms and dived in a long, graceful arch that experts later asserted would have rated 8 or 9 in competition. She disappeared for almost thirty heart-stopping seconds. When at last she surfaced, first the few eyewitnesses and later the whole nation thrilled to see that she had a very water-logged Senator in tow, heading for the shore.

I, Geneva Crenshaw, was the soon-to-be heroine. Explaining why I did it would be more difficult than the rescue itself. I had been driving to an NAACP meeting in a rural town and had had no intention of saving anyone, particularly not a politician who had built his career by tormenting black people. But when I was a young girl, I often daydreamed about rescuing from grave danger a person who would lift up the black race. When that big sedan swerved across the road in front of me and went through the rail, those dreams all flooded back, totally captured my thinking, and literally shouted at me: "This is your chance! This is your chance! This is your chance!"

It was hypnotic. Before I knew what I was doing, I had stopped and was out of my car and sprinting to the break in the bridge railing. Kicking off my shoes, I gauged the distance from the bridge to the river below. Then I jumped.

Actually, I only thought I jumped; the video cameras showed me pushing off from the bridge into what became a swan dive. I do not remember the dive, but the cold water was a shock. Fortunately, the car was right side up and only about ten feet or so below the surface. The doors had come open on impact. Somehow, I hit the water, found the car, and dragged the one occupant to the surface almost automatically. I remember realizing that I was not strong enough to haul him to shore, but then others who saw the accident were scrambling down the riverbank and swimming out to help me.

At first I was too disoriented to understand the significance of the person I had rescued. As I stood, in my sopping dress, shivering from cold and shock, everyone's attention was focused on efforts to revive the Senator. Finally, one of the paramedics handed me a blanket and hot coffee, and told me to sit down. Accepting the blanket and drink, I ignored the advice and tried to make my way back up the riverbank to my car. By then, though, the news people were everywhere and were not about to permit a Lone Ranger tactic to rob them of a good story. When they learned who I was, their main question couched in various guises was, as one reporter bluntly put it: "Would you have gone in and saved him if you had known who he was?"

I gave the reporter the hardest look I could muster, and said, "A human life is a terrible thing to waste." I refused to make any other comment and steadfastly turned down all subsequent invitations to be interviewed by the national television news programs. It made little difference. What they could not get firsthand, they manufactured by means of that wonderful journalistic tool—conjecture.

Within twenty-four hours, most of the country's television viewers had seen the dramatic rescue sequences countless times in close-ups and in slow motion. Tabloid editors, denied the visual drama of the films, tried to compensate with lurid headlines:

BLACK WOMAN SAVES A LIFE, DOOMS HER RACE

BLACK WOMAN WINS THANKS OF WHITE RACISTS

LAWYER LEAPS TO AID OF FALLEN FOE

Media columnists and editorial writers stretched reality to the breaking point to find connections between the always-salable news of an exciting rescue and the growing national interest in the heightened racial tensions in the state as civil rights groups resisted conservative efforts to neutralize the increasingly influential black vote.

The national sympathy and support blacks had generated in the voting rights campaigns of the 1960s had evaporated, and beyond the civil rights community's opposition, there was little public protest against the state's increasingly blatant efforts to dilute black voting power. Even so, the media seemed to feel some need to transform my action into a symbolic statement about the faithful black people who return good for even the most vicious racial evils. Forgotten was the fact that, at the time, I had had no idea whom I was saving. I was a model of behavior that one editorial writer and commentator after another suggested, not very subtly, might well be emulated by all black people "during this tense time of transition." I was helpless to counteract this updated version of the loyal slave/servant routine and determined not to make matters worse by accepting any of the rewards offered me for "doing the right thing."

Why, I wondered, do whites so readily visit on blacks the worst possible motives for actions that may have been well intended despite what whites may have deserved? The fact that I had saved a man committed to emulating the worst characteristics of every race-baiting politician of the last century did not make me less grateful that I had been able to rescue a human being from almost certain death by drowning.

And while, as expected, I had to grin and bear a range of sarcastic comments, that is how the black community viewed it.

"Come on, Sister Geneva," a woman said the day after the accident, at the beauty parlor where I had taken refuge from the constant phone calls. "That sure was quite a dive you made to save that S.O.B!"

"Well," I said, as women in the other booths joined in the friendly chiding, "I did not want the Senator to get out of paying for all his sins by drowning himself. The Lord probably has an appropriate reward waiting for him."

"Right!" the woman said, still smiling. "And the Lord might have been putting His plan into effect when you butted in."

Everyone laughed, including my friend Faith Ann Courage, who stays so involved in her race work, as she calls it, that she seldom sees the humor in anything even remotely touching on the subject. Actually, I had come to the state in response to Faith Ann's urgent call. For years, the Senator had been her major antagonist as she worked to make black voters a meaningful political force in the state.

"You know," Faith Ann said thoughtfully, "the Senator is probably more than a little ambivalent about Geneva saving him from drowning. On the one hand, he's still alive, but on the other, he's going to have a hard time preaching the inherent worthlessness of a people one of whom the whole country watched save his life at the risk of her own."

"Maybe," I replied, "but the media is pitching the rescue as a morality play whose message is that black people should protect and save whites no matter how vicious they are."

"What else would you expect?" Faith Ann said with disdain. "But that antebellum propaganda doesn't fool anyone nowadays. Had the Senator died in the crash, his legislation would have passed overwhelmingly as a memorial to him. But as things stand, he may have difficulty holding his racist support. So, when you saved the Senator, you may have rescued us after all. The question is what should we do now?"

"Watch out, white folks!" one of the beauticians said, unwilling to see the mirth go out of the conversation. "Sister Faith Ann is plotting again."

Faith Ann did not crack a smile. "We will beat them," she said, "if we're not too afraid to be serious at least some of the time."

The hush that followed her comment was not caused by it. Faith Ann's total seriousness was viewed as an acceptable fault by those who knew her. Rather, a young, well-dressed white man had entered, and all turned suspiciously on the intruder, who had arrived in a black limousine now visible in the shop's big front window.

"Yes?" the shop owner asked the visitor, who looked as though he feared he would be devoured on the spot.

"I work," he stammered, "in the Senator's office. He is very anxious to see Lawyer Crenshaw and asked me to bring her to the hospital."

I hesitated. Faith Ann did not. "You better go and see what he wants. And," she said only half in jest, "tell him if he feels the need to express his thanks, we would be much obliged if he would support our ultimate voting rights proposal."

That suggestion broke the tension, and everyone in the beauty shop burst into laughter. Even the Senator's aide managed a wan grin. For years, Faith Ann had been advocating a plan that would guarantee blacks a percentage of elective offices in the state equal to their percentage of the population. No one took her seriously. As one community comic had told her, "Forget it, Faith Ann. Seeking proportional representation in this state where black folk are barely able to vote is like asking the leader of a lynch mob to let you sleep with his mama. It ain't goin' to happen."

As I was soon to learn, the Senator did not agree. When I was ushered into his palatial hospital room, he went pale. Then with a nervous gesture, he dismissed nurses, secretaries, and hangers-on, but never took his eyes off me. Dressed in pajamas and an expensive robe, his head wrapped in bandages, he was reclining on a large chaise lounge. He did not look at all well.

Only after the room was empty did he ease himself to his feet and extend his hand and mutter, "Thank you." Then he motioned at a chair and rather painfully returned to his seat. I sat down, and we both looked at one another. He had barely spoken, and I certainly was not going to say anything. This was *his* meeting.

"Who are you and what do you want from me?" he asked. The plaintiveness in his voice was completely foreign to his character.

"You know who I am, Senator," I responded quietly.

My calm seemed to agitate him. "Please," he pleaded, for likely the first time in his life to anyone, white or black, "I know your name, but who the hell are you really?"

I stared at him, puzzled. Perhaps the concussion he suffered was more serious than the media had been told.

The Senator shook his head. Still watching me, he said slowly, "I have driven that road a thousand times at high speed and never even came close to missing that bridge turn. Know it like my own driveway. Yesterday, suddenly," he pointed at me accusingly, "I couldn't see the road because your face filled my window."

I looked at him, amazed. "Are you feeling well, Senator?"

He ignored my question. "And as my car sank to the bottom, I could see you dressed in a radiant gold gown and repeating over and over in a voice that I could hear even under water, 'This is your chance! This is your chance! This is your chance!' "

I tried not to allow my shock to show. There were powers at work in this incident beyond the control of either of us. For a long time, the Senator said nothing. Then he almost whispered, "Lawyer Crenshaw, I'm a politician. It's my business to know how people will react in any given situation. My accident was not an accident, and your rescue was not a normal reaction either. Nothing in the Good Samaritan rule requires a passing motorist—and a woman at that!—to jump off a damn bridge to save someone she's never seen before."

"Senator," I replied, "what happened just happened. Why don't we both just forget it? Soon the media and your constituents will tire of the subject and go on to something else."

"I wish it was that easy, girl," the Senator's manners had deserted him, "but I don't think whatever caused me to run off the road'll let me just forget it. All last night, and even as I talk, a voice that sounds like yours is pounding in my head repeating over and over, 'This is your chance! This is your chance!' Meantime, every dirty trick I've ever played on black people keeps coming back. When you spoke just now, the voice in my head stopped for the first time since the crash. I'm convinced you folks have mastered some new technology that's causing my harassment, and I'm ready to make a deal. Just tell me what you want."

If ever a man was speaking honestly, he was. But his reputation made sympathy hard, trust impossible. "There is no technology, Senator. Surely, you did not bring me here to rescue you from voices."

Whatever scheme he had in mind, the look of desperation on his face seemed genuine. "Lawyer Crenshaw," he began again, his manners returning, "Mamie, the black lady who raised me, often used to warn me that 'the Lord don't like ugly.' The public thinks my losing control of my automobile was an accident, and your rescue is seen as a heroic act. Only you and I know what really happened. If all of this is not some electronic trickery, is the Lord trying to tell me old Mamie was right?"

"Well, Senator," I replied, mustering all my courtesy and control, "I can't speak for your Mamie, but the black people in this state would say that you waited a long time to get sensitive to what the Lord does and does not like."

It was likely the most direct statement anyone had made to him since he left Mamie. It was clear he did not like it. His face got some color in it for the first time, and he leaned forward, saying, "I don't need a lecture about my political career. I did what thousands of other politicians, North as well as South, have done to get ahead. White people are the majority in this country, and they basically distrust blacks, always have, likely always will. All I've done, like governors George Wallace of Alabama and Orval Faubus of Arkansas, and Mississippi senators James Eastland and Theodore Bilbo, is build on how white people feel about your race."

He caught himself, took a deep breath, and continued more calmly. "It's nothing personal against your people. Fact is, I developed my speaking style listening to records of black preachers. Figured if the Beatles and all those white groups could get rich singing like they was black, I could do the same with my stump speeches. Worked pretty well if I do say so myself."

"Senator," I interrupted, "I am fully aware of the secrets of your political success. I came to North Carolina to try and stop your latest anti–voting rights scheme, and should be out working on it right now unless you have something else you want to say."

"Lawyer," he said angrily, "I told you why I brought you here. Your damned voice is blasting through my head. I want it to stop, and I believe you know what I must do to get some quiet."

It was then that I remembered Faith Ann's perception of my rescue as an opportunity rather than another burden for black people.

He noticed the hint of a smile on my face. "I'm not surprised that you take pleasure in seeing me like this, but your people will get scant benefit from my downfall. There's a long line of others ready to take my place using the same 'nigger-baiting' techniques."

"I am sure you are right, Senator. I was thinking about a black-vote organizer, Faith Ann Courage, who predicted my saving you would create a serious obstacle to your political aims."

"That woman is one helluva fighter. If even one-tenth of your people fought as hard as she does, we whites couldn't get away with what we do to you, that's for sure."

"Perhaps, but you don't know Faith Ann. If one-tenth of blacks were like her, most of us might have been killed by whites who could not stand the threat of even that many truly militant black folks. As a matter of fact, Faith Ann urged me to ask you to switch political gears and support what she calls an 'ultimate voting rights' bill, actually a racial proportional-representation plan that would guarantee blacks a percentage of legislators equal to their percentage of the population."

"Does she want me to join the NAACP, too?" the Senator asked sarcastically.

"I doubt Faith Ann would accept your membership application, and I am certainly not here to help you save a career that has brought so much misery to black people, but if you think about it, Senator, you may discover that the measure Faith Ann believes will help blacks will help your constituency as well."

"Sort of a racial version of the view that what's good for General Motors is good for the nation?"

"A lot of whites have benefited from laws supposedly enacted to help blacks," I reminded him. "By the way, how are the voices?"

"You probably already know. When you started talking about that proportional representation nonsense, your voice booming in my head stopped entirely. What does it mean, Lawyer Crenshaw?"

"Well, Senator, Faith Ann would say it means that if you want permanent relief, you should give her plan some serious thought." I turned to leave.

"I hope, Lawyer Crenshaw," he said hastily, "I can count on you not to mention our talk."

"All I can say is, Senator," I replied, opening the door, "I try not to tell folks things they will not believe."

A week later, the Senator left the hospital and was driven directly to the delayed joint session of the state legislature. The circumstances of his accident and rescue seem not to have affected his hold on that body's members, most of whom were beholden to him for long lists of political favors rendered. So for reasons of either fraternal fidelity or political allegiance, they greeted him with a prolonged standing ovation.

"Damn!" Faith Ann said as we watched the televised proceedings. "You go and save the S.O.B.'s life, and the media, and all those hacks who need him to raise money for their campaigns, save his reputation. He's now so popular he can recommend we be returned to slavery, and those fools would have us back in chains before we could catch our breath."

For once, though, Faith Ann's political foresight was wrong. The Senator began his speech with a melodramatic account of how he had lost control of his car after it was filled with a heavenly light. The steering wheel was yanked from his hands by an "invisible force," and when the car went through the bridge rail, a booming voice told him that he must alter the course of his life as radically as his car's direction had been altered.

"I felt like Paul on the road to Damascus," the Senator intoned in a not-half-bad facsimile of the sermon styles of black preachers he had been copying for so many years. "As my car went under for the last time, the Lord showed me the light for the first time. My body sank with the car, but my soul was lifted up. Everyone watching feared I was dead—but I was being born again. My sins were forgiven and a heavenly voice spoke to me, repeating over and over, 'This is your chance! This is your chance!'

"Tonight, I begin my new career committed to helping white people gain an equal opportunity for heavenly salvation."

Shifting oratorical gears, the Senator spoke confidentially to his thoroughly stunned audience. "Now, my friends, you know where I've always stood on the race question. I don't hate black folks, but I have devoted my life to protecting the good white people of this great state by ensuring they got the priority on whatever was up for grabs. But in that great moment of underwater revelation, I realized it was the white people I was keeping down, while the blacks in their persecution were able to enjoy the heaven-on-earth satisfaction of suffering that comes to all those who labor under the lash of their fellow men."

I looked at Faith Ann. She seemed dazed, a condition she likely shared with the legislature and most of the national television audience. "Watch out!" she warned. "He's leading up to something." Here, she was clearly right.

"Sure," the Senator continued, "we can keep them from the polls today, just as our great grandparents did after Lincoln freed them over a century ago. They used the three Cs: the black codes to take away their citizenship rights, chicanery to take their lands and their labor, and coercion to take their lives if they complained too loud about the first two. We can do the same. But now as then, the blacks will keep strivin' to get up, and we will spend our days and nights schemin' how to keep them down.

"Read your history! Oppressors are always overcome by those they oppress. Eventually, the brutality of the oppression becomes the measure of the oppressor's destruction. We must not condemn our children to playin' keeper in the prison of racism where they will, like we do, spend their lives in spiritual chains of fear, guilt, and hate.

"Because I have seen the light," the Senator proclaimed, "I am withdrawing my reapportionment bill which would have made it almost impossible for black voters to elect one of their own. This act would have been challenged in the courts, and if its validity was upheld, black voters would continue to push for their right to vote and elect representatives of their choice. The racial turmoil in our great state would continue, our difficulties in attracting new business and investments would increase, and we would remain the whipping boy on racial matters for sections of this country with worse race relations than ours.

"As the voice told me, my friends, I am telling you that this is your chance to change, to bring peace and prosperity to all the citizens of this great state and avoid a fate that might send any of you spinnin' off the road of justice to drown in a river of racial bitterness."

"Well! Do tell!" Faith Ann exclaimed. "Diving off that bridge to save that fool may have done more good than I thought."

Usually at this point in one of the Senator's sermon-speeches, the audience would have been on its feet cheering, and the hall filled with applause—and the Senator paused, stepped back, and waited for the familiar sound. It did not come. The legislature seemed in collective shock, as though Ronald Reagan had joined the Communist party or the Pope had renounced the Church's celibacy strictures for the priesthood.

Ignoring the silence, the Senator pushed on. "Tomorrow morning, I will introduce what I consider the ultimate voting rights act, my No Taxation Without Representation Voter Bill. I have intentionally named my plan after the earliest battlecry of red-blooded Americans committed to fairness at all costs. My bill has two indivisible sections that will guarantee that the hope of our first patriots will live and thrive in every hamlet in our great state.

"First, I want to make sure that all our citizens, black and white, will be able to afford to get out on election day and cast their ballots for the candidates of their choice. But in the good ol' American way, I want to encourage the vote, not coerce it. So, under part I of my bill, every voter who casts a ballot in a primary or general election will receive a hundred-dollar state tax rebate to cover travel and other expenses. Those voters who pay no taxes will receive their voter travel costs in cash."

This time when the Senator paused, there was sustained, if tentative, applause. It was probably just as well that he made no mention of the provisions in his bill requiring candidates for public office to contribute one-half of their campaign contributions to a special Voter Travel Fund out of which voter rebates would be paid.

"Second," the Senator continued, "my No Taxation Without Representation Voter Bill ensures that all our citizens will have a fair chance to elect representatives of their choice. Let me explain part II of my bill by asking you a question: Why do people take the time and go to the effort to vote? The answer, of course, is to elect a candidate to represent their interests. Now, my friends"— and his voice fell to a conspiratorial whisper—"how has that process promoted the vote in this great southern state of ours? I'll tell you how: by encouraging the white majority to vote to keep whites in office and discouraging the black minority from even trying because they know they're outnumbered from the start.

"That, my friends"—his voice rising and arms outstretched "—may be majoritarian democracy, but it ain't fair and therefore it ain't American. It's nothing less than what our forefathers deplored: taxation without representation."

The audience was stunned into quiet. But Faith Ann was on her feet, clapping her hands. "That sure is the truth! Praise the Lord! He knows how to make even a devil tell the truth." She turned to me, laughing with joy, "Sister Geneva, what did you do to that so-and-so while you had him under the water?"

I shushed her. "He is not finished yet."

"Follow me now, friends," the Senator was admonishing his stunned audience. "Follow me! If the reason for voting is to elect representatives who will support your interests, how do you ensure a large minority does not get locked out and discouraged? Again, the answer is simple. You amend the voting laws so that the minority race is *guaranteed* to elect representatives of their choice in numbers equal to their portion of the population eligible to vote.

"So part II of my plan is called the Racial Proportionate Representation Bill. I intend it as my proudest legislative achievement, and it is my hope that it will win the support of our great citizenry for it will guarantee our black citizens their fair share of all elective legislative seats and provide the means for a fair rotation of executive positions up to and including the governorship of this state."

"Geneva!" Faith Ann cried out. "That damn man has stolen my plan for an ultimate voting rights act! Do you hear him? That's the same remedy I tried to get our civil rights lawyers to push for over the years. They always tell me it's too radical and would never be approved by the legislature or the courts."

"Our great state," the Senator was winding up, "is facing chaos and great economic loss, perhaps even bloodshed over the electoral processes that serve now, and have always served, either to keep our black citizens away from the polls or to frustrate their desire to elect their people to participate in the governance of this country. They are twenty-three percent of our population. They deserve that percentage of our elective offices. They may find that number insufficient, but we will have done that which by rights we should do. We can do no more. But, by God, we must do no less! Think on it, my white friends. This is *your* chance. Thank you and good night."

The smattering of applause, much of it from the few black and liberal white representatives, did not worry the Senator. He knew he controlled enough votes to gain passage of virtually any legislation he supported. He also knew that he would work hard to implement his No Taxation Without Representation Voter Bill. His conversion was real. White people, too, must be saved. The fact that he no longer heard my voice reverberating in his head was simply a welcome bonus.

U NCERTAIN what Geneva wanted of me, I observed that, while the Chronicle of the Ultimate Voting Rights Act had some interesting characters, its conclusion left something to be desired—a remark on which Geneva pounced.

"It is your legal and not your literary expertise I want," she said coolly. "I want your opinion on whether, if the Senator were to get the state legislature to enact his voting rights bill, it could survive a court challenge; and whether, if it passed constitutional scrutiny, it would serve as the ultimate voting rights act we were discussing—one that might motivate blacks to really participate in expectation of actually electing representatives of their choice."

"Well, Geneva, if you put at my disposal the supernatural powers on display in your Chronicle, then I can straighten out this country without a No Taxation Without Representation Voting Act."

"You could have fooled me!" she replied. "Your every comment since arriving here ascribes supernatural authority to the Constitution and your precious rule of law. I would not think you needed more power than that."

"You needn't be sarcastic, Geneva. The fact is that I would need supernatural help to force the established political powers to enact part I of the Senator's bill providing a hundred-dollar tax rebate or payment to every voter who casts a ballot. Constitutionally, however, it wouldn't be a problem; and practically, it would help get to the polls thousands of poor voters for whom registration and voting can be expensive, time consuming, and often traumatic."

"A good point!" Geneva agreed. "We in the middle class tend to forget that registration and voting for the poor or the working class often means a long trip to the courthouse—still an alien place for many—and perhaps the loss of two days' wages: first to get registered, and later to vote. Many voters are intimidated by voting procedures and hostile officials. And if the percentages of voters who actually vote are disappointing among the middle class because of apathy and the sense that voting is a worthless exercise, how much more deeply ingrained such feelings must be among those for whom putting food on the table and keeping a roof overhead is an ongoing, lifelong ordeal."

"Actually," I said, "the tax rebate might overcome the apathy of the large numbers of middle-class citizens who haven't darkened a voting booth for years. Of course, that's just supposition. What is virtually assured is the fierce opposition to such a measure by many politicians who fear they might not be able to control these new voters. Paradoxically, resistance would come even from legislators whose campaigns regularly spend the equivalent of one hundred dollars a vote to get them elected."

"But no constitutional problems?" Geneva asked again.

"As you know, in 1966, the Court struck down state poll taxes under a Fourteenth Amendment–based principle denying the state the right to dilute a citizen's vote on account of economic status and ability to pay a fee or failure to pay a fee.[1] Were a state to encourage voting by paying voters to compensate for expenses and inconvenience, that measure would be sustained."

"Bravo!" Geneva cheered. "May I count on your similarly enthusiastic support for part II of the Senator's bill, the Racial Proportional Representation Plan, guaranteeing blacks a proportion of the elective seats equal to their percentage of the population?"

"Well, while I welcome the chance to come in out of the cold of your criticism and bask in the unfamiliar warmth of your praise, part II of the Senator's plan poses both political and constitutional problems that may require powers of advocacy beyond either my ability——"

"Or your inclination." Geneva saw I was hedging.

"Before you return to your critical mode, Geneva, let's set the record straight. The use of designated seats to ensure minority-group representation is not an idea the Senator had to steal from Faith Ann Courage. But many civil rights advocates agree with the late Justice William O. Douglas that such schemes 'have no place in a society that honors the Lincoln tradition . . . [where] the individual is important, not his race, his creed, or his color.' "[2]

"You are ever the idealist," Geneva said, shaking her head in frustration. "Though you know the sorry history of black people and the ballot as well as I do, you persist in your fairy-tale beliefs so removed from reality they make the Chronicle I just told sound like a presentation of hard, verifiable fact.' "

As she talked, I reached up and pulled down the Supreme Court Reports volume with Justice Douglas's warning that separate racial constituencies, like those the British established along religious lines in colonial India, would be a divisive force in our country, and would emphasize differences between candidates and voters which are irrelevant in the constitutional sense. Finding the passage, I reminded Geneva that Justice Douglas conceded that race, like religion, plays an important role in the choices voters make at the polls; and warned that 'government has no business designing electoral districts along racial or religious lines.' "And listen to this," I said:

> When racial or religious lines are drawn by the State, the multiracial, multireligious communities that our Constitution seeks to weld together as one become separatist; antagonisms that relate to race or to religion rather than to political issues are generated; communities seek not the best representative but the best racial or religious partisan. Since that system is at war with the democratic ideal, it should find no footing here.[3]

"If Justice Douglas is correct," I said, closing the volume, "then the proportional-representation remedy may increase the sense of racial difference and threat that underlie the historic resistance of white society to black voting and political power."

"That is hardly a criticism, friend. Many whites have seen as a threat every remedy intended to protect blacks against American racism from the Emancipation Proclamation on. Moreover, it is past time for us to stop basing our strategies on an assumption that whites will be fair. The whole history of black suffrage efforts belies any such faith. Consider the policy patterns from the beginning to the present day and then tell me we do not need proportional representation in this country:

- "In the periods before and after the Revolutionary War, 93 percent of the Northern free black population lived in states that excluded them completely or practically from the right to vote.[4] Only states with relatively few blacks—Massachusetts, New Hampshire, Vermont, and Maine—extended the franchise to blacks.

- "And during campaigns to eliminate voting qualifications to extend the ballot to all males, the loss of black voting rights was often the *quid pro quo* exacted by those opposed to universal suffrage before they would support unrestricted voting for white males.[5]

- "The Fourteenth Amendment was an insufficient mandate for most states that had barred blacks from voting. And despite the fact that ensuring the right of blacks to vote would guarantee Republican majorities for years to come, the idea of black suffrage was so unpopular that the Fifteenth Amendment was approved only because its ratification was demanded as a condition of readmittance for those few Southern states still out of the Union. New York rescinded its adoption of the amendment, and it was rejected outright by California, Delaware, Kentucky, Maryland, Oregon, and Tennessee.[6] Blacks were thus put on notice that when the political advantage to whites that was the amendment's real motivation came to an end, the amendment would not be enforced.

- "Legal scholars point to *Dred Scott* (1857) as the Supreme Court's most shameful decision, but Chief Justice Roger Taney's opinion finding that blacks were not included in the Constitution's definition of citizen, and striking down the politically wrought Missouri Compromise on the extension of slavery, was written without a clearly contrary mandate in the Constitution's text. But in terms of sheer outrageousness, *Dred Scott* pales beside the series of post-Reconstruction decisions in which the Court ignored the clear intentions of the Civil War amendments and condoned every practice including murder, all of which were openly used by Southerners to disfranchise blacks.[7] Regrettably, these cases are not much taught in law schools even though they offer a clear lesson in how Supreme Court decisions are influenced by the political environment.

• "Justice Oliver Wendell Holmes's opinion in a seldom-mentioned 1903 voting-rights case provided definitive proof that the Fifteenth Amendment was moribund. In denying relief to five thousand blacks who had sought to vote in Alabama, Holmes candidly acknowledged that if 'the great mass of the white population intends to keep the blacks from voting,' ordering them to be registered, as the petition requested, would be pointless because the order would be ignored at the local level. Holmes then proceeded to lecture the blacks that 'relief from a great political wrong, if done, as alleged, by the people of a State and the State itself, must be given by them or by the legislative and political department of the government of the United States.'[8]

• "And as for the hard-fought litigation beginning in the 1930s and culminating in the Voting Rights Act of 1965, one can credit the courage of blacks determined to vote, aided by the dedicated work of civil rights lawyers, for their persistence in invalidating every imaginable anti-black voting scheme from 'grandfather clauses' (exempting whites from stringent literacy tests if their forebears were voters at a time when blacks were slaves) to a myriad of white primary plans. Nevertheless we can conclude that the long campaign did little more than put whites to the task of designing newer, more subtle, but no less effective means of barring blacks from the polls or ensuring that their votes, once cast, would not much alter outcomes favoring the maintenance of white power in the political structure."

Geneva paused, out of breath, letting me get a word in. "I share your disappointment that our hopes of the 1960s have not all been realized, but it's a mistake not to place in the balance the millions of blacks who now are registered and do vote, and the presence of more than six thousand black elected officials. These real gains represent monumental progress when compared with the bleak and totally hostile era of the late nineteenth and early twentieth centuries. Problems remain, of course, but like the old black lady said, 'We ain't what we want to be, but thank God, we ain't what we was.' "

"I do not expect old black ladies to recognize that the so-called changes you boast of are more cosmetic than real, that increased black voting has not much increased political influence or provided representation even close to the percentage of our population. And most of the six thousand–odd black elected officials are mayors and city council members of small, mainly black communities. Those officeholders are welcome, God knows, but they hardly represent black power in politics.

"And spare me a recital of all the major cities that have elected black mayors. Even mayors of major cities are hardly in a position to do more than preside over, rather than relieve, the increasingly serious economic plight of the black masses in urban areas whose eroded economic bases have placed them on the verge of bankruptcy."

"Granting all that you've said, Geneva, I still see reason for a hopeful future. At the least, you must concede that our condition would be worse than it is without the black participation in politics that now exists. And Jesse Jackson's run for the presidency in 1984 proved that a charismatic candidate can both harness the black vote and win a surprising percentage of votes from whites able to see beyond the difference in a candidate's race to the similarity of their views and his on the important issues."

Ignoring my comment, Geneva asked: "Are you so opposed to the concept of proportional representation for blacks that you are willing to see black political power limited to electing blacks in mainly black areas and making a difference in the election of whites, most of whom then ignore black needs until the next election?"

"Don't be both melodramatic and unrealistic! The fact is, no one knows that continued effort won't result in our slow but eventual integration into the political system. We have already discussed and, I assume, agreed that civil rights efforts in the voting field have broadened constitutional coverage for all citizens."

"But what I am proposing now," Geneva insisted, "is a plan that might enable blacks to improve political coverage for themselves. More to the point, I think we should be able to do via legislation what the courts have done fairly frequently in granting relief for proven voting violations."

"They certainly don't call them proportional-representation remedies!" I countered.

"Come on, friend, would you turn down a Brooks Brothers suit because the label had been removed? Several courts have fashioned a proportional-representation remedy for proven violations of the Voting Rights Act, albeit without explicitly stating they were doing so.[9] And one of these courts was all but explicit, stating (as it remanded a court-approved redistricting plan because it provided inadequate assurances of minority political representation): 'There is simply no point in providing minorities with a "remedy" for the illegal deprivation of their representational rights in a form which will not in fact provide them with a realistic opportunity to elect a representative of their choice.' "[10]

I thought of the possible barrier to Geneva's hopes in a section which has come to be called the "Dole Compromise" in the 1982 amendments to the Voting Rights Act, and which provides "that nothing in this section establishes a right to have members of a protected class elected in numbers equal to their proportion in the population."[11] I was about to mention this obstacle, but Geneva anticipated me.

"Of course, I am aware of the Dole Compromise—but, in addition to not labeling their proportional-representation relief as such, courts have not specifically ordered this relief and have avoided potential roadblocks by requiring governmental entities found liable under the act to propose a remedy that will cure the statutory violation. Compliance with that direction usually leads officials to adopt on their own a proportional-representation plan."[12]

"A result," I interjected, "about which the Court's four most conservative members—Chief Justice Burger and Justices Powell, Rehnquist, and O'Connor—complained in 1986 while agreeing that the state of North Carolina had violated the Voting Rights Act by drafting legislative district lines so as to dilute the black vote.[13] A part of their concern was that a judicial direction to the state to create districts that maximize the black vote does not always guarantee that blacks will be able to elect representatives of their choice. Such districting also submerges the interests of black voters not residing in the majority black districts. Moreover, even the election of candidates responsive to black interests at best will have only a moderate impact in local elections and will usually be even less than that at the state legislative level."

"You forget," Geneva replied, "that the Senator's measure does not rely on the uncertainties of districting, but rather guarantees blacks a percentage of elective seats equal to their population percentage."

"I'm not at all sure that will avoid the problem. Consider a city with a three-member city council and a one-third black voting population. Under a multimember or at-large districting plan where all city residents vote for three candidates, there is little chance, particularly in the South, for a black to gain a seat. If, perhaps after a successful Voting Rights Act suit, a city is ordered to create single-member districts, it may comply by creating one mainly black district—although this arrangement may be resisted by blacks who prefer that their influence be spread more broadly.[14] But assuming the adoption of a 'safe black district,' the influence of the blacks' representative will be minimal, particularly about the many issues where the interests of voters diverge along racial lines. And that," I warned, "would also be the case under the Senator's Racial Proportional Representation Plan."

"Are you, then, suggesting that even if blacks were to overcome the many legal and political objections to the open adoption of proportional-representation plans, the improvements they would make in the ability of blacks to participate in the political process would be minimal?"

"Let me simply say that they would be far from an ultimate voting rights act. The reason, as you've been reminding me almost every minute since I arrived, is the caste-like status of blacks in the society: that is, the conditions in fact and in strongly held belief that together convince many whites that blacks as a class are somehow irreparably different from and less worthy than whites. This American mindset renders it impossible for blacks to participate in the political give-and-take with any real expectation that their basic goals can prevail."

"Are you saying that blacks can never profit from political participation?"

"Of course not. It's simply that their gains are almost always the gratuitous dividends of policies favored by a controlling white interest or group. When no such fortuitous arrangements are possible, blacks have found political participation quite difficult and unrewarding."

"Well, I'm pleasantly surprised to hear you take a more radical stance and lead me away from an optimistic posture influenced, I fear, by my friend Faith Ann Courage's enthusiasm for proportional-representation schemes."

"I certainly don't object to their use as relief mechanisms, Geneva, but they're not the representational millennium for black people who remain a minority in a still-hostile majoritarian society."

"Would you see more potential for black voting power if a state restructured all of its electoral districts along racial lines and in accordance with proportional-representation principles?"

"That brings us back to Justice Douglas's objection," I warned. "It would, I fear, worsen racial tensions because it distorts the political process in order to create targeted entities less likely to engage in the coalition building that is the hallmark of American politics. In 1977, Justice William Brennan, another liberal, expressed the same concern while approving the creation of a mainly black congressional district in Brooklyn."[15]

"Now, you are contradicting yourself," Geneva pointed out with ill-concealed irritation. "You just said that dominant white factions can and do ignore discrete and insular minorities."

"And that's true," I answered sharply, "but it is also a truth your irritation will not dissolve that guaranteeing some black representation through the creation of safe black districts constitutes a facsimile of a discrimination-free polity at a considerable cost to the fairness and integrity of the political process as it is viewed by those whose political power is diluted in this process."

"You seem caught up in theory," Geneva accused, "but *representation* as we define the term in this country is a distinctly practical notion. And, even on a theoretical plane, some scholars maintain that if 'one emphasizes political entitlements to vote as derived directly from notions of rights, whether individual or group, proportional representation becomes attractive, for it may well be the most rights-sensitive system of legislative selection available to us.' "[16]

"In theory, yes," I agreed, "but, as I see it at work in countries like Israel, proportioning political representation gives power to small splinter groups able to supply marginally essential votes far out of proportion to their numbers. It offers representation to lunatic fringe and hate groups of which, as you know, this country has more than its fair share. So, Geneva, while it sounds attractive and may have value in remedying the effects of past racial discrimination, as a solution or, as the Senator put it, as an ultimate voting rights act, I fear it would create a political structure that would make the maintenance of other central constitutional values difficult and perhaps impossible."

"As I recall," Geneva mused, "the Framers were afraid of majoritarian government; and in the *Federalist Papers*, James Madison urged a large, diverse electorate composed of many factions as the best defense against majority tyranny[17]—a persuasive approach if coalition building occurs freely across racial lines, but when blacks are consistently excluded from the coalition-building process, 'the ostensible protection against majority tyranny provided by Madison's theory becomes strained.'[18] So—if the coalition-building aspect of the current electoral system doesn't work for blacks and if, as you maintain, proportional representation would not be a better scheme—what kind of voting rights law would you recommend?"

"All things considered, I think blacks should keep up their pressures for enforcement of the existing Voting Rights Act; and, despite all the disadvantages, we should work harder to get our folks registered and out to vote on election day. Again, it'll be difficult, but there are no shortcuts in the struggle to overcome resistance to blacks voting and exercising political power."

"I swear, friend," Geneva said, more as diagnosis than as criticism, "given the dimension of those disadvantages, your refusal to face the facts borders on the idiotic."

"It's a matter of perspective. To those Africans who jumped from the slave ships to death in the shark-filled seas, those who failed to join them must have seemed idiotic. And yet, but for their idiotic 'refusal to face the facts,' we would not be here now."

"Now who is melodramatic? The facts are that the reapportionment cases tie the constitutional standard for review to the traditional American idea of representation by geographic location—an idea acquired at a time when real property was the basis of power, and governmental councils had to be responsive to landed interests.[19] But, contrary to Justice Douglas's assumption, geographic apportionment is not a prerequisite of representative government. John Stuart Mill once complained:

> I cannot see why the feelings and interests which arrange mankind according to localities should be the only ones thought worthy of being represented; or why people who have other feelings and interests, which they value more than they do their geographical ones, should be restricted to these as the sole principle of their political classification."[20]

"Well," I responded, "there's no indication in that quotation that Mill was thinking about districts based on race. So—even if through savvy political leadership and the chance to make one hundred bucks for voting as in the Senator's plan, a racial proportionate plan was enacted—it would hardly survive a judicial challenge given all the language in civil rights decisions speaking of the Court's abhorrence of racial classifications in the voting area."

"I am familiar with many of those cases, and each addressed an effort by whites to bar or limit black voting. The decisions and their language would seem distinguishable on that basis. Why would not the Senator's plan constitute a voluntary affirmative-action policy, voluntarily adopted by the state to address the effects of long years of discrimination against blacks in the electoral process?"

"Designating it an affirmative-action plan in the current racial climate, Geneva, isn't likely to help you win either political acceptance or judicial approval."

"You keep telling me why it cannot be placed in effect and I am more interested in whether, if implemented, it would work as Faith Ann Courage thinks it would."

"I see no reason to speculate about the impossible."

Noting my growing irritation, Geneva suggested we take a break. She went to the kitchen and returned a few minutes later with a tray that reminded me—not wholly with pleasure—that she had been a devotee of natural foods long before they were fashionable. But, having skipped breakfast that morning, I was ready to eat almost anything I could identify on the tray—which was not much.

Suddenly my tolerance began to slip and, despite my past fondness for Geneva, I began to regret my decision to come.

Turning off my tape recorder, I said, "Instructive as it always is, Geneva, to discuss racial issues with you, it's clear that our views differ a great deal, and I doubt my comments on your Chronicles are of help. So, unless you tell me what absolutely requires my presence, I really should start back."

"You misunderstand," Geneva said seriously. "I asked you to trust me, but I never said that I would not tell you why I invited you here. The question is whether you really want to know. The decision is yours. If you want to know, I will tell you."

Geneva stopped eating, pushed her chair back from the table, and looked at me with great kindness and even greater intensity. I felt a sense of foreboding, but could hardly back out now. With as much vigor as I could muster, I said, "Having come this far, I'm quite ready to share whatever trouble you're facing."

"Very well," and Geneva relaxed for the first time since I arrived. "I was never very good at secrets anyhow, and they did not order me not to tell you."

Suddenly, on what had been a beautiful fall day, the room felt warm and stuffy. I swallowed uneasily. "Who are *they?*"

"The members of the Curia, of course. I did not tell you the end of the Chronicle. After completing their agenda, the two Curia Sisters requested me to stay after the audience departed. They told me that they had proposed the Conservative Crusader role simply so that I could get to know them, and so the audience—the Curia Sisters called them the Chorus—could become acquainted with me. They said that the empty chair between them was reserved for me, and they felt that, upon taking it, I would resolve the long-standing dispute on reform strategies that divide them and dilute their powers.

"Right then, I understood the strange nature of the illness that had befuddled my doctors. During my effort to recover, I felt myself fighting, like the Senator, a great pressure to surrender to some strong force. Intermittently the pressure would diminish, and I would experience one of the Chronicles I am sharing with you. Fighting the pressure and living through the stories required all my strength, leaving me unable to communicate with anyone—a state the doctors interpreted as either coma or brain damage.

"The Curia members chided me for being neither a revolutionary ready to commit violence for my beliefs nor a traditional civil rights lawyer committed to legal outcomes no matter what. As one of them, they promised I would have real power to effect racial reform. Finally, I admitted that their offer was challenging, and agreed to accept on condition that I could return here and discuss the Chronicles with someone able to help me puzzle out their significance and perhaps evolve a new vision for achieving racial justice—one that would not rely on violent revolution nor require a black exodus.

"I thought of all the civil rights lawyers I had known and worked with, and came up with you."

"And now," I suggested, "you must regret your choice."

"Not at all," she said quickly. "Of course, when I selected you, I did not know that you had left civil rights work and become a law teacher. Your interpretations clearly are different from mine, but discussing those differences helps me clarify my views and also provides a firmer basis for the policy I hope to evolve as an alternative to those urged by the Curia members."

Whatever my doubts, it was clear that she was deadly serious about all she was telling me. I wondered whether I was being helpful by simply going along with her delusions. "Geneva, this is all quite——" I caught myself, feeling the awkwardness that comes when I am in the presence of a person who is detached from the reality I know. It pained me that this could happen to Geneva. I tried to speak firmly. "You're talking as though all of this really happened. It didn't. It was something you envisioned during your illness."

"The Curia was right," she said, "in warning me that Western peoples simply reject anything not explicable in scientific terms. But, for me, friend"—Geneva spoke slowly, emphasizing every syllable—"it was neither vision nor dream, and no more fantasy than some of the beliefs that you have said you hold."

When I offered no response, she continued. "In our years together at the Legal Defense Fund, I remember you were more committed to our cause than to any dogma regarding how we might best achieve our goals. Now I hope you will stay and hear the other Chronicles. I am sorry to be so argumentative, but I honestly believe the fate of our people may depend on what comes out of our discussions."

Leaving now was unthinkable. I unpacked my papers and turned my tape recorder back on. "Why don't we get started with the next Chronicle?" I reached over and touched her hand. "I'll do what I can," I promised.

Chapter 4

Neither Separate Schools Nor Mixed Schools

The Chronicle of the Sacrificed Black Schoolchildren

ALL THE BLACK school-age children were gone. They had simply disappeared.

No one in authority could tell the frantic parents more than they already knew. It had been one of those early September days that retain the warmth of summer after shedding that season's oppressive humidity. Prodded perhaps by the moderate weather, the pall of hateful racial invective that had enveloped the long desegregation battle lifted on what was to be the first day of a new school year. It was as well implementation day for the new desegregation plan, the result of prolonged, court-supervised negotiations. Plaintiffs' lawyers had insisted on what one called a "full measure" of racial balance, while the school board and the white community resisted, often bitterly, every departure from the previous school structure.

Now it seemed all for nothing. The black students, every one of them, had vanished on the way to school. Children who had left home on foot never appeared. Buses that had pulled away from their last stop loaded with black children had arrived at schools empty, as had the cars driven by parents or car pools. Even parents taking young children by the hand for their first day in kindergarten, or in pre-school, had looked down and found their hands empty, the children suddenly gone.

You can imagine the response. The media barrage, the parents' anger and grief, the suspects arrested and released, politicians' demands for action, analysts' assessments, and then the inevitably receding hullabaloo. Predictable statements were made, predictable actions taken, but there were no answers, no leads, no black children.

Give them credit. At first, the white people, both in town and around the country, were generous in their support and sincere in the sympathy they extended to the black parents. It was some time before there was any public mention of what, early on, many had whispered privately: that while the loss was tragic, perhaps it was all for the best. Except in scruffy white neighborhoods, these "all for the best" rationales were never downgraded to "good riddance."

Eventually they might have been. After all, statistics showed the life chances for most of the poor children were not bright. School dropouts at an early age; no skills; no jobs; too early parenthood; too much exposure to crime, alcohol, drugs. And the city had resisted meaningful school desegregation for so long that it was now possible to learn from the experience of other districts that integrating the schools would not automatically insulate poor black children from the risks of ghetto life.

Even after delaying school desegregation for several years, the decision to proceed this fall with the now-unneeded plan had been bitterly opposed by many white parents who feared that "their schools" would have to have a 50 percent enrollment of black children to enable the school system to achieve an equal racial balance, the primary goal of the desegregation plan and its civil rights sponsors. So high a percentage of black children, these parents claimed, would destroy academic standards, generate discipline problems, and place white children in physical danger. But under all the specifics lay the resentment and sense of lost status. Their schools would no longer be mainly white—a racial status whites equated with school quality, even when the schools were far from academically impressive.

Black parents had differed about the value of sending their children to what had been considered white schools. Few of these parents were happy that their children were scheduled, under the desegregation plan, to do most of the bus riding—often to schools located substantial distances from their homes. Some parents felt that it was the only way to secure a quality education because whites would never give black schools a fair share of school funds, and as some black parents observed: "Green follows white."

Other black parents, particularly those whose children were enrolled in the W. E. B. DuBois School—an all-black, outstanding educational facility with a national reputation—were unhappy. DuBois's parents had intervened in the suit to oppose the desegregation plan as it applied to their school. Their petition read:

> This school is the fruit of our frustration. It is as well a monument of love for our children. Our persistence built the DuBois School over the system's opposition. It is a harbor of learning for our children, and a model of black excellence for the nation. We urge that our school be emulated and not emasculated. The admission of whites will alter and undermine the fragile balance that enables the effective schooling black children need to survive societal hostility.
>
> We want our children to attend the DuBois School. Coercing their attendance at so-called desegregated schools will deny, not ensure, their right to an equal educational opportunity. The board cannot remedy the wrongs done in the past by an assignment policy that is a constitutional evil no less harmful than requiring black children to attend segregated schools. The remedy for inferior black schools sought by others from the courts we have achieved for ourselves. Do not take away our educational victory and leave us "rights" we neither need nor want.

The DuBois School's petition was opposed by the school board and plaintiffs' civil rights lawyers, and denied by the district court. Under the desegregation plan, two-thirds of the DuBois students were to be transferred to white schools located at the end of long bus rides, to be replaced by white children whose parents volunteered to enroll them in an outstanding school.

In fact, DuBois School patrons were more fortunate than many parents whose children were enrolled in black schools that were slowly improving but lacked the DuBois School's showy academic performance. Most of these schools were slated for closure or conversion into warehouses or other administrative use. Under a variety of rationales, the board failed to reassign any of the principals of the closed black schools to similar positions in integrated schools.

Schools in white areas that would have been closed because of declining enrollment gained a reprieve under the school-desegregation plan. The older schools were extensively rehabilitated, and the school board obtained approval for several new schools, all to be built in mainly white areas—the board said—the better to ensure that they would remain academically stable and racially integrated.

Then, in the wake of the black students' disappearance, came a new shock. The public school superintendent called a special press conference to make the announcement. More than 55 percent of the public school population had been black students, and because state funding of the schools was based on average daily attendance figures, the school system faced a serious deficit during the current year.

There were, the superintendent explained, several additional components to the system's financial crisis:

Teacher Salaries.   Insisting that desegregation would bring special stresses and strains, the teacher's union had won substantial pay raises, as well as expensive in-service training programs. A whole corps of teacher aides had been hired and trained to assist school faculties with their administrative chores. Many newly hired teachers and all the aides would have to be released.

School Buses.   To enable transportation of students required by the desegregation plan, the board had ordered one hundred buses and hired an equal number of new drivers. The buses, the superintendent reported, could be returned. Many had made only one trip; but the new drivers, mechanics, service personnel, and many of the existing drivers would have to be laid off.

School Construction.   Contracts for rehabilitation of old schools and for planning and building new schools had placed the board millions of dollars in debt. The superintendent said that hundreds of otherwise idle construction workers were to have been employed, as well as architectural firms and landscape designers. Additional millions had been earmarked for equipment and furniture suppliers, book publishers, and curriculum specialists. Some of these contracts could be canceled but not without substantial damage to the local economy.

Lost Federal Funds.   After desegregation had been ordered by the courts, the board applied for and received commitments for several million dollars in federal desegregation funds. These grants were now canceled.

Lost State Funds.   Under the court order, the state was obligated to subsidize costs of desegregation; and, the superintendent admitted, these appropriations, as well as the federal grants, had been designated to do "double duty": that is, while furthering school-desegregation efforts, the money would also improve the quality of education throughout the system by hiring both sufficient new teachers to lower the teacher-pupil ratio, and guidance counselors and other advisory personnel.

Tax Rates.   Conceding that the board had won several increases in local tax rates during the desegregation process, the superintendent warned that, unless approval was obtained for a doubling of the current rate, the public schools would not survive.

Annexations.   Over the last several years, the city had annexed several unincorporated areas in order to bring hundreds of additional white students into the public school system and slow the steady increase in the percentage of black students. Now the costs of serving these students added greatly to the financially strapped system.

Attorney Fees.   Civil rights attorneys had come under heavy criticism after it was announced that the court had awarded them $300,000 in attorney fees for their handling of the case, stretching back over the prior five years. Now the superintendent conceded that the board had paid a local law firm over $2,000,000 for defending the board in court for the same period.

Following the school superintendent's sobering statement, the mayor met with city officials and prepared an equally lengthy list of economic gains that would have taken place had the school-desegregation order gone into effect. The president of the local chamber of commerce did the same. The message was clear. While the desegregation debate had focused on whether black children would benefit from busing and attendance at racially balanced schools, the figures put beyond dispute the fact that virtually every white person in the city would benefit directly or indirectly from the desegregation plan that most had opposed.

Armed with this information, a large sum was appropriated to conduct a massive search for the missing black children. For a time, hopes were raised, but eventually the search was abandoned. The children were never found, their abductors never apprehended. Gradually, all in the community came to realize the tragedy's lamentable lesson. In the monumental school desegregation struggle, the intended beneficiaries had been forgotten long before they were lost.

A MOST disturbing story, Geneva! Symbolically, the sacrificed black children in the Chronicle represent literally thousands like themselves who are the casualties of desegregation, their schooling irreparably damaged even though they themselves did not dramatically disappear. It certainly calls into question the real beneficiaries in the thousands of school-desegregation cases that the former Legal Defense Fund director, Jack Greenberg, aptly called the 'trench warfare' of the civil rights movement."

"Why are you taking it so hard?" Geneva asked. "In our discussion following the Chronicle of the Celestial Curia, you cited both Lewis Steel, the civil rights lawyer, and Professor Arthur S. Miller for arguing that the Supreme Court's decision in *Brown* v. *Board of Education* should be seen as furthering the nation's foreign and domestic interests far more than it helped black people gain the critically important citizenship right to equal educational opportunity. In fact, you noted that both the NAACP and the federal government briefs argued the value of ending constitutionally supported racial segregation in our competition with communist governments" (see pages 60–62).

"That's true," I admitted, "but——"

"But what?" Geneva interrupted. "If your self-interest approach is a valid explanation for the change in constitutional interpretation—as you and others insist on viewing the *Brown* decision—then why wouldn't the same self-interest have to be present before that decision could be implemented?"

"I'm not sure many people lacking the intellectual insight of a W. E. B. DuBois recognized the factor of self-interest in the first several years after the *Brown* decision," I replied. "Moreover, the early problem, as I remember it, was that resistance to desegregation was so fierce and came from so many directions that any progress we made in overcoming it was simply accepted as a victory without much thought of *how* we—always the understaffed, underfinanced underdogs—had prevailed. We knew we were in the right, that God was on our side, and all of that, but while we spoke and thought in an atmosphere of 'rights and justice,' our opponents had their eyes on the economic benefits and power relationships all the time. And that difference in priorities meant that the price of black progress was benefits to the other side, benefits that tokenized our gains and sometimes strengthened the relative advantages whites held over us."

"And that," said Geneva, "is precisely the Chronicle's message."

"Indeed," I said, "the Chronicle portrays in dramatic terms the thesis of Daniel Monti's *A Semblance of Justice*, which reviews the long history of school desegregation in St. Louis. Professor Monti reports that St. Louis school officials staunchly resisted any liability for segregation in their schools. Then, after court orders were finally entered, the same individuals utilized school-desegregation mandates to achieve educational reforms, including magnet schools, increased funding for training, teacher salaries, research and development, and new school construction."[1]

"Amazing! And probably at the same time, they were calling the civil rights people everything but a child of God."

"Probably," I agreed, "but according to Monti, school officials accomplished all of these gains for the system without giving more than secondary priority to redressing the grievances of blacks. This did not seem to bother the officials who candidly told him that the only sensible way to deliver educational resources to the metropolitan area of St. Louis was through a metropolitan school system, and they also used desegregation to accomplish that end."

"Would Professor Monti be able to build a similar case of school-desegregation benefit for the system rather than for the blacks in other school districts?" Geneva asked.

"I'm afraid he could. Moreover, Monti's book explains how school officials used the school-desegregation controversy to increase their legitimacy as the proper policy-making location for public education—an accomplishment furthered by the fact that civil rights lawyers did not call for the abandonment of the school board, even though it and its predecessors in office were responsible for the discriminatory policies attacked in the courts."

"That is certainly an accurate statement, but I doubt that it is fair," Geneva said. "School boards do not make policy as much as reflect in their policies the wishes of those in their constituencies whom they really represent. The society was willing, albeit reluctantly, to drop school-segregation policies after *Brown*. But that decision did not require nor did the public want to dismantle the structure of public school systems. Even when courts placed absolutely recalcitrant school systems into a form of judicial receivership,[2] there was criticism that the courts had gone too far."

"A real catch-22 that made every step painful," I recalled. "When districts finally admitted more than a token number of black students to previously white schools, the action usually resulted in closing black schools, dismissing black teachers, and demoting (and often degrading) black principals. There was some effort to stem this practice via litigation,[3] but our main emphasis was on desegregating the schools. Black faculty, in all too many cases, became victims of that desegregation."

"I gather," Geneva commented, "that the desegregated schools did not provide educational compensation to black children for the involuntary loss of their former teachers and schools."

"It was tough, though for a long time we kept pointing to the strong kids who made it rather than to all those who did poorly or dropped out of school. But in the early days, the experience, even when there was little overt hostility, was much as reported in Ray Rist's *The Invisible Children* (1978). Rist, a social scientist, followed every day for a full school year a group of young black children bused to an upper-class, mainly white school.[4] The principal's policy was to 'treat all the kids just alike.' This evenhanded policy meant—in practice—that the handful of black children from the ghetto were expected to perform and behave no differently than did the white children from comfortable suburbs in this mainly white school where the curriculum, texts, and teaching approaches were designed for the middle-class white kids. As you can imagine, the results of this evenhanded integration were disastrous."

"Do you think," Geneva asked, "that we could have avoided some of the tragedy if educators had been more involved in planning the litigation that led to *Brown*?"

"That's what our former associate Robert L. Carter, who played a major role in planning school-desegregation strategy, seems to think. I'm happy to report that, unlike many of our old colleagues who read any criticism of desegregation strategy as a personal attack, Bob Carter, now a federal judge, has remained objective about his role. In a thoughtful article, he wrote that, if he were preparing *Brown* today, 'instead of looking principally to the social scientists to demonstrate the adverse consequences of segregation, [he] would seek to recruit educators to formulate a concrete definition of the meaning of equality in education.' "[5]

"Interesting—but how did he intend to use the definition effectively?"

"Carter said that he would have based his argument on that definition, and tried 'to persuade the Court that equal education in its constitutional dimensions must, at the very least, conform to the contours of equal education as defined by the educators.' "[6]

"Perhaps," Geneva said, "Carter's approach would have enabled us to avoid some of the pitfalls, but it is lawyer's conceit to think that one tactical approach rather than another will over-come society's strong resistance to a particular racial reform as opposed to gaining a favorable outcome in a case."

I smiled. "Knowing Bob Carter as well as we both do, I'd love to hear his response to your observation."

"Don't misunderstand me. Judge Carter's point is well taken. We civil rights lawyers attacked segregation in the public schools because it was the weak link in the 'separate but equal' chain. Our attack worked. But to equate integration with the effective education black children need—well, that was a mistake."

"Again, Geneva," I said, with some annoyance, "that's easy for you to say—but remember how many devices school boards and their lawyers worked out to convey the sense of compliance with *Brown*, while in fact the schools remained segregated. 'Pupil as-signment plans' (requiring black parents to run an administrative gauntlet of forms and requirements),[7] 'grade-a-year' plans (which maintained the pace of desegregation at a glacial rate),[8] 'freedom-of-choice' plans (which relied on community pressures and coer-cion to limit the number of blacks who dared choose white schools),[9] and on and on. Unraveling the seemingly neutral proce-dures contained in these plans to get at their segregation-maintaining intent proved a challenge for both civil rights lawyers and for many federal judges who were ostracized and abused for carrying out the *Brown* mandate."[10]

"I remember how difficult it was," Geneva acknowledged, "but, for the life of me, I can't understand how you allowed school-board resistance to trap you into relying on racial balance as the only acceptable remedy for segregated schools. If you ask me, it was the civil rights' lawyers' personal commitment to racial integration that trapped them into a strategy that could not succeed."

"Criticism based on hindsight is easy," I said heatedly, "but what would you, Geneva, had you been around, have recom-mended as an alternative strategy?"

"I see that, unlike your friend and mentor, Judge Carter, you are a bit sensitive about criticism of your legal tactics. Or," she added, with a wry smile, "is your apparent anger really advocacy at work?"

"I'll ignore that, Ms. Know-it-all," I sputtered. "But let's assume that, instead of refusing to clarify its mandate to desegregate the public schools 'with all deliberate speed'[11]—a refusal that, in effect, gave the South ten years of delay—the Supreme Court in 1955, in addition to sensing the strong opposition to desegregation, had recognized that the separation of students by race was actually not an end in itself but a convenient means of perpetuating the primary aim: the dominance of whites over blacks in every important aspect of life."

"Fine!" Geneva said, "but where would they have gained that insight? Probably not from most of you who were convinced that, once we got the damned Jim Crow signs removed, the racial-integration millennium would roll in with the next tide."

"Please stop rubbing it in! We did what we felt was right at the time, and I haven't heard of an alternative that had a better chance of success, given the hostility of the climate."

"Well, I don't agree that a better desegregation policy was beyond the reach of intelligent people whose minds were not clogged with integrationist dreams. For example—if we recognize that the real motivation for segregation was white domination of public education—suppose the Court had issued the following orders:

"1.   Even though we encourage voluntary desegregation, we will not order racially integrated assignments of students or staff for ten years.

"2.   Even though 'separate but equal' no longer meets the constitutional equal-protection standard, we will require immediate equalization of all facilities and resources.

"3.   Blacks must be represented on school boards and other policy-making bodies in proportions equal to those of black students in each school district.

"The third point would have been intended to give blacks meaningful access to decision making—a prerequisite to full equality still unattained in many predominantly black school systems. For example, an 'equal representation' rule might have helped protect the thousands of black teachers and principals who were dismissed by school systems during the desegregation process."

"In other words," I asked, "under this 'educational policy' approach, the courts would have given priority to desegregating not the students but the money and the control?"

"Exactly. And rather than beat our heads against the wall seeking pupil-desegregation orders the courts were unwilling to enter or enforce, we could have organized parents and communities to ensure effective implementation for the equal-funding and equal-representation mandates."

"How can you be sure that black parents—as well as some of their integration-crazed lawyers—would not have become demoralized by the ten-year delay and simply done nothing until the courts were willing to take direct action on pupil desegregation?"

"The proof," Geneva answered quickly, "is in the number of black schools like DuBois in the Chronicle where neither personnel nor parents have accepted the argument that black schools must be inferior. Even in the pre-*Brown* era, some black educators, without equal resources and with whites controlling school-board policy, managed to create learning environments that encouraged excellence, motivated ambition, and taught the skills and self-assurance that have produced scores of successful blacks in business and the professions.[12] The educational sociologist Professor Sara Lightfoot, in her *The Good High School*, provides an impressive report of an all-black high school in Atlanta, Georgia—George Washington Carver—and the policies that enabled it to gain a reputation for academic quality."[13]

"It does happen," I conceded, "but good schools in a hostile environment are always fragile, subject to constant stress and continuing challenge. Look what happened to the DuBois School in the Chronicle. Despite the fact that it was effective and the pride of the black community, and that blacks wanted to send their children to its schools, it was sacrificed to school desegregation."

"By the way," Geneva asked, somewhat sarcastically, "had you been the judge in the Sacrificed Black Schoolchildren Chronicle, how would you have ruled on the DuBois School parents' petition?"

"It was a moving petition, I will admit, but——"

113

Geneva was on her feet. "Oh no you don't! You are not going to sit there and tell me that you would have denied their petition, disavowed the justice of their cause, and dismissed their claim?"

"The problem," I observed in my most measured tones, "is that you black women get so emotionally involved in tactical matters that you fail to see that some must pay a price so that all may advance"—and then I ducked as Geneva rose with a vase in her hand.

But then she smiled and placed it back on the table. "Thought you would taunt me into forgetting my question, did you? *Black woman, emotional*—my foot! Now, Mr. Professor, I am waiting for your answer. What about the black parents' petition to save the DuBois School?"

"I'm shocked," I said in mock horror, "that you'd ever resort to violence over a simple jest and even think I'd resort to trickery to evade an answer on so important a question. A question of that magnitude would require a court, particularly a district court, to check the case law carefully for binding precedents. And, in fact, the DuBois School situation is much like the facts in a case brought by black parents in Chicago whose children had been assigned by lottery away from their integrated neighborhood schools because the percentage of nonwhites in those schools exceeded 60 percent, a figure the board feared would trigger white flight."[14]

"Surely, the district court told the board to amend its plan to reflect better the wishes of the black parents?"

"I'm afraid not. The court did insist that the schools to which the black children were assigned be integrated, and then approved the amended plan. And let me hasten to add that other courts facing similar issues have reached similar results.[15] So, you see, if the issues in the Chronicle suit are viewed primarily from a doctrinal viewpoint, it is a difficult case."

Geneva sighed. "It sounds like you want to play law professor rather than judge. Can you justify the Chicago decision in the next few minutes?"

"It shouldn't be hard. The board's lottery scheme involves an obvious racial classification. That is, when the percentage of nonwhites reaches 60 percent, the number of students—selected by race—exceeding that percentage will be selected by lottery for assignment to other integrated schools farther from their homes. Ordinarily, racial classifications of that type are deemed by courts inherently 'suspect' and can survive judicial scrutiny only if justified by a 'compelling state interest' and if there's a close connection or 'fit' between the classification and the compelling interest to be served."

"And," Geneva anticipated me, "the Chicago school board maintained that stable racial integration is the compelling state interest and that the lottery plan is closely tailored to achieve that interest with the least possible harm."

"Well, they will use that argument if their primary argument is rejected. Basically, they'll contend that their lottery plan involves a benign racial classification. Since race is being used to further an appropriate goal—integrated schools—only an intermediate level of scrutiny is required."

"What is benign about excluding students from the schools they want to attend solely on the basis of their race?"

"The board might respond, 'Look, Miss, you civil rights types got us into this school-desegregation business. Now we've looked at the "white flight" studies, and if we do nothing to change the balance of these schools, they'll soon be all black, and you folks will be back in court screaming that the board allowed the schools to become all black. We don't want that to happen, but we can't force whites to go to the public schools. So, as the percentage of nonwhites increases, we must reassign some of the black kids. Do you have a better plan?' "

"I doubt," said Geneva, "that any court would base its approval on grounds that the society's racism required them to withhold a group's rights."

"I wouldn't bet any serious money on that doubt. One court wrote: 'Although white fears about the admission of minority students are ugly, those fears cannot be disregarded without imperiling integration across the entire system. . . . The exodus of white children from the public schools would disadvantage the entire minority community and nullify this voluntary desegregation effort.' "[16]

"And would you feel bound by these decisions?"

"Given your likely reaction, I hesitate to say this, but I think both courts reached the only decision they could for the reason pointed out in the decision I just quoted. While my sympathies are with the black parents, the school board plans are the only way to maintain racial balance."

"That, of course," Geneva chided, "is precisely the problem with equating the 'equal educational opportunity' right established in the *Brown* decision with racial balance. The racial-balance goal can be met only in schools where whites are in a majority and retain control. The quality of schooling black children receive is determined by what whites (they of the group who caused the harm in the first place) are willing to provide—which, as we should not be surprised to learn, is not very much."

"And you, Geneva? Let's just suppose that you were on the bench, sitting there without the vaunted power of your Curia friends, and with all the restraints of legal doctrine that bind a judge. How would you rule on the DuBois School parents' petition?"

Geneva's eyes flashed. "I cannot imagine anyone offering me or my accepting a judgeship, but were I somehow to find myself up there in a black robe instead of a Curia gold one, I sure as hell would not dismiss their petition out of hand, either because there was precedent for such action or because both the plaintiffs and the defendants urged me to do it. In fact, a petition like that filed by both a sizable and an articulate portion of the plaintiff class should put any judge on notice that the plaintiffs' class-action suit does not represent all the plaintiffs."

"In defense of the judge," I interjected, "these petitions by portions of the class do not come to light until long after the suit is filed and at a time when formal intervention would be both difficult and unfair to the parties."

"If *I* were the judge, I would hope to employ either judicial imagination or some good old mother wit in the situation."

"Such as?"

"Such as calling for testimony from the petitioners and perhaps holding a nonbinding referendum in the affected community regarding the plan."

"I fear you'd expose yourself to criticism for turning the judicial process into a popularity contest."

116

"I would not be afraid of criticism, and I think black parents—and likely some white parents as well—would welcome an opportunity to engage in a discussion that has been taken over by the lawyers weighing inappropriate legal standards to reach unjust results."

"You're a tough woman!"

"I assume that *tough* is intended as a grudging compliment and not as a synonym for *evil*, which I would take as an affront. Howsomever," she continued, smiling at her "down home" expression, "my action would not be a precedent. As you know—but likely do not approve—several courts have become more sensitive over time to the fact that the plaintiffs' class in school desegregation is not a monolith, particularly on the issue of relief. Moreover, a few courts have come to recognize both the importance of the educational potential in desegregation remedies, and the fact that racial balance is not synonymous with, and may be antithetical to, effective education for black children. As a result of their tardy but still welcome awakening, a few courts have responded to black parents' preference for relief intended to make the schools more educationally effective rather than simply more racially balanced."[17]

"It's unwise," I cautioned, "to read those decisions for more than they're worth."

"Spoken like the law teacher you are!" Geneva replied, in friendly disdain. "You tell me how I should 'read' the 1981 *Dallas* school-case decision rejecting a civil rights request that a mainly black subdivision of the district be broken up in order to maximize desegregation with neighboring subdistricts that were mainly white.[18] The black subdistrict, like the DuBois School parents, intervened in the case and put on testimony that convinced the district court of the wide difference of opinion within the minority community on the issue of relief.[19] Based on that testimony, the court observed: 'Minorities have begun to question whether busing is "educationally advantageous, irrelevant, or even disadvantageous." ' To illustrate his concern, the judge's lengthy opinion referred to what I consider a classic statement by the school-board president, one of three minorities on the board, who had said:

I don't think that additional busing is even the issue. . . . It has never been the issue. . . . The issue is whether we are going to educate the children and youth. . . . I think that the whole question around the whole busing issue just loses sight of why we are here and what the schools are about now. I think it was a noble idea in 1954 . . . but what I envisioned and I'm sure what other black parents envisioned in 1954 just never happened.[20]

"The witness could extend that comment to cover virtually every aspect of civil rights," Geneva added. "Now, given our general agreement that the Chronicle's message is tragic, how can we use its insight to formulate more effective civil rights strategies in the future?"

"Well, Geneva, my feeling is that while whites continue to use their power to allocate to themselves the best educational resources, and to honor our pleas for justice only when there is further profit for the system, it will be difficult to gain more than limited benefits—whether in racial balance or in improved resources."

"Of course," Geneva said, "neither strategy will be easy! But if the issue and the goal are as the Dallas witness suggested— 'whether or not we are going to educate the children and the youth'—then you simply have to agree, first, that racial balance and integration—what the witness called 'a noble idea in 1954'— is of very limited value today; and, second, that our priority must be to gain educationally effective schools for our children."

Geneva's eyes were bright, her black skin had a warm glow, and perspiration was trickling down her forehead. She caught me staring as she looked for her handkerchief. We both laughed.

"Friend," she asked, "if white folks ever decided to straighten up and do right, what would we black folks have to talk about?"

"Lord only knows," I answered. "Take our debate over school policy. It has been going on for two hundred years. In 1787, Prince Hall, the black Revolutionary War veteran and community leader, urged the Massachusetts legislature to provide funds for an 'African' school because, in his words, 'we . . . must fear for our rising offspring to see them in ignorance in a land of gospel light.'[21] That petition was urging separate schools for black children who, while admitted to the public schools in Boston, were treated so poorly that their parents withdrew them."

"I bet your forebears were critical of Hall's action and urged black parents to return their children for more insults and mistreatment."

"Listen, Geneva, I'm not going to swell the ranks of the multitudes of black folks in Boston who claim their forebears were never slaves. Suffice it to say that I'd be proud to be a descendant of such a prophetic critic for, after the black community built a school for themselves which later the school committee assumed responsibility for, parents were soon complaining that the schoolmaster was an incompetent teacher and guilty of 'improper familiarities' with female students—all of which charges the school committee ignored. The result was a suit to desegregate the schools—which the black parents lost in 1850."[22]

"Yes," Geneva agreed, "but the legislature came to the rescue of that nineteenth-century school-integration movement and, a few years later, voted to desegregate the Boston schools. The blacks were likely overjoyed, but they should have listened to one Thomas P. Smith, whom I would like to adopt as an ancestor. On Christmas Eve in 1849, Brother Smith spoke to the 'Colored Citizens of Boston' urging them not to abolish the colored schools. He warned that if the schools were desegregated, black children would have to be assigned to white schools, where the space would be inadequate, necessitating the construction of new schools which would again be all black. Sure enough, within a dozen years, the Boston public schools were totally segregated."[23]

"Despite the Boston setbacks, though, black people continued over the succeeding decades to file dozens of suits either to desegregate the schools or to gain equal facilities in the black schools."[24]

"All that proves," Geneva responded, "is that some truths come hard. In his 1849 speech, Thomas Smith argued that the black school was in good condition, and added that 'the order and discipline of the scholars, their cheerfulness and spirit, are unsurpassed by any school in the city.' Smith said further that if the black school was abolished at the request of blacks, the inference would be drawn that 'when equally taught and equally comfortable, we are ashamed of ourselves, and feel disgraced by being together; but the proverb says, "Respect yourself ere others respect you." ' "[25]

"Well, Geneva, I don't think Mr. Smith really understood how the segregation he supported undermined the self-respect he espoused."

"You sound like one of the civil rights stalwarts who castigated W. E. B. DuBois when he said much the same thing in the 1930s. He had serious misgivings about the massive school-desegregation litigation campaign the NAACP was contemplating. In urging a more flexible strategy, Dr. DuBois advised that blacks need neither segregated schools nor mixed schools. What they need is education."[26]

"With all due respect to Dr. DuBois who, as you know, is one of my heroes, I think he was begging the question. We agree our children need education. The issue debated over two centuries is how blacks can best obtain it in a still-resistive society."

"Like too many black folks," Geneva scolded, "you spend more time doing homage to his memory than reading his words. DuBois argued that the priority for blacks should be the educational goal rather than the means of achieving that goal. He also suggested that effective schooling for black children might be possible even though the socializing aspects of integrated classrooms were not available."

"Geneva, we've heard it all before, but the NAACP did proceed with its school-desegregation campaign. After years of trying, they won, and the *Brown* decision settled the matter of our approach to quality schooling for black children—desegregated schools."

"You sound as though the schools were *in fact* desegregated, as though you are still committed to 'the noble idea of 1954.' You need to start paying tardy heed to your hero. What Dr. DuBois said over half a century ago is still pertinent to all the black parents in this damned country who care more about their children's schooling than about their long-lost noble dreams. Listen!

A mixed school with poor and unsympathetic teachers, with hostile public opinion, and no teaching of truth concerning black folk, is bad. A segregated school with ignorant placeholders, inadequate equipment, poor salaries, and wretched housing, is equally bad. Other things being equal, the mixed school is the broader, more natural basis for the education of all youth. It gives wider contacts; it inspires greater self-confidence; and suppresses the inferiority complex. But other things seldom are equal, and in that case, Sympathy, Knowledge, and Truth, outweigh all that the mixed school can offer."[27]

"The man was a powerful writer," I acknowledged. "Black kids with his ability would make it whatever the school they attended."

"True, but no group produces more than a few persons of Dr. DuBois's caliber. Most children will benefit from good schooling and will suffer if their educations are poor. They are the real subjects of our debate, the real victims of our mistakes, the innocent sacrifices to our continued refusal to face up to our real problem as black people in a white land."

"I thought our real problem was education, Geneva."

"Nonsense. If that were so, you and I would not encounter the discrimination we and even the best educated of us continue to experience. And statistics would not continue to report that, on average, white high school dropouts earn more than blacks who have finished high school, white high school grads earn more than blacks who have finished college, and so on, and on."[28]

"Are you suggesting that the attainment of 'equal educational opportunity' must await a time when we are at least moving in the direction of 'equal economic opportunity'?"

"In a country where individual rights were created to protect wealth, we simply must find a means to prime the economic pump for black people, particularly those of us living at the poverty level."

"That statement," I warned, "will win you several awards from conservative groups who oppose further 'benefits' for blacks and urge that they roll up their sleeves and make it the way immigrants from Europe did several generations ago—and the way some Hispanic and Asian groups seem to be doing today."[29]

"I don't care who agrees with me," Geneva said militantly. "Those conservatives are right about the need for blacks to get into jobs and off welfare. And, whatever their handicaps, Hispanics and Asians are not burdened with the legacy of slavery and segregation in a land of freedom that, over time, has undermined the sense of self-worth for many black people. Nor will these immigrants face, at least initially, obstacles based on the deeply held belief that blacks *should* be on the bottom. Furthermore, white ethnics were helped up the socio-economic ladder by several rungs that have seldom, if ever, been available to blacks."

"A point Professor Martin Kilson made quite well," I said, "reminding us that the white ethnics' experience with upward mobility required no special individualism as far as obtaining government assistance:

> Jews, Italians, Irish, Slavs, Greeks, and other white ethnic groups exploited every conceivable opportunity, including extensive corruption, to bring government—the public purse and public authority—into the balance, providing capital for construction firms and new technological industries, city and state colleges and technical institutes, educational grants and loans, among other government benefits."[30]

Geneva clapped her hands. "Well stated! But it leaves open the question of how those blacks for whom civil rights statutes are mostly meaningless will get a start at a time when unskilled jobs hardly pay a living wage, and manufacturing is leaving the country for so-called off-shore sites where employees can be hired for very low wages."

"You ask the question as though you have an answer."

"Not an answer—but a way of testing the viability of such an economic answer. Bear with me, friend, for the next Chronicle."

Chapter 5

The Racial Barrier
to Reparations

The Chronicle of the Black Reparations Foundation

AFTER MONTHS of excitement, the big day had arrived. The news conference was packed and hot. Television spots, like tiny orbitless suns, bathed the big stage where two dozen civil rights luminaries sat on folding chairs in a blinding glare of hot light. None of them seemed uncomfortable or even slightly put out that all eyes at this media event were on the large, balding white man who walked purposefully to the podium bristling with microphones, shuffled through a stack of notes, and then, in a deep, firm voice, began to give details of what had been rumored for months.

Given his status as one of the world's richest men, Ben Goldrich was accustomed to attention. To paraphrase a popular television commercial, "when Ben Goldrich spoke, people *really* listened"— but not always. Goldrich was here now, he told the televised news conference, because so few had heeded his warnings that the growing black underclass represented both a disgrace to the nation and a potential danger far more serious than any foreign enemy.

The son of an immigrant Jewish tailor, Goldrich said that the familiar statistics regarding the ever-worsening plight of roughly ten million black people living at or below the official poverty level provided a poignant proof that "for those whose ruined lives

123

are reflected in these statistics, the oft-heralded Supreme Court decisions and civil rights laws protecting against overt discrimination had come too late." He quoted a famous economist's conclusion that the "pattern of racial oppression in the past created the huge black underclass, as the accumulation of disadvantages were passed on from generation to generation, and the technological and economic revolution of advanced industrial society combined to insure it a permanent status."[1]

"I credit my success to hard work, faith in my ability, and the opportunity this country provided me when I was young. But," Goldrich asserted, "were I both poor and black, starting out in today's economy, I would fail: my hard work exploited by dead-end service jobs, my faith exploded by the society's still-virulent racism, my promised opportunity exposed as an unobtainable myth for all but a few people of color.

Whatever the benefits of affirmative action for blacks with educational skills and potential, Goldrich warned, again quoting the economist, these programs "are not designed to deal with the problem of the disproportionate concentration of blacks in the low-wage labor market. Their major impact has been in the higher-paying jobs of the expanding service-producing industries in both the corporate and government sectors." As a result, there is indeed, Goldrich feared, a "deepening economic schism . . . developing in the black community, with the black poor falling further and further behind middle- and upper-income blacks."[2]

As Goldrich spoke, the black leaders on the platform nodded, more out of courtesy than surprise. For years Goldrich had been making similar statements, to which few beyond the civil rights community had listened very closely. No government or industry leader believed that anything more was needed than the existing social welfare programs. While expressing concern about the growing black underclass, their main commitment remained with their personal and corporate "bottom lines"—their *sine qua non* for success and achievement and worth. It was, his critics pointed out, easy enough for Ben Goldrich to play humanitarian, but he was speaking as a man whose wealth was reputed to exceed five billion dollars. "Let him put *his* money on the poverty firing line. Then, perhaps, we'll take him seriously."

Frustrated by this response and convinced of the reality of the dangers he warned against, Goldrich had withdrawn from active involvement in his many business holdings to dedicate his life to righting what he believed was the nation's crucial sin. "I have been mightily disappointed in those liberals who, in the 1960s—when it was fashionable—joined blacks in their churches to sing 'We Shall Overcome,' but refuse to make way for them in the workplaces of the 1980s. All of Jewish history," he said, "counsels my commitment to defend any group designated as society's scapegoat, and condemns those long the victims of oppression who now feel so accepted in America that they can join in—even lead—the hypocrisy that urges blacks to forgo government help and pull themselves up on rungs of the economic ladder that no longer exist."

"Today," he said, "with the active participation of those sitting behind me, I am responding to the righteous need of blacks and the sorry hypocrisy of whites by establishing the Black Reparations Foundation, whose simple purpose is to bring economic justice today to the least fortunate of those black people whose forebears were refused such justice after the Civil War. It is with great humility and a strong sense of purpose that I stand here to carry on the work of the greatest abolitionist of them all, the nineteenth-century Radical Republican Thaddeus Stevens of Pennsylvania.[3] You all remember"—Goldrich gave most of his listeners undue credit for a knowledge of American history—"how, in and out of Congress, Congressman Stevens, known as the 'Great Commoner,' urged the nation to break up all the Confederate-owned plantations and, under what was called the 'Forty Acres and a Mule' plan, distribute the land to the freedmen in forty-acre lots. The great Massachusetts senator Charles Sumner made a similar fight in the Senate. But neither of these men were able to persuade the Congress or the country to act. Land that the Freedman's Bureau, the federal agency set up to administer the emancipation process, had distributed to the former slaves was reclaimed and given back to the original Confederate owners.

"The historian Lerone Bennett has written that, when Thaddeus Stevens was seventy-four years old and gnarled as an oak tree, he rose in the House and, always a realist, admitted that his dream of providing reparations to the former slaves was stillborn. In pronouncing the eulogy for his plan, Stevens said:

> In my youth, in my manhood, in my old age, I had fondly dreamed that when any fortunate chance should have broken up [the institution of slavery, we would have] so remodeled all our institutions as to have freed them from every vestige of human oppression, of inequality of rights. . . . This bright dream has vanished like the baseless fabric of a vision.[4]

"Here," said Goldrich, with a dramatic flourish, "I pause to allow you to consider the enormous price this country has paid over the last century because the pleas for economic justice so eloquently voiced by Stevens and Sumner and other ardent abolitionists were not heeded. Though I, too, have tasted the bitter defeat on the issue of black reparations which these men knew so well, I am convinced that their goal was right, but their vehicle, government, was wrong."

Goldrich quickly went on to explain his reason for rejecting federal funding—the twentieth-century version of the rejected nineteenth-century reparations plan the reporters had anticipated. "First," he said, "for better or worse, we live in an era when there is great public support for spending billions for military defense to protect against foreign threats, and equally great opposition to any spending for social programs to guard against domestic disruption."

As he deplored this attitude, he acknowledged its existence and strength. "Moreover," he said, "even if our sensitivities to justice for blacks and real security for us all were greater, my second reason for eschewing government in a reparations plan would retain its validity." Referring to the motivations and the performance of Germany in paying $820 million in reparations to Israel for the resettlement of five hundred thousand Jews, Goldrich referred to the warning of a scholar who had studied the Jewish experience: "Moral commitment to redress of historic wrongs against humanness can be badly compromised in the political and legislative process by which moral commitment is translated into programs and financial support."[5] "This means," Goldrich explained, "that politics and moral rhetoric tend to become confused in the legislative process. We talk about the 'good' reason, while that reason is contradicted by the 'real' reason for political action reflected in the legislation. As a result, 'we are caught off guard, and the legislative actions supposedly designed to correct social and political injustice actually result in greater injustice.' "[6]

Looking up from his text, Goldrich noted that the reporters were getting nervous, looking at their watches, feverishly dashing off to phone their editors and program directors. This, after all, was not simply news; it was racial drama—a subject, more likely than any, save perhaps sex, to hold the attention of readers and viewers.

Goldrich sensed that it was time for specifics. "For the reasons I have just described, I have decided that this program must be privately funded. I'm pleased to report that several wealthy individuals who wish to remain anonymous have contributed to this effort, and it's my fervent hope that many others will join in it. But whether or not such assistance is forthcoming, I am prepared to proceed and have transferred virtually all of my resources—the total assets will exceed twenty-five billion dollars—to the Black Reparations Foundation."

Although Goldrich announced his gift without any special emphasis, the enormous sum shocked even seasoned reporters, who spontaneously joined the blacks on the platform in applause. Not waiting for the applause to die down, Goldrich continued. "With the help of experts in several fields, the Black Reparations Foundation has prepared a complex reparations formula that will move blacks at the poverty level and below up to the economic levels they likely would have held but for the impediments of historic slavery and the continuing disadvantages of racism.

"As should now be clear, while I earnestly believe that black people are entitled to racial reparations, I am concerned about the corrupting effect of any windfall wealth, such as raffles and lotteries. Experience shows that the sudden acquisition of large sums can be destructive to the recipients and endangers relationships with family and friends. For this reason, entitlement to reparations grants will be based on free-enterprise models in which monthly payments are a percentage of currently earned income.

"The grant formula is carefully calibrated to reward enterprise and discourage sloth. Minimum-wage workers will receive grants supplementing their pay by an amount representing what they would have been paid had they been unionized and their wages set through collective bargaining rather than the disadvantageous economies of an overcrowded market of unskilled workers. And as to unemployed blacks or those unable to work, the grants will raise above poverty level the income of each such individual in the underclass. Additional sums will be provided to enable grantees to obtain remedial schooling, job training, job placement, and child care."

Pointing to Black Reparations Foundation associates who were now distributing informational reports to the media members, Goldrich explained that the brochures contained program details as well as answers to their questions. "You will find that the complicated computer algorithms used in the grant formula will not turn the poor into fat cats, but will produce some satisfying results. For example, sharecroppers, exploited over the generations by their landowners, may come into sufficient sums to gain real independence in bargaining, and some may be able to buy the land on which they have labored so long for little return.

"As another example, little-known rhythm and blues singers and jazz musicians, whose work has been systematically copied and presented by whites over the years, may suddenly become wealthy. As they invest earnings to get exposure once denied them, they may also achieve the recognition their talents and skills justify. On the other hand, some well-known white singers and musicians, whose work is simply derivative, may be rejected and fall swiftly not only in fame but in income. The same phenomenon may occur," he predicted, "in other areas where the social vulnerability of black people has made them ready targets of exploitation by whites and, sometimes, by other blacks."

Some in the audience laughed nervously, but Goldrich did not smile. "I want to make clear that the purpose of the Black Reparations Foundation is to do justice to blacks and not cause mischief or sow misery among whites. We must expect readjustments in our social status and in our expectations. It isn't possible to do justice to a long-exploited minority without cost to the majority, all of whom have benefited directly or indirectly. With the understanding and cooperation of all, the dislocations will prove minimal and will soon be forgotten as all our citizens prosper in an environment not involuntarily subsidized by some based on their race. I thank you."

Blacks at all economic levels were overjoyed by the announcement that the Black Reparations Foundation was scheduled to begin functioning in one year. One observer noted that, in black communities across the country, "optimism is up and blood pressure levels are down." "Thanks to the Black Reparations Foundation," a black construction worker said, "I feel now I can make it in America." "The racism remains," a civil rights leader cautioned, while acknowledging that "the economic component of that racism has been neutralized for the black poor."

Predictably, the reaction of much of white America was far less positive. Indeed, there was growing opposition to the scheme. The government launched an official investigation of Ben Goldrich's holdings and scrutinized his reparations plan for legal flaws. None were found. Still, there was concern and growing resentment despite the foundation's expensive, low-key advertising campaign designed to broaden awareness of blacks' historic disadvantages.

The implications and threat to the socio-economic status quo was not lost on the nation's policy makers, who tried to dissuade Goldrich with arguments that his reparations program would disrupt the economy and increase racial hostility as white workers saw their black counterparts doing the same work but in effect earning more money through reparations grants.

Opponents were planning several legal attacks. One challenge would assert that the Black Reparations Foundation was practicing racial discrimination and thus was not entitled to its charitable status under the tax laws. These opponents also contended that, while the foundation was not a government entity bound by the Fifth and the Fourteenth amendments, the scale of the Goldrich holdings was so large, its potential impact on people's lives so mammoth, that it was both appropriate and necessary to bring the foundation under governmental control. In addition, several state legislatures were studying anti-reparations bills which, while racially neutral on their face, would prohibit foundations from distributing assets according to the race of the recipient. Both approaches were characterized by their supporters as upholding integration.

Concerned black groups met with Black Reparations Foundation officials about the opposition. Some representatives recommended canceling the program and agreed with its opponents that it would do more harm than good. Others urged broadening it to include all economically disadvantaged Americans, even though this change would substantially dilute the benefits slated now for poor blacks. Most urged the foundation to go forward with its plans.

Ben Goldrich, now condemned by many people as both a traitor to his class and an enemy of his race, determined even more vigorously to proceed with the implementation of his reparations plans. As he put it, "only an act of Congress sustained by a definitive U.S. Supreme Court decision will bring the program to a halt."

AFTER several minutes, I decided to break the silence. "Did the Black Reparations Foundation survive the legal attacks?"

Looking a bit embarrassed, Geneva shrugged. "I am afraid there is no ending to this Chronicle—or at least none that I now remember."

"That's strange," I said, somewhat annoyed. "There must be more to the story. Reparations claims as compensation for both slavery and discrimination have often been discussed as a remedy for the victims of racism. Proponents have pointed to the abortive post–Civil War effort to give blacks land discussed by Ben Goldrich in the Chronicle, and have also used the precedent of reparations paid by this country to American Indians[7] as well as

German relocation costs of Jews seeking to emigrate to Israel after the Second World War.''[8]

"Not only that," said Geneva, "but, in 1948, a federal law, the Japanese American Evacuation Claims Act, was enacted that paid $38,000,000 in claims made against the government by Japanese-Americans evacuated from the West Coast in the early years of the war. Of course, that sum represented less than ten cents for every dollar claimed lost by Japanese-American evacuees,[9] but it does provide a precedent."

"For a time, it appeared that their story might have a more just ending," I remarked. "As you know, the government forcibly removed 120,000 citizens of Japanese descent from their homes and placed them in internment camps, where they remained as long as four years. In 1944, the Supreme Court determined that the internment policy was valid as a proper exercise of federal war powers.[10] But, on the basis of information in newly uncovered documents, Japanese-American citizens interned during the Second World War, or their representatives, brought suit in federal court charging that the U.S. Government fraudulently concealed the fact that there was no military necessity for the internment program, and thereby violated several of these citizens' rights. The court of appeals—in an opinion written in 1986 by that old civil rights warrior J. Skelly Wright[11]—found that, despite the passage of forty years, plaintiffs may still maintain an action for damages."[12]

"Any idea how the Supreme Court will rule?" Geneva asked.

"It will certainly be divided, as was the court of appeals; but the issue for the Japanese-Americans will be, as it has been for blacks, less whether injustice was done than whether serious procedural—that is, political—difficulties can be removed. The dissenting judge in the Japanese-American case admitted, for example, that the 'internment of fellow Americans on the basis of race, and out of what now appear to have been an excessive enshrinement of military necessity, sets a scenario for retributive justice.'[13]

"Also, the reparations concept was given a good deal of attention when, during the late 1960s, James Forman, then president of the Student Non-Violent Coordinating Committee (SNCC),

131

disrupted the Sunday-morning service at New York's liberal Riverside Church and read a 'black manifesto' statement condemning racism in the church and the country and demanding five hundred million dollars from the 'Christian white churches and the Jewish synagogues.' "[14]

"How were Forman's claims handled?" Geneva asked.

"It was a wonderful publicity ploy. One writer reported that 'Forman's violation of the most sacred hour of the week and his violent anti-American rhetoric against America, capitalism and the church touched millions of nerve ends like a multi-pronged cattle prod.'[15] Although the disruption was universally condemned, and other black militant groups who tried similar tactics won little support from the courts,[16] during the next year or so, various churches and denominational groups gave several million dollars to black churches for social-reform programs."

"I will bet," Geneva interrupted, laughing, "that the gifts all carried provisions that the funds not go to Forman or the group he represented."

"You're exactly right. This predictable reaction to black demands that are other than gentle would be funny if it weren't so sad. But the historic evidence on the willingness of those in power to provide a reparations remedy for past injustice is mixed. Are you sure," I asked again, "that you don't remember the conclusion to this Chronicle?"

"Not so far," Geneva confessed. "My mind simply went blank—but the many attractive components in the Ben Goldrich proposal would seem to give it a far better chance than Forman's threatening demands."

"I'm surprised, Geneva. Are you, the arch racial pessimist of all time, actually suggesting that the Black Reparations Foundation wasn't doomed to fail from the start?"

"I am," said Geneva. "Look, my pessimism reflects my current assessment of our racial condition. It will shift to enthusiastic optimism when I discover a strategy with promise that justifies my faith. That is why I am studying these Chronicles with such care. You would be of more help if you were more objective about the continuing worth of those obsolete litigation approaches to which you remain so devoted."

"Just a minute, Geneva, it's you, not I, who forgot the Chronicle's ending. And without an ending, how can we really know what message the Chronicle intends to convey?"

"I apologize, but the alternative outcomes are apparent. Either opponents of the reparations plan would prevail and no foundation grants would be made, or Ben Goldrich would put his plan into operation on schedule and millions of blacks would begin to receive carefully calculated compensation for discrimination suffered by them and their forebears. As a prerequisite to the latter possibility, the foundation would have to obtain some pretty good lawyering to ward off the hostile lawsuits suggested by the Chronicle. Do you think you could handle those cases, Professor?"

"Taking the cases wouldn't be difficult, Geneva, but winning them in the atmosphere of public resentment and fear generated by the mere announcement of the plan—that might be a formidable task. The public was outraged by Forman's disruption of a church service, but the Chronicle reports an uproar when the public learns that perhaps the nation's richest man has donated his whole fortune to help remedy wrongs the society has ignored for years."

Geneva interrupted. "Please stop bemoaning the usual resistance to any program promising gains for blacks, particularly if— as Goldrich admits—they might involve dislocations for whites. Simply tell me how you would represent the Black Reparations Foundation."

"Assuming its officers would have more faith in my legal acumen than present company does," I replied, "I'd counsel the following:

"First, as to the charge that the grants reflect a policy of racial discrimination, we must argue that the foundation grants do not represent an invidious discrimination against whites barred by civil rights laws. Rather, eligibility is based on previous condition of servitude because of race. Since only blacks were held in slavery and only blacks have suffered the injustice of racial discrimination, it would be appropriate and not invidious to target grants intended to remedy the continuing harm done on the basis of race.

"I would argue vigorously against the judicial tendency to

use—in order to forestall effective remediation of discrimination already suffered—standards established by blacks to end discrimination. The Supreme Court's 1978 decision in the *Bakke* case is an unhappy example of this practice.[17] Similarly, I would distinguish the situation of only blacks being eligible for Black Reparations Foundation grants from cases like *Bob Jones University* (1983),[18] where the Court found it appropriate for the government to deny charitable tax status to a private church school that bars students or staff involved in or advocating interracial marriage."

"And would you expect to win on at least that aspect of the legal challenge?" Geneva asked.

"I would hope so, but there would be some difficulty. Remember that *Bob Jones University* became a major case even though the legal issues it raised had apparently been settled a dozen years earlier.[19] To take seriously the church school's claim that its opposition to intermarriage—based on the inferiority of blacks—is a part of its religious belief, one must assume, as much of the country does, that the deity is white. Given that assumption, we must not be surprised that 'racial discrimination' prohibitions are applied to obviously remedial programs even as the prohibitions themselves are evaded to perpetuate discrimination against blacks.

"Even so," I continued with more confidence than I felt, "the Black Reparations Foundation should survive this test. And if Congress or state legislatures were to carry out plans suggested in the Chronicle to enact laws barring such grants, a similar argument responding to the alleged racially discriminatory character of those grants could be raised. Foundation giving has traditionally been allowed broad discretion. There must be thousands of programs whose mission was to aid blacks in one way or another. To prohibit Black Reparations Foundation grants as discriminatory while acquiescing in many similar programs would raise serious due-process questions that I think courts would be unable to ignore."

"None of those programs," Geneva pointed out, "has the coverage and potential impact of the Black Reparations Foundation's twenty-five billion dollars."

"But the size of a program shouldn't determine its validity."

"Not logically, but politically it would make a major difference out of which a legal distinction could be carved."

It still did not seem to me to pose a problem. "Not too long ago, a New York businessman told students finishing the sixth grade at a Harlem school that, if they remained in school and graduated, he would pay for their college educations.[20] The promise received wide and positive media coverage, and the businessman was almost canonized as a living saint. Other businessmen made similar promises,[21] I would imagine to similar acclaim."

"That's a very different thing," Geneva interrupted. "The scope of the New York businessman's beneficence on behalf of blacks is limited and takes the form of scholarships to students that improve their potential. Goldrich planned to raise the actual status of blacks as compared with their white counterparts, and that is why in the Chronicle he was more condemned than canonized. Suppose for a moment, though, that the grants did not have a racial character and, as some advised, were made on the basis of poverty. Would there then be any basis for legal attack or motivation for legislative prohibition?"

"I'd think not, but spreading the resources so broadly as to dilute dissent means that the basic racial remediation is lost. After all, if everyone moves up one notch on the ladder, blacks will remain below their white counterparts, vulnerable to all the disadvantages of their subordinate status."

"But there might," Geneva suggested, "be opposition other than racial. In a competitive society, all are threatened by any aid to those deemed lower on the economic scale that exceeds bare minimum subsistence—as in the resentment to the food-stamp program when a recipient is seen purchasing a steak or other luxury food."

"That's a social phenomenon," I said. "Many social reformers find that any improvement in the status of the poor requires a bigger improvement in the status of the middle and the upper classes. Take the Tax Reform Act of 1986, where long-sought reform was gained when six million poor taxpayers were dropped from the rolls—but the price was a major reduction in tax rates for higher-income taxpayers."[22]

135

Geneva glanced at the big wall clock, as she had been doing every few minutes. "To get back to the point, let me ask you this. We know that today there would be broad opposition to any modern reparations plan like the 'forty acres and a mule' of the 1860s. Considering all the components of this opposition, do you see a theme or point around which to center an argument that the plan is unconstitutional?"

"I'd like a week in the library to prepare a response to your question, curbstone opinions being worth no more when they come from law professors than from lawyers in practice."

"Some of us would maintain that they are worth less," Geneva said, smiling, "but I will consider your status with your answer."

"Your generosity is overwhelming," I murmured, trying to organize my thoughts. "It seems to me that, even without a major legal theory, the Black Reparations Foundation program could be seriously undermined by petty harassments."

"For example?"

"Suppose employers, concerned that the presence of reparations grantees among their employees would create dissension in the workplace, intensify racial divisions, and thus threaten productivity and profits. Acting on those fears, employers might refuse to employ blacks receiving grants, rejecting them not on the basis of race, but because of their disruptive potential. An anti-foundation employment policy would likely spread swiftly and might even be incorporated into state and federal laws."

"Such a policy would seem to violate fair-employment laws," Geneva said indignantly.

I looked at her with amusement. "Shall we prepare a list of all the policies like those requiring teacher applicants to gain a certain level on standardized tests—policies that are held valid even though they seriously disadvantage black applicants?"[23]

"I get the point. At the least, foundation funds and energies would be sidetracked into fighting legal battles, and more than a few blacks would conclude that the grants, helpful as they might be, were not worth risking a job—even a low-paying job."

"Exactly. But I doubt the country would be satisfied with coercion on an employer-by-employer basis. Ben Goldrich's proposal makes him, as his critics claim, a traitor to his class. This is not philanthropy, but a major redistribution of the wealth, a danger even if carried out according to class alone. Limiting the redistribution to the black poor would upset or at least threaten the long-standing arrangement, no less fixed because it is unspoken, that whites are to be taken care of first in this society—on the ongoing assumption that they, not blacks, are America's chosen ones."

"But is that motivation and belief so strong that the nation would accept all the dangers of black poverty, crime, and degradation? Until now, such dangers have been tolerated, as was slavery, because no one has offered to pay the price of remedying the evil. But if the government or someone like Ben Goldrich were to come forward and accept the bill, wouldn't that make a big difference?"

"Paying the financial cost is only one component of opposition. Protecting the vested interest of superior status is of equal importance."

"You sound convincing, but somehow I do not agree, perhaps because I do not . . ." Her voice trailed off, as a perplexed look came over her face.

"What is it?" I asked. "Are you OK?"

Geneva put her head in her hands. "Just give me a few minutes. I think the end of the Chronicle is coming back to me."

Five minutes passed. Ten. Geneva sat motionless, almost in a trance. When I mentioned the time, she did not respond and seemed not to hear me. In fact, I felt I was in the room alone. It was more than a little unnerving. What, I wondered, had all the years done to this brilliant woman? She was not, I thought, insane, but she was far from normal, whatever that is. I sighed in resignation. She was one of my best friends. She had been ill for a very long time and now viewed herself in some sort of serious trouble, which seemed to me—I hesitated to raise the word even to myself—*crazy*.

At that point she recovered herself, her expression far from happy. "You are right," she said, shaking her head, "and I have been foolish.

"It must have been two years after Goldrich announced his plan. The Black Reparations Foundation had been undermined by lawsuits, and recipients had been harassed as un-American and worse. I recall seeing Goldrich, now old and beaten down, in court standing before a judge. Apparently, in the Chronicle, Congress has enacted a statute barring from interstate commerce the distribution of any funds, from public or private sources, that have the effect of providing a financial advantage to recipients based on race—programs providing such assistance to fewer than one thousand persons not being covered, I assume, to save traditional aid programs."

"And the Supreme Court has approved this law?"

"According to the Chronicle, yes. I remember many references to the broad power of Congress under the Commerce clause to regulate commerce between the states: that this power had been utilized by Congress to eliminate racial discrimination in privately owned businesses under Title II of the Civil Rights Act of 1964;[24] and that programs prohibited by the act have a potential for racial disruption and injustice no less than had the Jim Crow laws."

"That's ridiculous!" I spluttered.

"Save your anger," Geneva warned, "until you hear this. In the Chronicle, the Supreme Court's opinion spends some time with the Black Reparations Foundation argument that, while the grants have been targeted to blacks, that is the only means of remedying the disadvantage of slavery and the badges of servitude. The Court responds that not only are the origins of the slavery standard of eligibility too remote in time to justify their continued validity at a period when nondiscrimination is the acknowledged legal standard, but the fact that the ancestors of blacks were black is no more justifiable as a criterion for receiving grants than was the right to vote without taking any tests justified in the 1915 grandfather-clause cases (see page 92)[25] because a white applicant's grandparents had voted at a time when blacks were barred from voting."

"Well," I said with resignation, "legal critics who claim that doctrinal rules are indeterminate and can be used to reach any result the courts choose, would have a field day with this decision. But," I asked, "you spoke of Ben Goldrich as being before a court himself on some matter related to the Black Reparations Foundation?"

"Apparently, a flaw has been found in the structure he created in giving his wealth to the foundation and reserving a few million for his personal needs. He now has to choose between giving everything he has to the foundation or dissolving it."

"A demand, I assume, that he make the supreme economic sacrifice to atone for his sin of showing up the rest of society. What is his decision?"

"I'm not sure. I remember black people, many of them crying, crowding into the court to offer Goldrich support. He himself insisted on prefacing his choice by reading the speech Thaddeus Stevens gave in the House when he acknowledged defeat of the original 'forty acres and a mule' idea. Then I recall a lot of commotion, the judge furiously pounding his gavel, and—at the last— all of the other blacks drowning him out and raising their voices in a spiritual: 'Nobody Knows the Trouble I've Seen.' "

Chapter 6

The Unspoken Limit on Affirmative Action

The Chronicle of the DeVine Gift

IT WAS a major law school, one of the best, but I do not remember how I came to be teaching there rather than at Howard, my alma mater. My offer, the first ever made to a black, was the culmination of years of agitation by students and a few faculty members. It was the spring of my second year. I liked teaching and writing, but I was exhausted and considering resigning.

I had become the personal counselor and confidante of virtually all the black students and a goodly number of the whites. The black students clearly needed someone with whom to share their many problems, and white students, finding a faculty member actually willing to take time with them, were not reluctant to help keep my appointments book full. I liked the students, but it was hard to give them as much time as they needed. I also had to prepare for classes—where I was expected to give an award-winning performance each day—and serve on every committee at the law school and the university where minority representation was desired. In addition, every emergency involving a racial issue was deemed my problem. I admit I wanted to be involved in these problems, but they all required time and energy. Only another black law teacher would believe what I had to do to make time for research and writing.

So, when someone knocked on my door late one warm spring

afternoon as I was frantically trying to finish writing final exam questions, I was tempted to tell the caller to go away. But I did not. The tall, distinguished man who introduced himself as DeVine Taylor was neither a student nor one of the black students' parents who often dropped by, when in town, just to meet their child's only black teacher.

Mr. Taylor, unlike many parents and students, came quickly to the point. He apologized for not having made an appointment, but explained that his visit involved a matter requiring confidentiality. He showed me a card and other papers identifying him as president of the DeVine Hair Products Company, a familiar name in many black homes and one of the country's most successful black businesses. By that time, I recognized Mr. Taylor's face and assured him I knew of his business even if I did not use his products.

"You may also know," Mr. Taylor said, "that my company and I haven't been much involved in this integration business. It seems to me that civil rights organizations are ready to throw out the positive aspects of segregation with the bad. I think we need to wake up to the built-in limits on all the 'equal opportunity' they're preaching. Much of it may prove a snare that will cost us what we have built up over the years without giving us anything better to take its place. Personally, I'm afraid they will integrate me into bankruptcy. Even now, white companies are undercutting me in every imaginable way.

"But," he interrupted himself with a deep sigh, "that is not why I'm here. You have heard of foundations that make awards to individuals based on their performance rather than on their proposals. Well, for some time my company has been searching for blacks who are truly committed to helping other blacks move up. We have located and helped several individuals over the years with what we call the 'DeVine Gift.' We know of your work and believe your efforts merit our support. We want to help you help other blacks, and we can spend a large amount of money to fund your endeavors. For tax and other business reasons, we can't provide our help in cash. And we don't wish anyone to know that we're providing the help."

He was clearly serious, and I tried to respond appropriately.

"Well, Mr. Taylor, I appreciate the compliment, but it is not clear how a black hair products company can be of assistance to a law teacher. Unless"—the idea struck me suddenly—"unless you can help locate more blacks and other minorities with the qualifications needed for membership on the faculty of this law school."

Mr. Taylor understood at once. "I was a token black in a large business before I left in frustration to start my own company," he said. "With our nationwide network of sales staff, I think we can help."

When I had been hired, the faculty promised that although I was their first black teacher, I would not be their last. This was not to be a token hire, they assured me, but the first step toward achieving a fully integrated faculty. But subsequent applicants, including a few with better academic credentials than my own, were all found wanting in one or another respect. Frustration regarding this matter, no less than fatigue, had brought me to the point of resignation before Mr. Taylor's visit.

With the behind-the-scenes help from the DeVine Gift, the law school hired its second black teacher during the summer—a young man with good credentials and with some teaching experience at another law school. He was able to fill holes in the curriculum caused by two unexpected faculty resignations. The following year, we "discovered," again with the assistance of Mr. Taylor's network, three more minority teachers—a Hispanic man, an Asian woman, and another black woman. In addition, one of our black graduates, a law-review editor, was promised a position when he completed a judicial clerkship.

We now had six minority faculty members, far more than any other major white law school. I was ecstatic, a sentiment that I soon learned was not shared by many of my white colleagues. While I am usually sensitive about such things, I so enjoyed the presence of the other minority faculty members, who eased the burdens on my time and gave me a sense of belonging to a "critical mass," that I failed to realize the growing unrest among some white faculty members.

Had we stopped at six, perhaps nothing would have been said. But the following year, Mr. Taylor's company, with growing expertise, recruited an exceptionally able black lawyer. The aca-

demic credentials of this, the Seventh Candidate, were impecca-
ble. The top student at our competitor school, he had edited the
law review and written a superb student note. After clerking for
a federal court of appeals judge and a U.S. Supreme Court Justice,
he had joined a major New York City law firm where, after three
years of work they rated "splendid," he was in line for early election to partnership. Now, though, the DeVine people had inspired
him to teach.

When the dean came to see me, he talked aimlessly for some
time before he reached the problem troubling him and, I later
gathered, much of the faculty. The problem was that our faculty
would soon be 25 percent minority. "You know, Geneva, we
promised you we would become an integrated faculty, and we've
kept that promise—admittedly with a lot of help from you. But I
don't think we can hire anyone else for a while. I thought we
might 'share the wealth' a bit by recommending your candidate
to some of our sister schools whose minority-hiring records are
far less impressive than our own."

"Dean," I said, as calmly and coldly as I could, "I am not interested in recruiting black teachers for other law schools. Each of the
people we have hired is good, as you have boasted many times,
publicly and privately. And I can assure you that the Seventh
Candidate will be better than anyone now on the faculty without
regard to race."

"You could be right, Geneva, but let's be realistic. This is one
of the oldest and finest law schools in the country. It simply would
not be the same school for our students and the alumni with a
predominantly minority faculty—as I thought you, an advocate
of affirmative action, would understand."

"I am no mathematician," I said, "but 25 percent is far from a
majority. Still, it is more racial integration than you want, even
though none of the minorities, excluding perhaps myself, has
needed any affirmative-action help to qualify for the job. I also
understand, tardily I admit, that you folks never expected that I
would find more than a few minorities who could meet your academic qualifications. You never expected that you would have to
reveal what has always been your chief qualification—a white
face, preferably from an upper-class background."

To his credit, the dean remained fairly calm throughout my tirade. "I've heard you argue that black law schools, like Howard, should retain mainly black faculties and student bodies, even if to do so they have to turn away whites with better qualifications. We have a similar situation in that we want to retain our image as a white school just as you want Howard to retain its image as a black school."

"That's a specious argument, Dean, and you know it! Black schools have a remediation responsibility for the victims of this country's long-standing and, from what I am hearing, continuing racism—a responsibility different from schools like this one, which should be grateful for the chance to change its all-white image. And," I added, "if you're not grateful, I'm certain the courts will give you ample reason to reconsider when my seventh candidate sues you for the job he earned and is entitled to get."

The dean was not surprised by my unprofessional threat to sue. "I have discussed this at length with some faculty members, and we realize that you may wish to test this matter in the courts. We think, however, that there are few precedents on the issues such a suit will raise. I don't want to be unkind. We do appreciate your recruitment efforts, Geneva, but a law school of our caliber and tradition simply cannot look like a professional basketball team."

He left my office after that parting shot, and my first reaction was rage. Then, as I slowly realized the real significance of all that had happened since I received the DeVine Gift, the tears came, and kept coming. Through those tears, over the next few days, I completed grading my final exams. Then I announced my resignation as well as the reasons for it.

When I told the Seventh Candidate that the school would not offer him a position and why, he was strangely silent, only thanking me for my support. About a week later, I received a letter from him—mailed not from his law firm but, according to the postmark, from a small, all-black town in Oklahoma.

Dear Professor Crenshaw:

Until now, when black people employed race to explain failure, I, like the black neoconservative scholars, wondered how they might have fared had they made less noise and done more work. Embracing self-confidence and eschewing self-pity seemed the right formula for success. One had to show more heart and shed fewer tears. Commitment to personal resources rather than reliance on public charity, it seemed to me, is the American way to reach goals—for blacks as well as for whites. Racial bias is not, I thought, a barrier but a stimulant toward showing *them* what *we* can do in the workplace as well as on the ball field, in the classroom as well as on the dance floor.

Now no rationale will save what was my philosophy for achievement, my justification for work. My profession, the law, is not a bulwark against this destruction. It is instead a stage prop illuminated with colored lights to mask the ongoing drama of human desolation we all suffer, regardless of skills and work and personal creed.

You had suggested I challenge my rejection in the courts, but even if I won the case and in that way gained the position to which my abilities entitled me, I would not want to join a group whose oft-stated moral commitment to the meritocracy has been revealed as no more than a hypocritical conceit, a means of elevating those like themselves to an elite whose qualifications for their superior positions can never be tested because they do not exist.

Your law school faculty may not realize that the cost of rejecting me is exposing themselves. They are, as Professor Roberto Unger has said in another context, like a "priesthood that had lost their faith and kept their jobs."[1]

But if I condemn hypocrisy in the law school, I must not condone it in myself. What the law school did when its status as a mainly white institution was threatened is precisely what even elite colleges faced with a growing number of highly qualified Asian students are doing: changing the definition of merit.[2] My law firm and virtually every major institution in this country would do the same thing in a similar crisis of identity. I have thus concluded that I can no longer play a role in the tragic farce in which the talents and worth of a few of us who happen to get there first is dangled like bait before the masses who are led to believe that what can never be is a real possibility. When next you hear from me, it will be in a new role as avenger rather than apologist. This system must be forced to recognize what it is doing to you and me and to itself. By the time you read this, it will be too late for you to reason with me. I am on my way.

Yours,
The Seventh Candidate

This decision, while a shock, hardly prepared me for the disturbing letter that arrived a few days later from DeVine Taylor, who evidently had read of my well-publicized resignation.

Dear Geneva,

Before you received the DeVine Gift, your very presence at the law school posed a major barrier to your efforts to hire additional minority faculty. Having appointed you, the school relaxed. Its duty was done. Its liberal image was assured. When you suggested the names of other minorities with skills and backgrounds like your own, your success was ignored and those you named were rejected for lack of qualifications. When the DeVine Gift forced your school to reveal the hidden but no less substantive basis for dragging their feet after you were hired, the truth became clear.

As a token minority law teacher, Geneva, you provided an alien institution with a facade of respectability of far more value to them than any aid you gave to either minority students or the cause of black people. You explained your resignation as a protest. But you should realize that removing yourself from that prestigious place was a necessary penance for the inadvertent harm you have done to the race you are sincerely committed to save.

146

I am happy to see that the DeVine Gift has served its intended purpose. I wish you success in your future work.

DeVine Taylor

A DEVASTATING NOTE," I murmured, imagining how it must have shocked Geneva, as I watched her pacing the room in agitation, oblivious of me. She said something about the foolishness of accepting a teaching position at a school where she would be so vulnerable.

I tried to reassure her. "I think that most black people, faculty as well as students, feel exposed and vulnerable at predominantly white law schools. And I know that most black teachers run into faculty resistance when they seek to recruit a second nonwhite faculty member."

"Why black law teachers more than blacks in any other occupation?" Geneva asked, finally taking notice of me.

"It is true," I said, trying to organize my thoughts, "that there are few black workers who do not experience some sense of exclusion because of race. For example, there's plenty of discrimination in professional sports where ability can be measured accurately by performance.[3] The sense of unease to which I refer, though, is blacks' experience in positions where it's difficult to objectify job performance. In elite, academic settings, an applicant without outstanding grades, earned preferably at a major educational institution, is usually given little consideration. Law schools adhere to this fixation on grades even for applicants who have done extremely well in law practice."

"Well do I know it," said Geneva. "My faculty colleagues insisted that, in the hiring of law teachers, grades are a better indicator of intellectual ability and predictor of scholarly potential than is success in law practice."

"A response that simultaneously insults law practitioners—in-

147

cluding those trained at the law schools where the policy is followed—and raises questions about the real value of legal scholarship which could be the subject of a separate discussion. But the unease I want to focus on is that experienced by the black faculty member who did not earn the highest grades or graduate from a top school. Reports from minority law teachers who are 'firsts' at their schools parallel your experience in the Chronicle. When they suggest the names of other blacks and Hispanics, often with grades as good as, even better than, their own, the usual response is: 'We want more minorities, but those you recommend just don't seem to have the intellectual background we need at this school.' "[4]

"Tell me about it," Geneva said.

"Even with all the problems, law teaching has many wonderful advantages whether you're black or white—but for blacks, it's also the perfect environment in which to develop paranoia. Your black friends who want to get into teaching wonder why you're never able to follow through on your promises to help. And you know that the black applicant your faculty rejects out of hand today would be hired tomorrow if you suddenly suffered a fatal heart attack."

"Before I gained the questionable advantage of the DeVine Gift," Geneva confessed, "rejection of the minorities I recommended would send me into a depression. What were they trying to tell me? Was it that I was doing such a great job that they saw no need to hire others like myself? Or was it, rather, that my performance was so poor that they refused to hire anyone else for fear of making another serious mistake?"

"Happily," I said, trying to steer the discussion back to the Chronicle, "our question is whether the Supreme Court would view the law school's rejection of a seventh eminently qualified candidate as impermissible racial discrimination. I would guess from the Chronicle that the law school's action was not challenged in court."

Geneva thought for a moment. "That part is fuzzy. I probably knew all along, but repressed, what the school really thought about its minority faculty members. I guess I was naïve, but even with all the problems about who was qualified, and who was really smart—I had discovered that those questions bedevil even those whites on the faculty who have flawless academic credentials—I had come to feel a part of the school. The Seventh Candidate, according to his letter, was in no mood to challenge his rejection in the courts. But all I remember is resigning and that most troubling note from Mr. Taylor."

"That's too bad because, at first glance, I don't think the dean's justified in his confidence that the law would support the school's rejection of the Seventh Candidate. Although the courts have withdrawn from their initial expansive reading of the federal fair-employment laws,[5] I would think that even a conservative court might find for your seventh minority candidate, owing to his superior credentials and the hard-to-deny fact that his race was the major factor in his rejection."[6]

"Remember," Geneva cautioned, "that, despite what the dean told me, the law school would claim first that its preference for whites seeking the opening is based on their superior qualifications. I gather that the cases indicate that an employer's subjective evaluation can play a major role in decisions involving highly qualified candidates who seek professional positions."

"That's true. Courts are reluctant to interfere with upper-level hiring decisions in the absence of strong proof that those decisions have been based on an intent to discriminate. Judicial deference is particularly pronounced when the employment decision at issue affects the health or safety of large numbers of people. The courts, for example, have hesitated to interfere with decisions regarding the hiring of airline pilots.[7] But, more generally, courts have shown an unwillingness to interfere with upper-level hiring decisions in the 'elite' professions,[8] including university teaching.[9] Under current law, if there are few objective hiring criteria and legitimate subjective considerations, plaintiffs will only rarely obtain a searching judicial inquiry into their allegation of discrimination in hiring."[10]

"In other words," Geneva said, with a hint of sarcasm, "despite your optimistic opening, what you are now saying is that this would not be an easy case even if the plaintiff were the first rather than the seventh candidate."

"I never said it would be an easy case. I do think the Court could surprise the law-school dean if the school's action were challenged and the litigation record showed the Seventh Candidate's qualifications to be clearly superior to those of other candidates. It might be an attractive situation for the Court. The discrimination is clear, and the situation isn't likely to arise very often. The Court just might use the case to reach a 'contradiction-closing' decision: that is, one that narrows the gap between the country's equality precepts and its often blatantly discriminatory practices. In predictable fashion, minorities and liberal whites would hail a decision for the black applicant as proof that racial justice is still available through the courts."

Geneva gave me a look best described as stunned pity. "Having painted that scenario filled with rosy 'just mights,' are you now ready to tell me what the Court would be *most* likely to do in this case?"

Like most law teachers, I am ready to predict judicial outcomes even without being asked, but knowing how important this discussion was to Geneva, I thought it wise to review the situation realistically. "Well, weighing all the factors in the cold light of the current Court's conservative drift, the dean's belief that his law school would prevail in court may be justified after all."

"Well," Geneva slumped in mock exhaustion, "getting that out of you was like pulling teeth. And we have not yet considered the possibility that, even if the Court found that our candidate had the best paper credentials, the law school might have an alternative defense."

"I'm afraid that's also correct. The law school might argue that, even if its rejection of the Seventh Candidate was based on race, the decision was justified. The school might aver that its reputation and financial well-being were based on its status as a 'majority institution.' The maintenance of a predominantly white faculty, the school would say, is essential to the preservation of an appropriate image, to the recruitment of faculty and students, and to the financial support of alumni. With heartfelt expressions of regret that 'the world is not a better place,' the law school would urge the Court to find that neither federal fair-employment laws nor the Constitution would prohibit it from discriminating against minority candidates when the percentage of minorities on the faculty exceeds the percentage of minorities within the population. At the least, the school would contend that no such prohibition should apply while most of the country's law schools continue to maintain nearly all-white faculties."

"That," Geneva observed with a raised eyebrow, "was an effective summary, counselor. Are you sure you do not harbor a secret urge to represent the other side?"

"If that's supposed to be a joke, its humor is lost on me. What I am suggesting is less what a school would actually argue, but what most of them, in fact, believe—and what the courts believe as well."

"Well, then, how do you think the Court would respond to such an argument?"

"Given the outstanding quality of the minority faculty, courts might discount the law school's fear that it would lose status and support if one-fourth of its teaching staff were other than white."

Geneva did not look convinced. "I don't know. I think a part of the dean's concern was that, if I could find seven outstanding minority candidates, then I could find more—so many more that the school would eventually face the possibility of having a 50 percent minority faculty. And the courts would be concerned about that precedent. What, they might think, if other schools later developed similar surfeits of superqualified minority job applicants?"

"Well, the courts have hardly been overwhelmed with cases demanding that upper-level employers have a 25 to 50 percent minority work force, particularly in the college and university teaching areas. But perhaps you're right. A Supreme Court case involving skilled construction workers suggests that an employer may introduce evidence of its hiring of blacks in the past to show that an otherwise unexplained action was not racially motivated.[11] Perhaps, then, an employer who has hired many blacks in the past may at some point decide to cease considering them. Even if the Court didn't explicitly recognize this argument, it might take the law school's situation into account. In fact, the Court might draw an analogy to housing cases in which courts have recognized that whites usually prefer to live in predominantly white housing developments."

151

"I am unfamiliar with those cases," Geneva said. "Have courts approved ceilings on the number of minorities who may live in a residential area?"

"They have, indeed. Acting on the request of housing managers trying to maintain integrated developments, courts have tailored tenant racial balance to levels consistent with the refusal of whites to live in predominantly black residential districts. A federal court, for example, has allowed the New York City Housing Authority to limit the number of apartments it made available to minority persons whenever 'such action is essential to promote a racially balanced community and to avoid concentrated racial pockets that will result in a segregated community.'[12] The court feared that unless it allowed the housing authority to impose limits on minority occupancy, a number of housing developments would reach the 'tipping point'—the point at which the percentage of minorities living in an area becomes sufficiently large that virtually all white residents move out and other whites refuse to take their places.[13]

"You know, civil rights groups developed 'benign' housing quotas before most fair-housing laws were enacted. But the technique has always been controversial. Professor Boris Bittker examined the legal issues in a 1962 article written in the form of three hypothetical judicial opinions reviewing the constitutionality of an ordinance designed to promote residential integration by limiting the number of blacks and whites who would reside in a planned community.[14] The majority opinion struck down the ordinance on the rationale that the Constitution is 'color-blind.' The opinion relied on prior cases invalidating housing-segregation schemes,[15] and refused to examine the town's contention that this ordinance differed from invalid schemes because it was intended to promote racial integration. A dissenting opinion maintained that the Constitution 'may be color-blind, but it is not short-sighted.'[16] Distinguishing the cases that the majority cited, the dissent viewed the ordinance as a reasonable approach intended to remedy a vexing problem. Although the ordinance involved a racial classification, the dissent argued, it was not hostile toward blacks and should not be struck down. Finally, a concurring opinion noted that blacks are likely to resent the restrictions imposed by invidious segregation schemes. Emphasizing the odiousness of racial classifications, the concurring judge urged the town to seek integration through education and other voluntary means. The concurrence also expressed concern about the precedential potential of a decision approving the 'proportional representation' of blacks in housing, jobs, and elective offices.[17]

"The analogy is not perfect, but the 'tipping point' phenomenon in housing plans may differ little from the faculty's reaction to your seventh candidate. Both reflect a desire by whites to dominate their residential and nonresidential environments. If this is true, the arguments used to support benign racial quotas in housing could be enlisted to support the law school's employment decision."

"But," argued Geneva, "I do not view as in any way benign the law school's refusal to hire the Seventh Candidate. The school's decision was unlike the adoption of a housing quota intended to establish or protect a stable integrated community before most private discrimination in the housing area was barred by law. The law school did not respond to a 'tipping point' resulting from the individual decisions of numerous parties beyond the authorities' ability to control, but instead imposed a 'stopping point' for hiring blacks and other minorities, regardless of their qualifications. School officials, whose actions are covered by federal civil rights statutes, arbitrarily determined a cutoff point."

"Don't get trapped in semantics, Geneva! A so-called benign housing quota seems invidious to the blacks excluded by its operation. They are no less victims of housing bias than are those excluded from neighborhoods by restrictive covenants. Yet at least in some courts, those excluded by benign quotas have no remedy. In our case, the law school could argue that the Seventh Candidate should likewise have no remedy: he has made—albeit involuntarily—a sacrifice for the long-run integration goals that are often persuasive in the housing sphere.

"In any event, the Court would likely apply a rule that incorporates a desire for white dominance without, of course, admitting as much. Perhaps someone would resurrect and revamp Professor Herbert Wechsler's view that the legal issue in state-imposed segregation cases is not discrimination but rather associational rights.

Assuming, he said, that segregation denies blacks freedom of association with whites, then 'integration forces an association upon those for whom it is unpleasant and repugnant.' The task, according to Professor Wechsler, was to consider and balance these associational rights in accord with neutral principles of law.[18] Of course, courts originally ignored Professor Wechsler's call for a neutrally principled formulation of the antisegregation decisions, but they might now take up and distort his views in order to establish limits on the *level* of desegregation required by law. Specifically, courts might hold that once employers have achieved a certain compliance with civil rights laws, they may consider openly how hiring more minorities will affect the conditions and atmosphere of their workplaces. I don't believe Professor Wechsler would be pleased with this development, but his emphasis on associational rights in desegregation cases may be used to support just such a result."

"In other words," Geneva said, "if and when the number of blacks qualified for upper-level jobs exceeds the token representation envisioned by most affirmative-action programs, opposition of the character exhibited by my law school could provide the impetus for a judicial ruling that employers have done their 'fair share' of minority hiring. This rule, while imposing limits on constitutionally required racial fairness for a black elite, would devastate civil rights enforcement for all minorities. In effect, the Court would formalize and legitimize the subordinate status that is already a *de facto* reality."

"Indeed, affirmative-action remedies have flourished because they offer more benefit to the institutions that adopt them than they do to the minorities whom they're nominally intended to serve. Initially, at least in higher education, affirmative-action policies represented the response of school officials to the considerable pressures placed on them to hire minority faculty members and to enroll minority students. Rather than overhaul admissions criteria that provided easy access to offspring of the upper class and presented difficult barriers to all other applicants, officials claimed they were setting lower admissions standards for minority candidates. This act of self-interested beneficence had unfortunate results. Affirmative action now 'connotes the undertaking of remedial activity beyond what normally would be required. It sounds in *noblesse oblige*, not legal duty, and suggests the giving of charity rather than the granting of relief.'[19] At the same time, the affirmative-action overlay on the overall admissions standards admits only a trickle of minorities. These measures are, at best, 'a modest mechanism for increasing the number of minority professionals, adopted as much to further the self-interest of the white majority as to aid the designated beneficiaries.'[20]

"And one last point. Some courts have been reluctant to review academic appointments, because 'to infer discrimination from a comparison among candidates is to risk a serious infringement of first amendment values.' "[21]

"In other words," said Geneva, "the selection of faculty members ascends to the level of a First Amendment right of academic freedom."

"I'm afraid so, and the law school's lawyers would certainly not ignore Justice Lewis F. Powell's perhaps unintended support for this position given in his 1978 *Bakke* opinion, in which he discussed admissions standards in the context of a university's constitutional right of academic freedom.[22] He acknowledged that ethnic diversity was 'only one element in a range of factors a university properly may consider in attaining the goal of a heterogeneous student body.'[23] Given the importance of faculty selection in maintaining similar aspects of this form of academic freedom, it would seem only a short step to a policy of judicial deference to a school's determination that the requirement to surpass an already successful minority hiring policy would unbalance the ethnic diversity of its faculty."

"You assume," Geneva said, "that any faculty would react as mine did to an apparently endless flow of outstanding minority faculty prospects. But I would wager that if the Chronicle of the DeVine Gift were presented to white law teachers in the form of a hypothetical case, most would insist that their faculties would snap up the Seventh Candidate in an instant."

"What you're seeking," I replied, "is some proof that a faculty *would* respond as yours did, and then some explanation *why*. The record of minority recruitment is so poor as to constitute a *prima facie* case that most faculties *would* reject the Seventh Candidate.

And most black law teachers would support this view. Their universal complaint is that, after hiring one or two minority teachers, predominantly white faculties lose interest in recruiting minorities and indicate that they are waiting for a minority candidate with truly outstanding credentials. Indeed, as long as a faculty has one minority person, the pressure is off, and the recruitment priority disappears."

"No one, of course, can prove *whether* a given faculty would react as mine did," Geneva said, "but for our purposes, the more interesting question is *why* a faculty would if it did. You would think that whites would be secure in their status-laden positions as tenured members of a prestigious law school faculty. Why, then, would they insist on a predominantly white living and working environment? Why reject the Seventh Candidate?"

"Initially, it's important to acknowledge that white law teachers aren't bigots in the redneck, sheet-wearing sense. Certainly, no law teacher I know consciously shares Ben Franklin's dream of an ideal white society[24] or accepts the slave owner's propaganda that blacks are an inferior species who, to use Chief Justice Roger Taney's prescription in the 1857 *Dred Scott* decision, 'might justly and lawfully be reduced to slavery for his benefit.'[25] Neither perception flourishes today, but the long history of belief in both undergirds a cultural sense of what Professor Manning Marable has identified as the 'ideological hegemony' of white racism.[26] Marable asserts that all of our institutions of education and information—political and civic, religious and creative—either knowingly or unknowingly 'provide the public rationale to justify, explain, legitimize, or tolerate racism.' In his view, a collective consensus within the social order of the United States gives rise to the result that

the media play down potentially disruptive information on the race question; inferior schooling for black children denies them necessary information and skills; cultural and social history is rewritten so that racial conflict and class struggle are glossed over and the melting pot ideal stressed; religious dogmas such as those espoused by fundamentalist Christians

156

divert political protest and reaffirm the conservative values on which the white middle class's traditional illusions of superiority are grounded.[27]

"You'll notice, Geneva, that Professor Marable doesn't charge that ideological hegemony is the result of a conspiracy, plotted and executed with diabolical cunning. Rather, it's sustained by a culturally ingrained response by whites to any situation in which whites aren't in a clearly dominant role. It explains, for example, the 'first black' phenomenon in which each new position or role gained by a black for the first time creates concern and controversy about whether 'they' are ready for this position, or whether whites are ready to accept a black in this position."[28]

"Putting it that way," said Geneva, "helps me understand why the school's rejection of my seventh candidate hurt without really surprising me. I had already experienced a similar rejection on a personal level.[29] When I arrived, the white faculty members were friendly and supportive. They smiled at me a lot and offered help and advice. When they saw how much time I spent helping minority students and how I struggled with my first writing, they seemed pleased. It was patronizing, but the general opinion seemed to be that they had done well to hire me. They felt good about having lifted up one of the downtrodden. And they congratulated themselves for their affirmative-action policies.

"Then after I became acclimated to academic life, I began receiving invitations to publish in the top law reviews, to serve on important commissions, and to lecture at other schools. At this point, I noticed that some of my once-smiling colleagues now greeted me with frowns. For them, nothing I did was right: my articles were flashy but not deep, rhetorical rather than scholarly. Even when I published an article in a major review, my colleagues gave me little credit; after all, students had selected the piece, and what did they know anyway? My popularity with students was attributed to the likelihood that I was an easy grader. The more successful I appeared, the harsher became the collective judgment of my former friends."

"I'm glad," I replied, "I haven't experienced that reaction, but

I know many minority teachers who have. It is a familiar phenomenon. One of its forms is condescension thinly veiled as collegial-
ity. Professor Regina Austin's experience is an example. Shortly
after publishing two articles for which she was granted tenure,
one faculty member—the school's affirmative-action officer—
came into her office and draped himself on her couch ready for
conversation. He proceeded to inform me," she reports, "that he
was glad that it had been unnecessary for him to write a memo-
randum in support of my promotion because he really did not
know what he would have written about my articles.

"Professor Richard Delgado thinks that something like 'cogni-
tive dissonance' may explain this reaction:

> At first, the white professor feels good about hiring the mi-
> nority. It shows how liberal the white is, and the minority is
> assumed to want nothing more than to scrape by in the rar-
> efied world they both inhabit. But the minority does not just
> scrape by, is not eternally grateful, and indeed starts to sur-
> pass the white professor. This is disturbing; things weren't
> meant to go that way. The strain between former belief and
> current reality is reduced by reinterpreting the current reality.
> The minority has a fatal flaw. Pass it on.[30]

"The value of your Chronicle, Geneva, is that it enables us to
gauge the real intent and nature of affirmative-action plans. Here,
the stated basis for the plan's adoption—'to provide a more representative faculty and student body'—was pushed to a level its
authors never expected to reach. The influx of qualified minority
candidates threatened, at some deep level, the white faculty members' sense of ideological hegemony and caused them to reject the
Seventh Candidate. Even the first black or the second or the third
no doubt threatens a white faculty to some extent. But it is only
when we reach the seventh, or the tenth, that we are truly able to
see the fear for what it is. Get my point?"

"I do," said Geneva. "But the question is whether the Supreme
Court would get it and, if they understood, whether that understanding would help my case. I suppose we have already agreed
that it would not. We have both noted the judicial reluctance to
interpret Title VII requirements strictly in academic settings. And

we have agreed that the courts might view my law school's hiring efforts as a voluntary affirmative-action plan so impressively successful that it moved the school beyond the ambit of antidiscrimination law."

"That's all true, but I would still recommend that the seventh candidate take his case to court. We civil rights advocates don't give up so easily, Geneva. Assuming that the case could survive a motion to dismiss, the trial court would require the law school to *explain* its rejection of a highly qualified black man—a process that would educate the public, embarrass the law school, and at least provide a liberal judge with the factual support necessary to decide in our favor."

"Does your strategy," Geneva asked sarcastically, "for going ahead with litigation include an offer of representation on a contingent-fee basis?"

"Why not? I'd be willing to take the risk."

Geneva shook her head. "God help our people!" she said, lifting her eyes toward the ceiling in mock prayer. "You concede that consideration of 'The Chronicle of the DeVine Gift' is a helpful exercise for civil rights proponents. The Chronicle is a sharp reminder that *progress* in American race relations is largely a mirage, obscuring the fact that whites continue, consciously or unconsciously, to do all in their power to ensure their dominion and maintain their control. But what good is the lesson, if you evade the very points that the exercise is designed to teach?

"Let me try once more to reach you. Now we know that the disadvantages wrought by generations of racial discrimination cannot be remedied simply by enjoining discriminatory practices. In adopting affirmative-action plans, many institutions and governments have attempted to address this problem. But the controversy over whether and to what degree affirmative action is wise, legal, and moral has obscured the inherent limitations on the affirmative-action approach in particular and on the integration ideology in general. Perhaps because of my long absence, I see more clearly that racial integration is this era's idealistic equivalent of abolition in the pre–Civil War years. Each represented in its time a polestar by which those seeking reform could guide their course during a desperately hard journey—away from slavery in the last century and away from segregation in ours. While pointing the way, these beacons fail to provide us with a detailed blueprint of what to do upon arrival. They do not tell us how to ensure that those who have been long exploited by the evil now removed shall be recompensed for their losses in pocket, psyche, and public regard. Confusion arises from the failure to recognize the difference between the beacon we have and the blueprint we need. We inevitably lose our way and wander back to the situations of subordination from which we worked so hard to escape."

Finally, Geneva, who had been pacing back and forth again, sat down. "The DeVine Gift Chronicle illumines the reasons why affirmative-action remedies advance our frustration as much as our cause, and yet I sense a more viable blueprint hidden somewhere in its bleak message."

"While you were speaking," I said, "I thought of an observation that the Protestant theologian Reinhold Niebuhr made more than fifty years ago. He wrote that black people could not expect 'complete emancipation from the menial social and economic position into which the white man has forced him [the black man], merely by trusting in the moral sense of the white race.' He suggested that, although large numbers of white people would identify with our cause, the white race in America will not admit the Negro to equal rights if it is not forced to do so. Upon that point, Niebuhr said, 'one may speak with a dogmatism which all history justifies.' "[31]

"I know the passage," Geneva said, "and its note of deep despair, which rings as clear and true now as then, challenges even you to give it a positive twist."

"I'm not so sure. Remember, Niebuhr spoke at a time when progress would have been defined as a reduction in the number of blacks lynched each year.[32] You are right, Geneva, that the statement has meaning for our time—but a meaning suggestive rather than fatalistic. Even in his pessimism, Niebuhr assumed that, if whites perceive that substantive rather than symbolic racial reform is necessary, meaningful reform will take place—an assumption validated by history. What we need is some common crisis: war is the best example. Whenever the country has been engaged in armed conflict, beginning with the Revolutionary War, the need for manpower has enabled blacks to gain opportunities in the military as well as in domestic positions formerly closed to them. Other kinds of national crisis can have the same result. I am thinking of an event that captures the nation's imagination and makes clear how much our future depends on mutual effort—on our relating as equals, rather than as superiors and subordinates. In other words, I envision a common crisis that will serve as a catalyst to move us out of the traditional *we/they* racial thinking."

"Well," Geneva said, "I guess you're entitled to your modern-day equivalent of the slaves' Old Testament hopes that a Moses would come and rescue them—hopes that certainly helped them survive. But if your prayers were answered, a common crisis of the type you envision would be self-effecting. There would be no need for civil rights lawyers to go into court and seek the creation of new rights."

"I don't expect a common crisis to bring on the millennium. The post–Second World War conditions that prepared the way for an end to racial segregation were not self-effecting. We still needed years of litigation to gain any benefit from the *Brown* decision. I would expect a common crisis to do no more than to impress on policy makers on the Court and in government the necessity for further racial reform."

Geneva looked at me with both sympathy and sadness in her eyes. "The best response to your common crisis strategy is contained in my next Chronicle—which, I warn you, may strain your faith in this approach beyond the breaking point."

Chapter 7

The Declining
Importance of the
Equal-Protection
Clause

The Chronicle of the Amber Cloud

At midnight the Lord smote all the first-born in the land of
Egypt, from the first-born of Pharaoh who sat on his throne
to the first-born of the captive who was in the dungeon, and
all the first-born of the cattle. And Pharaoh rose up in the
night, he, and all his servants, and all the Egyptians; and there
was a great cry in Egypt, for there was not a house where one
was not dead.

—EXODUS 12:29–30

THE AMBER CLOUD descended upon the land without warning,
its heavy, chilling mist clearly visible throughout the long night it
rolled across the nation. By morning, it was gone, leaving disaster
in its wake. The most fortunate young people in the land—white
adolescents with wealthy parents—were stricken with a debilitating affliction, unknown to medical science, but whose symptoms
were all too familiar to parents whose children are both poor and
black.

The media called it Ghetto Disease, a term that made up in accuracy what it lacked in elegance. Within days, the teen-age offspring of the nation's most prosperous families changed drastically in both appearance and behavior. Their skins turned a dull amber color. Those afflicted by the disease could not hide it. Because its cause and contagious potential were unknown, its victims, after an initial wave of sympathy, were shunned by everyone not so afflicted.

Perhaps the victims' bizarre personality changes were a direct result of the Amber Cloud itself; perhaps they simply reflected the youths' reaction to being treated as lepers, both in public and in all but the most loving of homes. Whatever the cause, the personality changes were obvious and profound. Youngsters who had been alert, personable, and confident became lethargic, suspicious, withdrawn, and hopelessly insecure, their behavior like that of many children in the most disadvantaged and poverty-ridden ghettos, barrios, and reservations.

The calamity dominated all discussion. The wealthy felt the effects directly and were distraught. Before the crisis ended, more than one parent had publicly expressed envy for their ancient Egyptian counterparts whose first-born were singled out and slain during the night of the Passover. Attendance and achievement in the finest schools plummeted. Antisocial behavior rose sharply as parents whose child-rearing credo had been "privileged permissiveness" lost the status-based foundation of their control. Apathy was the principal symptom of the afflicted; but in many cases, undisciplined behavior in the home escalated to gang warfare in suburban streets. Police had difficulty coping with serious crimes committed by those who earlier had committed only minor misdemeanors. Upper-income enclaves, which had long excluded blacks and the poor, now were devastated from within.

Working-class whites, although not directly affected by the cloud, sympathized deeply with the plight of the wealthy. Long accustomed to living the lives of the well-to-do vicariously through television and tabloids, they reacted with an outpouring of concern and support for the distressed upper class.

Private efforts raised large sums of money to further Ghetto Disease research. At the same time, governmental welfare programs extended their operations from the inner-city poor to the suburban rich. No one questioned the role of government in the emergency. Even those far to the political right sounded themes of the necessity of state involvement. The proffered public aid was not "welfare," they said, for the nation's future—now in danger—must of necessity be secured.

The young victims did not blame their plight on blacks. But many of their well-to-do and powerful parents claimed that subversive black elements were responsible for the disaster—an accusation they supported by noting that no children of color were affected and by recalling that some civil rights leaders recently had expressed bitterness at the government's failure to improve the conditions in which ghetto children were raised and educated. Police officials soon responded to political pressures to "do something" about the crisis by rounding up civil rights leaders on a variety of charges. During the next few months, a growing number of whites urged even greater retaliatory measures against black leaders and those whom they represented.

Racial hostility did not extend to a group of black social scientists, all experts on the destructive behavior of black ghetto life, who worked with government experts to develop an effective treatment plan. During the search for a cure, hundreds of blacks volunteered for extensive psychiatric testing designed to determine the precise nature of Ghetto Disease.

After a year of strenuous effort, the president announced the development of a psychological-conditioning process and a special synthesis of mind-altering chemicals that appeared capable of curing Amber Cloud victims. Both the treatment and the new medicine were very expensive; together they would cost up to $100,000 per person. But a nation that had prayed for a cure "at any cost" proved willing to assume the burden.

Civil rights leaders hailed the discovery and urged that the treatment be made available to nonwhite youths whose identical behavior symptoms were caused by poverty, disadvantage, and racial prejudice. They cited scientific appraisals predicting that the treatment would prove as effective in curing minority youths as Amber Cloud victims. They also argued that society owed minorities access to the cure, both because blacks had been instrumental in developing the cure and because the nation was responsible for ghetto pathology afflicting poor minorities.

The public responded negatively to this initiative, criticizing the attempt to "piggyback" onto the Amber Cloud crisis the long-standing problems of minority youth. Moderate critics felt that minority leaders were moving too fast; the vehement openly charged that the problem with ghetto youths was not disease but inherent sloth, inferior IQ, and a life-long commitment to the "black lifestyle."

A presidential task force recommended legislative action authorizing the billions needed to effectuate the cure. Congress budgeted the costs largely by cutting appropriations for defense systems. "Defense," it was argued, "must begin at home." The Amber Cloud Cure bill included a "targeting" provision that specifically limited treatment to the victims of the Amber Cloud. Over the furious objections of minority-group legislators, the Amber Cloud Cure bill was quickly enacted.

Civil rights litigants prepared and filed lawsuits challenging the exclusion of minority youths from coverage under the Amber Cloud Cure Act. The lower courts, however, dismissed the suits on a variety of procedural grounds. The treatment program was carried out with maximum efficiency and patriotic pride, as the nation faced and overcame yet another emergency. Following the cure of the last Amber Cloud victim, a national day of prayer and thanksgiving was proclaimed, and the nation and its privileged youth returned to normality. The supply of the cure was exhausted.

I t was all too clear that The Chronicle of the Amber Cloud undermined my theory that progress for blacks might evolve out of a national crisis endangering whites as well as blacks; and, reluctant to accept all the Chronicle's implications, I confined myself to murmuring that it would make an interesting question for my constitutional law course.

"I surely hope I have not gone to all this trouble just to provide you with teaching aids," Geneva said angrily. "And I hope that asinine comment does not reflect any lingering illusion that this country would not respond any differently than in the Chronicle. Or have you forgotten the discriminatory way in which government benefits were distributed during the Great Depression? As the historian John Hope Franklin reports, 'Even in starvation there was discrimination, for in few places was relief administered on a basis of equality. . . . In many of the communities where relief work was offered, Negroes were discriminated against, while in the early programs of public assistance there was, in some places, as much as a six-dollar differential in the monthly aid given to white and Negro families.'[1] In that, the country's most serious economic crisis, there was widespread suffering and an unprecedented amount of government intervention to relieve it—but the usual racial priorities were scarcely altered. Furthermore, have you forgotten that, even during the Second World War, the meager gains made by blacks were not achieved in an atmosphere free of racial hostility and discrimination?"[2]

"No, I haven't," I assured her, my mind jumping ahead. "It's not easy to accept but there does seem to be more historical support for the Chronicle's conclusion than for a happier outcome. Even more recently, the nation's frantic response to the recession of 1980–81, when unemployment rose to double-digit figures for both whites and blacks, compares poorly with the lack of concern during the last few years when only the black unemployment rate has remained high."

"Given that evidence"—Geneva was pushing me—"what possible basis sustains your theory?"

"If any possibility remains of making progress during a common crisis, it's no more than an opportunity that fate may provide. It is not a promise around which blacks can plan a strategy. Still, I wonder what significance the Chronicle has as a predictor of how the Supreme Court would address issues like those the civil rights groups tried vainly to raise in the lower courts."

"Well, I am encouraged that you seem to have abandoned your idea that a common crisis would miraculously accelerate the pace of racial reform. But," Geneva continued, the sarcastic edge returning to her voice, "is your continued hope of success in the Supreme Court based on some major decisions that I have overlooked in my reading?"

"No, but I think that the Court might view as a racial classification the provision that effectively 'targets' the Amber Cloud Cure for whites. The Court must review with great care laws that burden a racial minority.[3] And to justify such discrimination, which otherwise could constitute a violation of the Fourteenth Amendment's equal-protection clause, the government must show a compelling state interest."

"Perhaps you know better than I," Geneva interrupted, "but it has always seemed to me that the application of the so-called strict-scrutiny test to determine the validity of racial classifications is more rhetoric than reality. When minorities most need the Fourteenth Amendment's shield, the Court does not seem to respond."

"I'm not sure I understand your problem, Geneva. You certainly remember the language in the Japanese internment case *Korematsu v. United States* (1944): 'all legal restrictions which curtail the civil rights of a single racial group are immediately suspect. . . . Courts must subject them to the most rigid scrutiny. . . . Although pressing public necessity may sometimes justify the existence of such restrictions, racial antagonism never can.' "[4]

"I remember it," Geneva acknowledged, "and its rhetoric is reassuring—but not, to my mind, as telling as the Court's application of its test. For example, I find it hard to forget the actual decision in the *Korematsu* case. The governmental rules excluded Japanese-Americans from their home areas solely on the basis of race, assuming 'that all persons of Japanese ancestry may have a dangerous tendency to commit sabotage and espionage and to aid our Japanese enemy in other ways.'[5] And yet while the Court claimed to review the regulations with super suspiciousness or strict scrutiny, that standard, as applied in *Korematsu*, did not prevent a majority of the Court from approving orders excluding Japanese-Americans from areas where they lived and worked and, in a companion case of the same time, from subjecting them to a curfew."[6]

"Well, the strict-scrutiny standard did have a rather shaky birth, but obtaining judicial protection of individual rights during a wartime crisis is always problematic."

"Problematic, hell! It was predictable racism. Justice Frank Murphy called it by its right name when he stated in dissent that whatever deference should be given to the military's judgment in its own sphere, the judgment here was premised on 'questionable racial and sociological,' rather than military, considerations."[7]

"Perhaps so, Geneva, but you must concede that reliance on the military's judgment in wartime, when the nation's very future is at stake, is a tendency the courts are likely to follow rather then defy. Remember Justice Felix Frankfurter's concurring opinion in the *Korematsu* decision: that the challenged rules were justified by the constitutional provisions authorizing the president and the Congress to wage war. In his view, 'to find that the Constitution does not forbid the military measures now complained of does not carry with it approval of that which Congress and the Executive did. That is their business and not ours.' "[8]

"It seems to me," said Geneva, "that blacks have always been treated like an alien force in this country, and that you are all too ready to rationalize judicial tentativeness on civil rights issues on just those occasions when courageous certainty has been most needed. You seem to forget, my friend, that blacks seeking to enforce their rights are always 'special situations' that courts must handle sensitively. 'Political sensitivity'—like 'wartime necessity'—acts as an unacknowledged barrier when we ask the Court to apply the strict-scrutiny standard. So much of the Court's sensitivity is reserved for white concerns that there seems to be little left for black needs. Have you forgotten *Brown II*'s 'all *deliberate* speed' formula of 1955[9] for implementing *Brown I*'s ringing mandate the previous year to save the 'hearts and minds' of black children?"[10]

"Geneva," I cautioned, "you're being too harsh. Long before the 'strict scrutiny of racial classifications' approach was formally announced, the Court struck down some racial classifications that prevented blacks from voting and living in white neighborhoods, barred Chinese from operating laundries, and limited jury service to white males."[11]

"I have not forgotten those decisions," Geneva said, "but I also recall that the same Court upheld segregation schemes that resulted in separate and equal facilities for blacks.[12] Not until 1954 did the Court recognize that separate facilities are 'inherently unequal.'[13] And since then, far too little has changed. Every law student is familiar with 'suspect classification' decisions such as *Loving* v. *Virginia* (1967)[14] in which the Court applied the standard to a statute barring interracial marriage. By the mid-1960s, a full decade after *Brown*, these rulings were generally accepted and, outside the deep South, even applauded. But I will bet that few law students know, and even fewer law scholars remember, that only a few months after *Brown*, the Court refused to review the conviction, under an Alabama antisegregation law, of a black man who had married a white woman.[15] Many of us do remember, of course—and remember, too, the procedural contortions that the Court used one year after *Brown* to avoid deciding another challenge to a state law barring interracial marriages."[16]

"You're a hard woman, Geneva. But you must agree with Professor Gerald Gunther, who, although not happy about the procedural process in the decision you speak of, conceded that 'there [were] strong considerations of expediency against considering the constitutionality of anti-miscegenation statutes in 1956.'[17] Moreover, I'm not sure how much light these old cases can shed on how the Court would handle equal-protection issues today."

"A strange statement," Geneva shot back, "for someone whose racial theories rely as much on history as yours do! And it becomes even stranger when we consider that modern cases have continued the pattern."

I was confused. "What is this pattern in the strict-scrutiny cases that you see as limiting the protection provided to blacks under the equal-protection clause?"

"It seems to me that the Court strikes down laws that contain racial classifications only if they (1) overtly discriminate on the basis of race, (2) cannot be justified by crisis needs or the protection of socioeconomic stability, and (3) can be invalidated without creating too much opposition either to the decision or to the Court."[18]

Geneva sat back, pleased with her summary, but I wanted to

put her three-part formula into perspective. "After 1937, when the Court abandoned its half-century of effort to protect economic rights,[19] it adopted a very relaxed standard of equal-protection review of social and economic legislation.[20] On the other hand, in 1938, the Court unofficially suggested that 'discrete and insular minorities' would receive a special measure of judicial protection[21]—a suggestion later spelled out in the language, although not in the outcome, of the Japanese-American exclusion cases. As a result, there were two standards for judicial review of claims that state laws violated the Fourteenth Amendment's equal-protection test.

"My point is that some legal commentators concluded that, under the Court's equal-protection test, the standard that was 'strict in theory' ended up being 'fatal in fact.'[22] That is, every challenge to a law containing a racial classification led the Court to strike down that law. Now you seem to be saying that racial classifications survived strict scrutiny unless they met your three-part test. Most people will want more evidence of the accuracy of your assessment than you have provided."

"At this point," Geneva said, "my first concern is not in convincing most people but in converting you. Keep in mind that, by the end of the 1960s, most states had abandoned enforcement of blatant segregation statutes—those requiring 'white' and 'colored' signs in rest rooms, and so on. It was the Court's record of invalidating these 'Jim Crow' statutes that gave rise to Professor Gunther's observation that, in practice, the strict-scrutiny standard was 'strict in theory, fatal in fact.'[23] Later cases tended to involve laws or policies that adversely affected blacks but did not explicitly mention race. Obviously troubled by such cases, the Court, after some uncertainty, shifted the focus of its review away from a measure's 'suspectness,' as determined by the harm a law caused blacks, and toward the 'intentions' and 'purposes' of those who enacted the measure.[24] The Court assures us that the harm to blacks, its 'disproportionate impact, is not irrelevant, but . . . is not the sole touchstone of an invidious racial discrimination forbidden by the Constitution.' "[25]

"What you're saying," I suggested, "is that in most contemporary cases, the Court, while perhaps mouthing the standard, actually applies strict scrutiny only after the plaintiffs have overcome the heavy burden of proving that an official action, ostensibly serving a legitimate end, was really intended to discriminate against blacks."

"Exactly," Geneva said, "and the burden of proving discriminatory intent in most of these cases is so great that blacks gain no benefit from the suspect-classification standard—and, without overwhelming proof that the challenged policy is an act of outright bigotry, will not prevail. Some decisions indicate that even evidence of obvious racial hostility may not be enough."

"Can you cite particular decisions that support your point?" I asked.

"Please," Geneva urged, "do not treat me like one of your law students. You know the cases as well as I do, though I imagine you would rather forget *City of Memphis* v. *Greene* (1981). There, the city of Memphis, at the request of a white neighborhood association, closed a street at the border between a white and a black neighborhood, forcing residents of the black neighborhood to take an alternate route to the city center. Blacks claimed the barrier's creation of racially separate neighborhoods was barred by the Thirteenth Amendment's prohibition of 'badges of slavery' that in this instance reduced property values in the black community for the benefit of the white neighborhood. The Court held that legitimate motives of safety and residential tranquillity justified the closure, and that the blacks had not suffered a significant property injury by the action.[26]

"The *Memphis* street-closing measure was challenged, under a civil rights statute based on the Thirteenth Amendment rather than the Fourteenth,[27] in an effort to avoid the tough-to-meet intent standard the Court was certain to apply under the Fourteenth Amendment. As it turned out, the Court applied the hard-to-meet standard by claiming there was not sufficient evidence of harm to reach the intent issue. Justice Thurgood Marshall, joined by Justices William Brennan and Harry Blackmun, filed a vigorous dissent, asserting that the Court's majority ignored evidence of historic segregation in Memphis, that there was evidence of discriminatory intent in this situation, and that the erection of a barrier to carve out racial enclaves within the city is precisely the

THE LEGAL HURDLES TO RACIAL JUSTICE

kind of injury that the Thirteenth Amendment–based civil rights statute was enacted to prevent.

"And, if you want an example involving the Fourteenth Amendment, take *Palmer* v. *Thompson* (1971), where the Court by a five-to-four vote refused to find unconstitutional the decision of Jackson, Mississippi, to close its public swimming pool rather than comply with a court order requiring desegregation of all public facilities. In response to claims that the city officials' motivation for closing the pool was a desire to avoid integration, the majority acknowledged evidence of some ideological opposition to pool integration but, contending that legislative motivation was difficult for a court to ascertain, concluded that 'no case in this Court has been held that a legislative act may violate equal protection solely because of the motivations of the men who voted for it.' "[28]

"Perhaps," I suggested, "this and the Memphis street-closing decisions reflect the Court's reluctance to antagonize large numbers of whites over minor matters, which do not involve crucial rights like voting, jobs, and schools."

"The Court is applying the same tough-to-meet intent standard in critical as well as in less important cases. Moreover," Geneva said sadly, "it is the 'minor matters,' as you call them, that I fear convey unintended signals to blacks and whites about how the Court weighs the relative interests of the two races. The Court's inclination to avoid upsetting whites any more than is necessary, combined with its use of a standard of review that encourages government officials to create 'neutral' rules that everyone knows will disadvantage blacks, in effect creates a property right in whiteness and the consequent loss of some cases that we should by all rights win."

"Proving discriminatory intent can be tough, Geneva, but on occasion, civil rights lawyers have enlisted historians to help them to prove that a challenged law is discriminatory despite its racially neutral text and arguably legitimate purpose. This technique was successful after remand in *City of Mobile* v. *Bolden* (1980),[29] where the Supreme Court approved an at-large districting plan even though it prevented blacks from electing representatives to the city commission. The city argued that its at-large method of elect-

172

ing city commissioners, adopted in 1909, could not have been motivated by racial discrimination because at that time blacks were
barred from voting by a 1901 state constitutional amendment.
Historical evidence, however, showed that the at-large system
was adopted to dilute the vote of blacks in the event the federal
government were to order their re-enfranchisement. The district
court invalidated the city's at-large elections."[30]

"We should applaud the civil rights lawyers' resourcefulness,"
said Geneva, "but we should also question more closely why the
Court's majority was willing to accept the city's argument that a
blatantly unconstitutional state provision—the Alabama constitutional amendment—should serve to insulate from close scrutiny an at-large scheme that had prevented any black from gaining election to a city commissioner's seat, despite the fact that
blacks constituted 35.4 percent of the voting population.

"But before I let you further apologize for the Court, I would
like to hear your response to my conclusion that, under the
Court's interpretation of the equal-protection clause, the targeting
provision of the Amber Cloud Cure Act would easily withstand
legal challenge."

"Why are you so certain litigation would fail?" I asked.

"Because, the Court might find that the targeting provision was
a racial classification and that strict scrutiny should be applied,
but nevertheless conclude that, in light of the crisis created by
the Amber Cloud, the government had shown a compelling state
interest justifying the limiting of the cure to victims of the
Cloud—to the exclusion of minority children. The opinion would
read much like the one in the wartime Japanese-American exclusion cases.

"Alternatively, the Court might conclude that the act did not
constitute a racial classification, but rather provided a remedy for
one distinct form of a widespread ill. In arriving at this conclusion,
the Court would focus on the different *sources* of the ailments—
the Amber Cloud and the sociological conditions of life in the
ghetto—and conclude that the racial differentiation of the act was
entirely fortuitous, rather than invidiously intended. With no
need to apply the strict-scrutiny test, the Court would find that
under its more relaxed equal-protection review standard, Con-

gress was justified in deciding to address one ill at a time.[31] Finally, at least one justice would not be able to resist the observation that if any racial discrimination was practiced in this case, it was by the unknown forces responsible for the Amber Cloud. The government, he or she would say, was simply aiding in a race-neutral way those who were the victims of that discrimination."

"Geneva," I said, as she paused, "I think your assessment of the equal-protection clause's value in contemporary civil rights cases has some validity. The current Court's interpretation of the clause, while certainly more helpful to civil rights litigants than was the interpretation in effect when we began the long struggle to overturn the 'separate but equal' doctrine, provides ample leeway for an adverse ruling in the Amber Cloud litigation. On the other hand, the facts are enough to shock the conscience of even the most conservative jurist, and might, reviewed against the backdrop of the black experience in this country, induce the Court to rule in our favor. Could a society burdened with the guilt of two centuries of slavery and another century of formal segregation survive the moral onus of withholding from the black community a tested cure for its devastating social ills? And if a concern for the image we as a nation presented to Third World peoples after the Second World War influenced the decisions to abandon racial segregation, then wouldn't the nation's policy makers be concerned about the message projected by the denial of medical treatment to poor black children?"

"You remind me," Geneva snorted, "of that typical response to nineteenth-century abolitionists: 'Certainly slavery is wrong, but who will pay to free the slaves?' Cost would be no less a barrier today."

"Well, Geneva, perhaps we might argue that the government's provision of health benefits to whites and its denial of the same benefits to blacks with precisely the same needs infringes on a fundamental personal right to a minimum level of health, triggering strict scrutiny review. Certainly health benefits are crucial to an individual's well-being—no less critical than the educational benefits to which Justice William Brennan referred when he wrote that we 'cannot ignore the significant social costs borne upon our

THE EQUAL-PROTECTION CLAUSE: DECLINING IMPORTANCE

Nation when select groups are denied the means to absorb the values and skills upon which our social order rests.' "[32]

"Interesting," Geneva conceded, "but in recent years the Supreme Court seems to have closed the ranks of fundamental rights in equal-protection review.[33] Do you have reason to believe that the Court will return to a more expansive approach?"

"Look, Geneva, we might lose the case for all the reasons you've mentioned. Suspect-classification doctrine has helped relatively powerless minorities, but only when the classification under review is so blatantly and arbitrarily discriminatory that the Court could strike it down under a much less exacting standard of review. Strict scrutiny under the equal-protection clause has not served to protect minorities against the operating laws and governmental policies that are racially neutral on their face but very burdensome in effect.

"The Court rightly sought to maintain heightened equal-protection review for minorities after its post-1937 adoption of a lenient 'reasonableness' standard of review for most governmental actions. What it perhaps could not have foreseen was that overt exploitation and subordination are not the only forms of racial discrimination, and that facially neutral social and economic legislation may wreak havoc on blacks because of their past deprivation. Thus, as it is with so many civil rights principles, the symbolic value of the suspect-classification standard, while reassuring, in practice provides no protection at all.

"I admit the prospects aren't good, but perhaps we could convince the Court to undertake a full-scale review of equal-protection jurisprudence and its usefulness in contemporary racial cases. Such a review, conducted in the dynamic and volatile context presented in the Amber Cloud Chronicle, could prove enlightening to everyone. Even in defeat, as we learned in *Korematsu*, the Court may yet gain new insight into the problems of modern racism and devise an improved method of addressing those problems in future cases."

Geneva smiled. "My friend," she said, "I remember when I shared your never-say-die enthusiasm. But now I am no longer certain that such earnest commitment is a help to our people in the absence of a still-to-be-discovered new approach to our age-old problem. In fact, I fear that your efforts to effect change through unthinking trust in the law and the courts place you not on the side of black people, but rather in their way."

I looked at her soberly. "We blacks have enough problems without charging one another with obstructionism simply for doing the best we can."

"You're right, friend, and I am sorry. I guess I am tired. It's been a long day and we must both be ready for a break. I do hope you have planned to stay over. That couch you're sitting on converts into a fairly comfortable bed."

"No, Geneva, I think not. Since you have no phone, I want to get back to town and call my wife, so she won't worry about me tramping around in the wilds of Virginia."

"Is it the wilds she minds—or the wild woman in the wilds?" Geneva inquired, raising an eyebrow.

"Oh," I said, smiling, guarding against her sudden irritation, "if she knew you the way I do, she'd know she has nothing to fear."

"If she knows me only as well as you do," Geneva said, her voice as flat as a large lake at high noon on a hot day, "then she knows nothing at all."

"What do you mean by that?" I, too, now defensive.

"Only that some things seem never to change. White folks want to run everything. And you want to act stupid about women."

"I wonder," I said, packing up my papers and tape recorder, "whether you and I are doomed by fate not to be able to talk more than two minutes about anything without an argument."

"Fate?" she asked, relentless. "Mother Nature may not like your blaming on fate your inability to function with women on other than a serious basis."

I stood up. "I always try to be a gentleman, Geneva. I am sorry if my efforts to treat you as a valuable human being entitled to respect seem cold and uncaring."

"Well," she said, her eyes flashing, "I resent your holier-than-thou posture of being interested only in my mind as much as I would were you one of those men who can't see me beyond my——"

"The problem with you strong, black women," I interrupted,

"is that there's no pleasing you. It's impossible to survive in this racist society and live up to your images of what you want us to be. You, above all, should know that the dilemma of black males from slavery until now is the same: we must either accommodate to white domination and live, or challenge it as males should, unceasingly and without compromise, and be ground down to dust."

"Have you forgotten, Mr. Male Ego, that black women live in this society, too, and must face the same racism as black men?"

"True enough, but, out of a combination of fears and guilt, it is black men who are deemed the threat, as indicated by any number of measures: lynching, arrest and sentencing disparities, prison populations, employment bias, and on and on."

"You know, friend, black men and women face interpersonal problems caused by this country's racism that are every bit as important as the law-related issues we have been discussing. I think we must explore them fully."

"Not tonight, Geneva, please."

"Not tonight—but it should be at the top of our agenda tomorrow. Do come early—nine at the latest."

Then we hugged, and I went down the steps and out to my car. Glancing back, I saw her standing in the doorway. She was still there as I drove off.

PART II

The Social Affliction of Racism

Prologue to Part II

EVEN HAD I not been preoccupied with thoughts of that last exchange with Geneva, my chances of finding my way back to town would have been no better than fifty-fifty. But I was somewhat groggy with the long day of talk, and the bright moon cast just enough light to enable me to see side roads not mentioned in Geneva's original directions. All of them looked promising, and none was marked by a sign that meant anything to me. I was totally lost in about twenty minutes.

Finally I came upon a paved road wide enough to seem likely to lead me back to town. Just as I stepped on the gas, I was passed by an old car that must have been doing at least eighty. One of those "good ole Southern boys," I thought, practicing the skills that produce so many champion stock-car drivers—and for a moment considered giving chase, on the chance he'd lead me to some outpost of civilization. But before I could act on the idea, I glanced in the car mirror and saw the revolving blue lights that every driver both recognizes and dreads. I pulled over immediately, braced for trouble, but the police cruiser sped by me and soon disappeared in the distance. I sighed with relief and tried to relax.

It was not easy. No driver welcomes being stopped by the police, but for blacks such incidents contain a potential for harm and abuse seldom experienced by whites save those who are actually wanted by the law. Few blacks ever feel so secure as to be free of such trepidation.

I thought back to another dark road many years before. I had graduated from college with a B.A. degree and a commission in the air force. Driving to my duty station in Louisiana, my new uniform in the back seat, I missed a turn and found myself on a dark country road where my worst fear became fact in the presence of a state policeman, huge and hostile, who stopped my car, refused to accept "lost" as the reason I was so far off the main highway, and threatened to hold me responsible for various thefts in the area reportedly made by, as he put it, "some damned nigger." It was only by showing him my uniform with its gold lieutenant's bars and my military orders that I managed to calm him. Finally, after a long look at the orders, comparing the name with that on my driver's license, he handed them back to me and, scowling still, told me how to get on the right road. Then he stamped back to his cruiser and roared away.

The lesson of that exchange was not lost on me. While air force officers were entitled to wear civilian clothes while off duty, I wore my full-dress uniform every time I left the base. Northern-born and raised, and insulated by my parents from the meanest manifestations of discrimination, my first trip South was traumatic. I felt clearly, and was convinced accurately, that my life and well-being lay totally at the whim of any white person I encountered. Even when they were not hostile, as many were not, I knew that the choice of courtesy or rudeness was theirs to make, mine to accept—or face the consequences. Gaining a measure of protection for my person through my officer's uniform was the first of many techniques I have adopted in my life as supplement— more accurately, substitute—for the respect racism denied me as a person.

Even now, a respected lawyer and law professor, I was fearful of being stopped and hassled because of my race—even now, with the many civil rights statutes protecting me against police violation of my right to due process of law. On that dark country road, any legal rights I had seemed remote and irrelevant.

Suddenly, topping a rise in the road, I could see far ahead the flashing blue light of a patrol car. Coming closer, I saw it was parked behind another car like the one that had flashed by me so fast. Two figures were standing in the light of the police cruiser's headlights. Thank God, it's not me! I thought, and prepared to drive past.

By then, I was close enough to make out the two figures. While one was, of course, a police officer, the other was not the "good ole Southern boy" I had imagined, but a black woman wearing what appeared to be a choir robe of some shade of gold. As my headlights picked up the scene, I saw the woman was crying, obviously in distress and, from the way the policeman was brandishing his flashlight at her, in some little danger as well. I had to stop, however little I wanted to. I eased the car to the side of the road, turned on the emergency flashers, fished the rental-car contract out of the glove compartment, and, getting slowly out, walked back to the two vehicles.

The policeman challenged me at once. "Mister, I ain't got time to give no directions. You want to go to town, you headed in the wrong direction."

Before I could say anything, the woman broke in, "Sir, he forced me off the road, claims I was speeding, and look what he made me do to my tire!" I had by this time noticed that her car, a vintage Pontiac, had a flat tire. "Now he's trying to turn me into a criminal, which he knows full well I am not."

"What is she charged with, officer?" I asked him, but it was the woman who answered.

"So far, he wants to charge me with speeding, driving a defective vehicle, and assaulting an officer."

"And," the officer interrupted, turning to me, "unless you move on right this minute, I'll charge you with interfering with a policeman in the performance of his duty. Now move!"

"But, officer, I'd like to help if I can. This lady is mighty upset."

Slowly and ominously he removed his service revolver from its holster and pointed it directly at me. "Look, mister, I don't know who you are, but you're not going to rescue this suspect. She's none of your business. Interfering with a police officer in the performance of duty is a violation of state law. Now I am ordering you to leave the area."

I was scared. Not for a long time—not since the early civil rights struggles—had anyone pointed a gun at me, and that empty feeling in my stomach didn't feel any better now than it did then. But the woman offered me an opening. Putting her hand on my arm, she said quietly, "I needs a lawyer, sir. Could you go and call someone for me?"

"Officer," I said, making an effort to keep my voice from shaking, "I am a lawyer, though not admitted to practice in Virginia. I want to represent the lady until she obtains local counsel."

"I don't care who you are, mister. This woman is my suspect. You're interfering with my questioning, and I'm warning you one last time to clear the area."

I began to have second thoughts. After all, I didn't know the woman or what she might have done. A married man with children in college, I felt my attempt to be a knight errant fade. Still, I could give it one more try.

"Officer, however easy it may be to put me down, I don't think you'll find it quite so easy to dismiss my friends in this area." I dropped the names of a prominent politician, the federal judge in the area, and the president of the local university. "I've known each of them for years, and I am sure they would state, on the witness stand if necessary, that I would never have threatened you so as to justify you in using your gun."

The news of my high-placed connections would not have deterred a policeman making a legitimate arrest. It clearly disconcerted the officer standing in front of me.

"Who the hell are you anyway?" he demanded, slipping his gun back in its holster.

I reached in my pocket for my wallet and handed him a card. "That shows I am a law professor, and I'm sure my faculty colleagues would support the president and the dean here in Virginia."

In that moment of silence, some of the tension went out of the scene. The officer said to no one in particular, "How the hell this country ever get in such a fix?" I was thinking the same thing, though I had come at it by a very different route.

"This lady got a heavy foot and a big mouth," he said, taking out his book and writing a ticket for speeding. After handing it to the woman, he stalked back to his patrol cruiser without another word and sped off.

"Thank you," the woman said. "He was real ugly, knowin' I belong to the church up the road, where we been petitionin' to stop police harassments around here, and he takin' his anger out on me."

After my scare, I was disgusted with myself, and the woman's thanks made me feel no less embarrassed. She had assumed me to be powerless—an assumption she'd seen verified when I hesitated and almost started back for my car until I thought to invoke the names of important white men.

"Don't thank me," I said. "You owe your thanks to my friends in high places."

"Those people not here tonight. You were, and it's you I'm thankin'—especially since you a friend of Geneva Crenshaw's."

"How do you know that?" I asked, taken entirely by surprise.

The woman giggled slyly. "Well," she said, "in this small Southern town, don't no one keep nothin' quiet, especially a big-time law professor payin' a call on our own Lawyer Geneva, who only got home herself a short time back. When you see her next, you can thank her from me for havin' a man with courage 'round when I needed him."

"I think you mean a man with contacts rather than courage."

"Far as I'm concerned, it amounts to the same thing. And most of our mens ain't got neither one."

Though I was anxious to leave, her comment demanded a response. "That's not fair. I'd bet that any black man driving by and seeing you stranded, with a state patrolman hassling you, would have stopped and tried to help."

"Now *you* mixin' up courage and contact," she said. "The only courage the black mens around here show is when they making contact with some white womens."

"I doubt that, too. But as a civil rights lawyer, I helped get rid of laws that barred marriage across racial lines. Black men have a constitutional right to marry whomever they please, white as well as black—a change in the law effected, in fact, by a 1967 Supreme Court decision in a case from this very state."[1]

"Not talkin' about marryin' no white womens—though that's bad enough. I'm mad at those who go pantin' 'round after them, ignorin' us women who black just because we ain't droppin' our drawers soon as they look our way. It just makes me sick. We black womens got the name of loose and lusty, and the white womens got the game."

"I think you exaggerate. The sexual revolution has affected all

185

races. But this is no place to discuss either law or morality. I need to get back to town and with that flat tire, you need a ride, Miss ——?"

"My name is Delia Jones, but just call me Delia. Now I could fix the tire, but I think I'll ride with you and come back for my car tomorrow."

After we got into the car and I'd started it up, Delia turned on me with all Geneva's intensity. "You married?" she asked.

"Yes."

"Your wife white?"

"What difference does that make given my rights under the laws I just told you about?"

Delia winced as though I had slapped her, and then was silent.

"Well?" I asked finally.

"Question like that," she said with some sadness, "take far more time than we have between here and town to answer. Why don't you take me on home and we talk it over there?"

"Well, I'll take you home, but likely your husband won't care for a stranger dropping in so late."

Delia laughed. "But I ain't got husband or boyfriend. I tried both but have about given up on you black mens ever gettin' your damn selves together in this country."

Delia was an ample woman built on the classic mold, and not at all unattractive. But I thought of my wife and said, "Thanks, Delia, but I can't." To change the subject, I asked whether the robe she was wearing meant she had been singing earlier in the evening—a question that left Delia tongue-tied. "It's a beautiful robe," I went on. "I'll bet it's for a gospel choir."

"It is, but I don't get out here to sing with them very often. My work keeps me busy."

"What do you do?" I was glad to have eased the conversation to neutral grounds.

"You bein' a friend to Geneva, you won't think much of my work. She don't."

"I don't understand."

"Well, I do a little cleanin', I work in the black school helpin' the teachers sometime, and do a little preachin' when the spirit moves me, but mostly I agitate for emigration."

"You do what?"

"You ever hear of Bishop Henry McNeil Turner, Martin Delany, Henry Bibb, or Marcus Garvey?"[2]

"Of course," I responded. "Each of them advocated black exodus from this country. I've read particularly about Garvey, the charismatic black nationalist from Jamaica who founded the Universal Negro Improvement Association and pushed his 'back to Africa' movement through his Black Star Line steamship company during the 1920s."[3]

"You know what happened to him then?"

"He raised millions of dollars and gained broad support among the black masses, but he was convicted—about 1925, I think—of mail fraud and later deported back to Jamaica."[4]

Garvey, Delia told me with obvious pride, was a distant relative, and she in her own way was committed to continuing his work. "That must be pretty hard to do in the rural South," I remarked. "Blacks are a conservative people, and the notion of leaving the country and starting over in a place foreign to them is a very radical idea."

"Life ain't suppose to be no crystal stair, professor," she said, "but white folks so mean, they do most of my work for me. I get to those blacks who tired of takin' low and do what I can to move them in the right direction. You know," she added, "Marcus Garvey said that racial prejudice was buried deep in the white man's nature, and that it's useless to talk to him about justice and all that high-soundin' jazz that nobody believes. Our only hope is to leave this place and start over."

"And even after all the progress made by blacks since Garvey's time, you still believe that?" I asked.

"All that progress, as you call it, didn't keep that white redneck cop from calling me outta my name and pointin' his gun at you when you try to help."

"Well, Delia, that could have happened to anyone interfering like I did."

"Not to your big-shot white friends. Mentionin' their names got that gun right back where it'd never have left if any of them had stopped to inquire why I was upset."

"Your point is well taken, Delia, but America is our home. We were born here."

She laughed. "You remember what Malcolm X said about blacks who boasted they was born here? He would tell them that 'because a cat has kittens in an oven, it don't make them biscuits.' "[5]

"Maybe not," I replied, "but humorous analogies don't alter the fact that we've invested a great deal in this country and gained some rights, and many of us are determined to continue the struggle of those who came before until we or our children have all the rights to which we're entitled by law and simple justice."

"Justice!" Delia mouthed the word in disdain. "Let me ask you something," she said. " 'If you believe that black people will gain their freedom in this racist land, *why* do you believe it? What is the source of your belief, your faith, your hope?' "

I recognized the questions as ones the abolitionist orator H. Ford Douglass asked of black folks who opposed emigration at a conference in 1854,[6] and told Delia so, while conceding their pertinence today. "You really know this subject, Delia."

"And I've got reason to!" she replied. "Livin' with the upper classes like you do, you may not have noticed, but things not gettin' better for the black masses, they's gettin' worse—fast. Unless you got two degrees, the right connections, and a lot of luck, jobs are just not to be had. Our schools about back to black after all that mess to integrate them. Only difference is whites now holdin' down teaching jobs that black folks would've had back in the old segregation days. We votin', but not electin' any of us to anything that counts. And the harassments by police is gettin' worse all the time, as you saw firsthand out here tonight."

Again she reminded me of Geneva, but was more extreme. "Are you advocating separate areas in the country where black people can settle and live?" I asked.

"It just ain't workable. Separatist groups, Black Muslims, New Republic of Africa, others too—they all tried that. It's too threatenin' to whatever white folks was around. No, sir, we got to get out of this America altogether."

"Have you stopped to think that the racism that moves you to leave might bar your departure?"

"Break that down, professor, so a poor home girl can understand."

"Think about it, Delia. When blacks in great numbers began migrating north during the First World War, white southerners, who had maintained that blacks were a liability rather than an asset to the region's economy, resorted to coercive tactics—including arrests, threats, and violence—in an effort to slow the exodus.[7] This country denied a passport to Paul Robeson in the 1950s because 'during his concert tours abroad, Robeson repeatedly criticized the conditions of Negroes in the United States.'[8] Federal law requires a passport for those leaving the country for any purpose, and a passport may be denied to any person whose activities abroad are considered to interfere with foreign relations or otherwise be prejudicial to the interests of the United States."[9]

"Are you tellin' me if I recruited a boatload of black folks who wanted to leave this country for good, the government could stop us?"

"I don't know of any precedents, Delia, but a country that feared what Robeson might do to its image would not waive any available restrictions if a boatload of blacks tried to depart, claiming they were forced to emigrate because racial discrimination in the nation of their birth rendered their lives unbearable.

"And another thing, Delia, assuming the country decided to let all the blacks leave who wished to go, where would we go? How would we get there? Who would finance this emigration movement and stake our claims in some new place?"

She had obviously heard all these questions many times. Her answer was quick and confident. "First, we decide to go. Once we make that decision, answers to your other questions will come to us."

"That sounds like another of your prepared responses, Delia. What specific plans do you have if and when you recruit blacks who are ready to join your emigration movement?"

Without hesitation, Delia launched into a surprisingly detailed outline of how she hoped to carry out a dream she had held for a long time. Viewing the establishment of a new nation as a long-term goal, for the present she advocated an emigration equivalent of the Peace Corps. Blacks with skills useful in African or Caribbean countries would commit themselves to live and work in those countries for a period of years, their work subsidized by funding from an emigration organization that would solicit money from across the country. After a corps of persons had found homes in their new countries, they would make it possible for others to follow. Both Africa and the Caribbean islands offered, she argued, great variety in life style, political and social organization, and economic opportunity. It was, she insisted, possible to go there and help rather than exploit, to contribute and not simply add to the immense burdens of countries still struggling in the postcolonial phases of their development. Every well-publicized departure, she assured me, would throw the country into a quandary of ambivalence and uncertainty that could not fail to benefit those blacks who remained.

"You're really committed to a black exodus," I observed as we drew up in front of her house in the black area of town.

"It's either exodus or extinction," she replied. "Not much of a choice. I just hope we not too late."

"As a gospel singer, you must know that old song with the refrain 'Please be patient with me, God is not through with me yet.' Think about that song when you think of me, Delia, and all those men who look like me—and you. If we're not worth saving here, we won't be worth taking any place else. Good night."

The motel sign, for all its neon garishness, looked like fine art. After calling my wife, I went to bed. It was very late, after midnight, but I couldn't clear my mind of thoughts about the incident with the policeman. It was just one more reminder of my inability to defend myself or another black against the racial hostility that any black person, but particularly men, can encounter at any moment, regardless of who we are. That knowledge of my powerlessness affects my relationships, and all relationships between black men and women, in ways no less hurtful because they are impossible to prove—or even discuss. Despite all my legal arguments, Delia might be right about the need to make a new start "any place but here."

Unable to sleep, I turned the options over and over in my mind: physical emigration, or accommodation of a kind most costly to self-worth. It is a dilemma as difficult to explain as it is painful to face. I recalled the lectures over the years in which I had attempted to explain to mostly unbelieving white audiences how vulnerable to the smallest aggressions of racial fear and hostility even the most successful black person remains. Income, professional achievements, and prestige, none of these is a certain defense.

And now I had another experience that would be hard to get my audiences to comprehend. To save one black woman from a white cop's verbal abuse and possibly worse, I had surrendered a bit more of my self-esteem. Using the names of well-known white men as a shield against the cop's anger was but a contemporary form of the shuffling my forebears had had to do, a form of the "scratchin' when it don't itch and laughin' when it ain't funny" tactic that generations of blacks have used to show subservience when whites have threatened their well-being or their lives. While what I had done was no worse, it surely was no better, than the stereotype of the beloved obsequious black so popular in this country.[10]

I remembered my early days at the NAACP Legal Defense Fund when the then general counsel Thurgood Marshall would regale the staff with stories about going to the South in the 1940s to represent some black man charged with rape or another crime against a white that had turned the community into a racial tinderbox. On such trips, the defendant's attorney from up North was the target of local scorn and risked being attacked. I was saddened more than amused when Thurgood, asked how he handled those situations, in mock humor gravely explained that when he got to town, he would take out his civil rights and fold them very carefully, and then put them down deep in his back pocket, and—pausing for effect—he would leave them there where they and their owner would be safe until he got out of that damned town.

It was hardly a comfort to realize many years later that Thurgood's self-deprecatory anecdote illustrated a survival formula used, in one form or another, by all of us. Of course, the law prohibits intimidating conduct by state officials, including police, but the sanctions always seem inadequate or, at the most, remote. Even today, for blacks as well as whites, the traditions of racial subordination are deeper than the legal sanctions. Such statutes, making racial harassment by law-enforcement officials a criminal offense, had been enacted after the Civil War and, after a long period of neglect, had received judicial rejuvenation in the 1960s;[11] while, in the 1970s, civil remedies also received more liberal interpretations enabling at least victims of particularly heinous police abuse to recover damages.[12] Geneva and I must surely discuss all of this tomorrow.

I awoke with a start, jarred back to consciousness by the bright sunlight that filled the room. Geneva would be furious. I dressed and after a quick breakfast at the motel to spare my stomach any more of her health food than was necessary, I set off for her cottage. As I feared, she was waiting at the door, frowning. She stood aside as I entered, but said nothing, nor did her frown soften.

"I ran into some trouble finding my way back to town last night," I apologized, "and overslept. But I had a dream associated with your Chronicles."

"Association based on one day?" Geneva interrupted. "Sounds more like guilt to me. I offer you a perfectly good couch to spend the night here—but, oh no! You have to rush off into the night like some male Cinderella about to turn back into a pumpkin. It was hardly a compliment to me. I certainly wasn't going to attack you, and I am equally certainly able to resist any untoward overtures of yours—though any such action on your part would have been quite a switch from our NAACP days."

"And what's that last comment supposed to mean?" I asked warily. "I thought we were friends, two lawyers committed to bringing our people out of the wilderness of racial segregation."

"You may not have noticed, but in the old days"—her sarcasm revealing some old resentment I had never suspected—"some of our colleagues found time, on occasion—how shall I put it?—to 'socialize.' " Her sarcasm slurred *socialize* into a paragraph of suggestive meaning.

"Of course, I noticed, Geneva—that whenever there was time for anything other than work, you were always surrounded by a panting pack of amorous males. And I wasn't going to be a part of that macho horde."

"You're simply brimming over with compliments this morning. Why in God's name do you think that you would have been 'part of that macho horde' had you expressed at least a tiny interest in anything other than my lawyerly skills?"

"I cannot be hearing Geneva Crenshaw talking—that woman of the fierce, feminine independence and stickler for gender equality. Are you saying you were waiting for me to make the first move, exhibit male dominance, assume a posture of patrimony in a patrimonial world?"

She looked me in the eye and said simply, "I am Geneva. And it would have been no crime had you at least once discussed something other than the cases, the clients, and the civil rights cause."

The Geneva I remembered had never seemed likely to make such a concession about her interest in anyone.

"But Geneva, at the risk of prolonging this less-than-joyous reminiscence, I would like to know why you of all people didn't at least suggest that I join the crowd of your male admirers?"

"Lord!" Geneva said, shaking her head slowly. "Why must black women be doubly cursed: victimized by white racism and black sexism?"

"I don't follow you."

She spoke cautiously. "Let me start with the suggestion that you may not have wanted to join those men chasing after me in New York because you saw in their stud type of behavior a not very praiseworthy compensation for all the other expressions of male power denied them as black men in a white world.

"And," she added before I could comment, "you have spent your life in self-assertion of one form or another, proving that a black man can challenge his subordinate place and survive. However praiseworthy the results, much of your life is spent teaching white folks a lesson about their racial stereotypes—namely, that those racist myths do not apply to you. At bottom, though, yours is just another form of compensation, little different—and certainly no less sexist—than the compensation affected by those New York characters you so despised."

Geneva's tone softened, though her words continued to sting. "You see," she explained, "neither approach is a compliment to women however much you and the macho men, each for your own reasons, think it is. And both approaches are manifestations of frustration at a society that refuses to acknowledge your personhood even though you accept its assumptions about male domination by behaving like sex-starved dogs or the most chivalrous of men."

"Must I feel privileged then that you saw sufficient difference in the compensatory mechanisms to invite me here rather than one of those New York characters?"

"Don't be peevish! The fact is that your claim that you wanted to treat me simply as a working associate is self-serving, a typical response from men unable to understand that professional women can be respected and loved simultaneously. For them, we must be aggressive 'bitches' to make it professionally, but servile or at least docile to be loved, and perhaps eventually married."

"You're entitled to your opinion," I told her, determined not to oppose the expression of that entitlement, as irrational as I found it. "But my question remains. If you identified what you thought was my misguided sense of male chivalry while we were working together, and were interested, why didn't you simply tell me so?"

She laughed. "It seemed to me that you were fond of me but were afraid to admit it lest you'd have to compete with those smooth-talking New York dudes. But had I said anything intended to encourage your interest, you would have concluded that I was another overly assertive woman, and fled in panic.

"You may not have realized it yourself but, unwilling to compete in the usual way, you tried harder to be a good friend—which, of course, I could appreciate at the professional level. You worked hard at your job, were serious about using your life well, showed real courage in the courtroom, and seemed always worried about principle rather than self in your decisions. I was impressed, but——"

"It seems," I interjected, "that with all your militant insistence on equality for women—an area you felt strongly about long before the national movement got started—your social standards resemble those of the Victorian era. And I have seen that lingering insistence on traditional courting in many of my black women law students."

"Precisely how most black women in what were considered middle-class families were brought up back then. And," she conceded, "I gather, some of that background lingers today in black women's desire for traditional courtship rituals. But my problem with you, friend, was not my upbringing but your well-intentioned but no less demeaning confusion of sex and sexuality with sexism. In an effort not to be sexist in a Don Juan way, you effectively denied that it was possible to respect my professionalism and love me as a person.

"Now let's move on. But before you tell me your dream, I would like to hear about the trouble you had on your way back to town last night."

"A state patrolman was harassing a black woman whose car had a flat tire. I stopped to help, and I got him to leave her alone—though not in a manner I want to boast about. Actually, the woman is an acquaintance of yours who knows you're here and that I'm visiting you."

"Impossible!" exclaimed Geneva. "I am absolutely certain no one knows I am here."

"Well, Delia Jones indicated that she grew up around here and that you know her."

Geneva looked blank. "I don't remember anyone by that name, but she may have been much younger than I. What did she look like?"

"Brown skin and solidly built, you might say on the heavy side. The heaviness, though, was all in the right places."

Geneva frowned. "Sexism does live in your heart unaccompanied, as far as I can see, by any compensatory characteristics. What else can you tell me?"

"She's probably in her forties, but looks younger. When I first saw her, she was crying and being harassed by a local cop. While I was driving her back to town, she told me she was a distant relative of Marcus Garvey and was trying to form a back-to-Africa movement in this area. But she's also a gospel singer and was wearing a beautiful gold robe."

"Oh, my God! Oh, my God!" Geneva sank down on the couch and put her head in her hands.

"Then you do know Delia?" I asked.

Geneva shook her head slowly. "My friend," she said, staring into my eyes, "I do not know Delia Jones, because there is no Delia Jones. You saw a woman who must have looked quite real as well as quite good, to judge by the gleam in your eye as you were describing her. But Delia Jones is, in fact, one of the Celestial Curia Sisters. Did she try to convince you that her black-exodus project was the only option left to our people?"

"That she did."

"Those women are not trustworthy," Geneva said furiously. "I am trying as hard as I can to decide what I believe we blacks should do to overcome racism, and they damn well know I chose you to help me in my evaluation. How dare they interfere and try to influence you to influence me?"

"It makes sense to me," I said, trying to remain calm in the light of this revelation. "You know that each of the Curia members are urging very different strategies, and you, in conflict, are looking for a third approach militant enough to meet the reality of our condition and yet humane enough to equate with the religious faith that helped sustain us through so many bad times."

"Well, if this Sister felt you might be able to win me to support a black-exodus strategy, she was mighty mistaken. With your commitment to legal reform, you're hardly the ideal recruit for an emigration scheme."

"I don't know about that. Delia's plans sounded pretty good. And you have such a poor opinion of my militancy that, had I returned here espousing a black exodus, the shock might have won you over."

Geneva laughed. "You may be right—but unless we get back to work, I may have to choose emigration by default."

"How about the other Curia Sister who advocates disruption and possibly violence?" I asked. "Is she likely to appear and try to influence your decision through me?"

"I doubt seriously that the other Curia Sister really cares whether or not I adopt her strategy. As far as she is concerned, increasing violence and eventual armed racial struggle is inevitable. It may be a long time, but she is willing to wait."

"That's frightening."

"What is really frightening is the apparent certainty of many conservatives that they can dismantle the few social welfare programs, and the civil rights agencies now providing inadequate protection against poverty and racism, without blacks reacting violently here as oppressed peoples have reacted elsewhere in the world—as, indeed, over two centuries ago, white Americans reacted to an oppressive government."

"We likely encourage that certainty," I said soberly, remembering last night's exchange with the policeman and Delia's diatribe against black men. "Given our history, it's understandable but no less deplorable that our automatic reaction—of both black men and black women—to white hostility is to accommodate, accommodate, accommodate. And then we let off our frustration by violence against one another and often unspeakable treatment of our women whom we can't respect because their very presence is a constant reminder of our inability to protect them against the racism that constantly challenges us either to accommodate or to pay the price. Indeed, the dream I spoke of bears on the society's racial pressures and their impact on black male-female relationships."

"If it were a Chronicle, what would you call it?"

"Well, it's influenced by your Chronicle of the Amber Cloud, but takes a quite different direction. Let's call it the Chronicle of the Twenty-Seventh-Year Syndrome."

Chapter 8

The Race-Charged Relationship of Black Men and Black Women

The Chronicle of the Twenty-Seventh-Year Syndrome

IT WAS NOT LONG after the terrible phenomenon of the Amber Cloud, when the nation had been totally preoccupied with saving its upper-class, white, adolescent youth from the devastating effects of Ghetto Disease, that it was discovered that the Amber Cloud had, after all, affected at least one category of the black population: able black women, many of them with excellent positions in government, industry, or the professions. Gathering the data was difficult, but it appeared that each month twenty-seven black women in this socio-economic group were falling ill without apparent reason, about three months after their twenty-eighth birthday.

The illness itself was bizarre in the extreme. Without any warning, women who had contracted the malady went to sleep and did not wake up. They did not die nor go into a coma. Their bodies functioned but at less than 2 percent of normal. Nothing known to medical science could awaken the women, save one natural remedy—time. After four to six weeks, the illness seemed to run its course, the women awakened, and, after a brief recovery period, all their physical functions returned to normal.

That was the good news. The tragedy was that, in a special form of amnesia, the women lost their professional skills and were forced to return to school or otherwise retrain themselves in order to continue their careers. In some cases, this meant several years of work and sacrifice that some of the victims were unable or unwilling to make. After some time, medical researchers were able to delineate more specifically the characteristics of the black women at risk. They had: (1) held at least one degree beyond the bachelor's and had earned an average of thirty-five thousand dollars per year over the three years prior to their twenty-seventh year; (2) completed their twenty-seventh year of life; and (3) had neither ever been married or entertained a *bona fide* offer of marriage to a black man.

Women who were or had been married to, or who had received a serious offer of marriage from, a black man, seemed immune to the strange malady. But not sexual activity, or a relationship outside of marriage, or even out-of-wedlock motherhood served to protect the victims. Marriages of convenience did not provide immunity, nor did a sexual preference for other women. Strangely, black women married to white men also contracted the disease. Public-health officials called the sickness the "Twenty-Seventh-Year Syndrome," while the tabloids referred to it, with an editorial snicker, as "Snow White's Disease."

For a time, the media followed the story eagerly. But gradually—because there were no fatalities, and the victims of the malady were spread across the country—the ailment slipped into the category of illnesses like sickle-cell anemia that strike mainly blacks and thus are of only passing interest to whites.

The nation's refusal to make the Ghetto Disease cure available to black young people barred all hope that a national mobilization would be undertaken to find a remedy for the Twenty-Seventh-Year Syndrome. And, as one high-placed government health official explained, there was little interest in searching for a medical remedy when a social remedy was at hand: these women should each find a black man who would offer to marry them. "It was," he said, "as simple as that."

But as virtually everyone in the black community knew,

the simple remedy was, in fact, extremely difficult. The Twenty-Seventh-Year Syndrome had added a dire dimension to what had long been a cause of deep concern to black leaders and a source of great pain and frustration to able black women. For many years before the strange disease made its appearance, the most successful black women had had a very hard time locating eligible black men with whom to have social relationships that might blossom into love, marriage, and family.

Social scientists have isolated several components of the social problem confronting all professional women, but exacerbated for blacks by the fact that the black population includes over one million more women than men, and by the high proportion of black men in prisons and among drug addicts compared with the very few who attend college and graduate school. In addition, those black men who survive, and achieve success comparable to that attained by black women professionals, have many more social choices. They may not marry at all, or can marry very young women without advanced degrees or professional skills. Some few of the otherwise eligible men are gay; and much to the chagrin of black women, a goodly number are married to white women.

For all of these reasons and more, many of the most talented, successful, and impressive black women remain single or do not marry until well into their thirties. As a result, at the very time when the black community is racking its wits about how to address the problem of teen-age black girls becoming pregnant and bearing children by young males unable to support them, many of those black women most qualified to raise the next generation of black children remain unmarried and childless.

The unhappy paradox produces disunity in the black middle-class community, where women tend to condemn the inadequacies of black men; and the men, resentful at being further burdened with society's faults, lash out at black women as being unsupportive and hard-hearted. With the onset of the Twenty-Seventh-Year Syndrome, this debate intensified as speakers claiming to represent the interests of men or of women demanded that the other "do something."

Federal health officials, still smarting from the attacks by blacks outraged at the government's failure to extend the Amber Cloud Cure to black youths, determined to act aggressively on the Twenty-Seventh-Year Syndrome. Lacking funds to search for a cure, they decided, with little or no consultation, to issue compulsory Syndrome Control regulations which would, as they said, "serve as a quasi cure by making known to the 'cure carriers' (black men) the identities of those persons at risk." In summary, single black women between twenty-four and twenty-seven years of age and deemed vulnerable because of their marital and socio-economic status were required to register with the government. If they had not established stable marriages with black men by the middle of their twenty-seventh year, the law required broad public disclosure of this fact along with detailed biographical information.

The populace in general and black people in particular were appalled and angered by the new regulations. The charges of "cruel and heartless" were not much reduced by amendments to the law providing that the records of a woman married to, or in a stable relationship with, someone other than a black man would not be made public. It was pointed out that while the Syndrome was disabling, it struck only 27 women each month, and 324 women each year—a serious matter, to be sure, but hardly justifying subjecting literally thousands of black women to a humiliating public display of their personal lives. Civil liberties lawyers seeking to challenge the constitutionality of the regulations as being in violation of First Amendment rights of privacy were stymied by procedural provisions that rendered it difficult for any woman to gain standing to challenge the rules until after she had been subjected to the compulsory publicity in the regulations.

As it turned out, the first woman whose name was selected in a special drawing to receive the publicity expressed little interest in challenging the regulations. Amy Whitfield, a well-known writer, said the law represented a particularly pernicious form of male chauvinism, one more indignity heaped on black women. Given the legacy of rape and degradation that her sisters had endured down through history, she assumed she should be thankful that a male-dominated society had not designed some still more odious process to harass those women already enduring the frightful knowledge that they might soon become a Twenty-Seventh-Year-Syndrome victim.

Ms. Whitfield explained that marriage was not the sole goal of her life, that she and her educated sisters had made contributions and lived full lives without the need to seek rescue from men who were not interested in them. "I am not opposed to marriage," she said. "There are men I would have married and men who would have married me—but they have never been the same person.

"Conjugal convergence," she went on, "requires more men than are available, particularly for black women, all of whom, owing to the horrors of American racial history, find it difficult to contemplate marrying a white man, while some consider it out of the question. Basically," she concluded, "if the public disclosure required by the statute serves to spotlight some of the dual burdens of racism and sexism black women carry, the humiliation may be bearable. But at this stage of my life, I am not interested in becoming any man's damned damsel in distress."

Most black men agreed. The frustrated anger they felt upon learning that the Twenty-Seventh-Year Syndrome attacked only black women turned to rage when government health officials announced their Syndrome Control regulations. Urged by a group of black ministers to vent their fury in positive ways, black men across the country organized "Together at Last" clubs to raise money for the medical research the government refused to fund, set up "sleep-care" facilities to nurse Syndrome victims, and established scholarships to assist recovered women in regaining their skills.

What black men did not do was rush out and propose to black women simply to save them from contracting the Syndrome. As one young black professional put it, "Black women have suffered enough because we have emulated the society's sexism. Now, in their time of need, we should not add to their Syndrome-caused despair by patronizing marriage proposals that are little more than romantic vaccinations."

But the Syndrome experience did cause many black men who had—"as one option"—taken black women for granted to begin recognizing them for the remarkable individuals they are: survivors in a tough, hostile world, who have overcome difficult barriers and seek men able to share their success and not be threatened by the strengths without which that success would not have been possible.

The change in black male attitudes was slow, halting, and produced no miracles of sex-role reformation. The Syndrome continued to claim its predictable number of victims, and there remained far more black women than eligible black men. But out of tragedy came a new awareness and understanding. And while the "black male versus black female" debate continued, the bitterness disappeared from discussions that looked toward reform and away from recrimination.

W ELL, I was wrong," Geneva began, "and you were right in predicting that I would not like your Chronicle. Despite some camouflage, it just brims with patriarchy and sexism. Sure, the society's racism is a substantial cause of the shortage of eligible black men. I rather doubt, though, that black women or the race will be much advanced if the only cure for racism's impact on black families is male domination of the sort implicit in the so-called cure for the Twenty-Seventh-Year Syndrome."

I raised both hands in defense against her harsh words. "It was only a dream, Geneva. I'm not personally invested in it. Still, it can serve as a vehicle for discussing the degree to which racism has exacerbated for blacks the always-difficult social relationships between men and women. The focus was narrow: namely, on those black women who, having overcome society's hurdles, find that their professional achievements present barriers to their hopes for personal happiness through marriage and family.[1]

"The Chronicle of the Twenty-Seventh-Year Syndrome does not disparage the fact that many, many women, regardless of race, live meaningful and entirely happy lives without either marriage or children. The simple point is that, in today's world, many white women and black women must choose the single road. And black women in particular are denied free choice on that important matter precisely because of society's erosion of the role of black men."

"And your Chronicle," Geneva burst out, "provides these societally disabled black men with their long-awaited chance to come riding to our rescue just as their white chauvinist prototypes do. Perhaps we should retitle it the 'Chronicle of the Black Male Castration Cure.' "

"You shouldn't condemn what you obviously don't understand," I cautioned. "Black men do feel castrated by the society and can be male chauvinists in some of the worst ways imaginable, as a whole cadre of black women writers have been reporting to the world for years.[2] I certainly don't want to condone wife cheating, wife beating, and all the other forms of abuse—even though one needn't be a psychologist to recognize that much of this conduct is the manifestation of frustration with racism."

"There are some acts we cannot blame on white people," Geneva said firmly, plucking a book out of a huge pile beside her chair and opening it to a page marked with a slip of yellow paper. "I agree with Grange Copeland, the character in Alice Walker's first novel who warns his son of the trap of blaming others for making a mess out of your life. Listen to this:

> I'm bound to believe that that's the way white folks can corrupt you even when you done held up before. 'Cause when they got you thinking that they're to blame for *everything* they have you thinking they's some kind of gods! You can't do nothing wrong without them being behind it. You gits just as weak as water, no feeling of doing *nothing* yourself. Then you begins to think up evil and begins to destroy everybody around you, and you blames it on the crackers. *Shit!* Nobody's as powerful as we make them out to be. We got our own *souls* don't we?"[3]

"That's a powerful statement," I said, "and it reflects a wisdom

Grange Copeland has to travel a bitter road to gain. But that's my point. There's a history here that cannot be ignored. A major component of slavery was the sexual exploitation of black women and the sexual domination of black men. The earliest slavery statutes devoted substantial attention to prohibitions on interracial sex and marriage.[4] The clear intent of these laws was to delineate the inferior status of blacks as much as to discourage interracial sexual activity, a goal furthered by the double standards generally followed in their enforcement.[5] And while slavery is over, a racist society continues to exert dominion over black men and their maleness in ways more subtle but hardly less castrating than during slavery, when male-female relationships generally weren't formalized and, even when a marriage was recognized, the black man's sexual access to his wife was determined by when the master or his sons or his overseer did not want her.[6]

"As Professor Oliver Cox observed," I continued, " 'If a Negro could become governor of Georgia, it would be of no particular social significance whether his wife is white or colored; or, at any rate, there would be no political power presuming to limit the color of his wife.' On the other hand, as Professor Cox has also said, if in what is supposedly a democracy, the state can insist that a black man have a black wife, it is then possible to have a structure in which not only can the black not become governor, but he can be required to do the dirtiest work at the most menial wages."[7]

Geneva was not impressed. "That is digging rather deep into history for racial injustices to explain current failures by black males. You seem to forget that black women as well as black men suffered the pains of slavery. The black activist Lucy Parsons said it all when she wrote that 'we are the slaves of slaves; we are exploited more ruthlessly than men.' "[8]

"I've not forgotten, Geneva. But I am suggesting that, while the racial injustice was shared, the sexual harm differed. Black women were exploited, abused, and demeaned, and that harm was serious. Forced to submit to the sexual desires of their masters or of slaves selected by their masters, these women then suffered the agony of watching helplessly as their children were sold off. But black men were also dealt a double blow. They were forced to stand by powerless and unable to protect black women from being sexually available to white men, and were denied access to white women as a further symbol of their subordinate status. The harm done black men by this dual assault has never been fully assessed. Moreover, the assault continues in less blatant but still potent forms."

"True, it was a serious problem," said Geneva, "but the wounds in present relationships caused by the nonfunctioning of black men seem self-inflicted, as Alice Walker and scores of less articulate but no less wronged black women have testified."

My patience was exhausted. "Ms. Crenshaw, I am not a sociologist. I agree that historically 'black women have carried the greatest burden in the battle for democracy in this country.'[9] If you and your black sisters achieve a perverse pleasure out of castigating black men, I can't stop you. I think, though, that there is value in trying to find an explanation other than the condemnation 'no good' to explain our admitted shortcomings."

"I am listening," Geneva replied, "but I hope you do not expect me to maintain a respectful silence during your effort to justify with words what is often unjustifiable behavior."

"Having your sympathetic and impartial ear will make my task easier," I said, teasingly. "Let me say again that unconscionable behavior by black men makes my point. For the physical restraints of slavery that rendered the black male powerless have been perpetuated in the present, with economic restraints, joblessness, and discrimination in all its forms today rendering many black men powerless to protect wives and family. Shame and frustration drive them from their homes and lead them to behavior that can be as damaging to black women as any actions by whites in this racist society.

"While you and many proponents of women's rights feel that it is sexist for a man to feel some special responsibility to protect his woman, in this society such feelings go with the territory. And by making it so damned difficult to fulfill that protective urge, the society has turned many black men into modern instruments of their own oppression, mistreating black women and disrupting the struggle for a semblance of family life. This is not our intent, but it is, in fact, the result of conduct growing out of our unconscious realization that we, as much as our slave forebears, are powerless to protect whatever or whomever whites decide they want."

"It all sounds rather melodramatic," Geneva observed, "particularly now that laws barring racial discrimination, including interracial marriage, have been struck down by the courts."

"Again," I explained, "we have to look at history. It's important to remember that economic exploitation, rather than an abhorrence of interracial sex, was the real basis for all the so-called anti-miscegenation laws that were contained in the first slavery statutes and remained on the books of twenty-nine states as late as 1951.[10] Professor Cox argued that these laws were motivated by the cultural advantage they secured for whites. By asserting that they were protecting the 'honor and sanctity of white womanhood,' white elites provided themselves with both a moving war cry and an excellent smokescreen for furthering and shielding their basic purpose: refusing blacks the opportunity to become the economic peers of whites."[11]

"In effect, then, white women became tools of white male oppression?"

"That at least is how one student of the problem, Calvin Hernton, characterizes it," I responded. "Hernton, who rejects Cox's 'economic' explanation as 'too mechanical,' believes that both white women and black men are in a 'semi-oppressed' class in terms of jobs, political power, money, property, and access to opportunities for higher status.[12] And as a predictable result, any number of black spokesmen—including Frantz Fanon, Malcolm X, and Eldridge Cleaver—have acknowledged the political implication in the black man's attraction for white women."[13]

"I wonder," Geneva interrupted, "whether you are not making too much of the economic and political functions of anti-miscegenation laws. Is not the main view that these sanctions were motivated by whites' basic fear and abhorrence of interracial sex?"[14]

"One need not deny that view," I said, "to agree with Frantz Fanon that it is reasonable to assume that attitudes about sex are embedded in a given cultural and historical context; and that even if sexuality is basically biological, its form of expression is influenced by variables including economics, status, and access to power.[15] And Cox, on this point, notes that whenever whites are in a ruling-class situation, there is a very strong urge among black men to marry or have sex with white women."[16]

"It is this seemingly ungovernable urge that many white men fear and a great many black women detest," Geneva observed.

"Don't I know it! But Professor Cox is, I think, on target with his comment that 'it must not be supposed that it is the white woman as a mere sexual object which is the preoccupation of colored men, it is rather her importance to him as a vehicle in his struggle for economic and cultural position.' "[17]

"Does all that sociological theory explain the vastly greater number of black men who marry white women than black women who marry white men?" asked Geneva.

"Well, I gathered the census data a few years ago, and the disparity you speak of does exist. As I recall, of 125,000 black-white couples in 1977, three-fourths involved a black husband and a white wife. And by 1981, the percentage of black husband–white wife couples had increased to almost 80 percent. I should add that interracial marriages of all types are on the rise, having jumped, between 1960 and 1970, by 108 percent (from 148,000 to 310,000). They increased 36 percent from 1970 to 1977, and even more from 1977 to 1981."[18]

"Those figures must put you in something of a quandary," Geneva remarked. "Wearing the sociologist hat you've been sporting for the last few minutes, you must view those interracial marriages as psychologically explainable but no less regrettable in the ammunition they provide for accusations and recriminations among black people. On the other hand, as an integrationist, I assume you applaud these figures as a happy fruit of civil rights victories in cases like *Loving* v. *Virginia* (1967) that struck down anti-miscegenation laws?"[19]

"I do feel some ambivalence," I admitted, "but I'm also aware that, as with other racial reforms, the removal of barriers against interracial marriage serves the needs of the whole society but not necessarily those of the blacks as a people within that society. Chief Justice Warren, speaking for a unanimous Court in the *Loving* case, dismissed the state's arguments for retaining the laws as 'obviously an endorsement of the doctrine of white supremacy.'[20] Of course, he was correct, but the remedy—opening the way for marriage across racial lines—cured only one evil while doing little to reconstruct the deeply damaged sense of what we might call 'black male wholeness.' "

"Evidently," Geneva said sarcastically, "it is sufficient cure for those black men who choose white women as wives or sexual partners."

"I'm not sure you're being fair," I responded. "White women must also choose black men. It is possible for a black man and a white woman to mate and marry for the old-fashioned reason: love. But my point is that, for whatever reason black men are drawn to choose white women, that attraction, and the Court's decision that made it legal, simply decreases the already inadequate number of potential mates for black women. And, as our discussion on this subject illustrates, the decision exacerbated tensions between black men and black women, particularly on the issue of black male responsibility to black women."

"A responsibility," Geneva observed, "that, according to your theory, they're too damaged by what happened in slavery even to recognize, much less assume."

I nodded. "But it's more complicated than that. The continuing powerlessness of black men affects black women as well, particularly strong black women. A strong woman doesn't achieve that status by accident. She knows her strength, has developed it over the years, appreciates it, perhaps even revels in it. It's her basis of survival. Her strength makes her intolerant of weakness, particularly in those whose weakness threatens her survival. Thus, even though she may love a man, her contempt for weakness will come out. And if her man is black, you can believe that in this society there will be many opportunities for that weakness to be all too obvious—no matter how successful he is and how strong he tries to be. No matter how hard she tries to accept him as he is, her true estimate of his strength comes out in ways that her man reads as a lack of respect—and resents precisely because he knows damn well that because of this society's racism he can never earn the respect his woman wants to give, and cannot."

I took a deep breath. "I haven't wanted to confess it, but I had one such reminder of my powerlessness last night when I stopped to help Delia Jones as she was being harassed by that policeman. He pulled his gun and threatened me in a way he would not have threatened a white man similarly dressed and behaving as I did— a lesson I reinforced in effect by shielding my race-based inadequacy and warning him that well-connected white men I knew would cause him grief if he didn't leave me alone. It worked, but it was a further proof, in my mind, of who is strong in this country and who is weak."

"That wasn't weakness," Geneva said. "That was using your head to keep from losing it. We have always been able to outsmart white folks. It was a key part of our survival technique. You're foolish to confuse it with a stupid macho image of how a 'real man' would have handled the situation. For the most part, real men of that type are either myth or dead."

"It's easy for you, Geneva, to dismiss the protective male urge as patriarchal in origin and suicidal when emulated by black men. But didn't you just admit that you accepted—*acquiesced* was your word—in male-dominant modes of courtship because, given the current patriarchal structure of our society, it was likely the only romantic approach I could handle?"

Geneva blushed. "Please don't confuse the subject of the male urge to protect his woman with your inability to deal with me as lawyer and lover. My problem with your Chronicle of the Twenty-Seventh-Year Syndrome is that it ignores all the black males with problems like yours, and elevates to the level of indisputable truth the sexist ideal of men as the natural protectors of women. So, while recognizing that society is patriarchal, your Chronicle does not analyze the harm that priority does to the black community's struggle against racist oppression. Rather, it encourages black men to assume a role equal to the white man within the patriarchal order. It does not even hint at—much less espouse—a more desirable option: that is, for black men to reject the whole 'protective role' concept and become one with black women in order effectively to confront the common enemy—racism."

"My Chronicle is based on the world as it is," I tried to explain, "not as some of us would like it to be. Within that context, it provides a dramatic situation intended to show black men that black women, even those who have demonstrated outstanding ability and survival strengths, cannot themselves create black mates with abilities and strengths equal to their own. To the extent this is a problem—and at the risk of being labeled sexist—I consider it damn serious, and a problem that only black men can cure."

"And are you saying that, before the crisis caused by the Twenty-Seventh-Year Syndrome, black men were unable to function in what you call a 'manly' way regarding these single black women?"

"Why do you find that so hard to believe?" I asked. "There have been many such transcendent events in black history—in fact, in all history. Consider the reaction of black people to the Emancipation Proclamation and the *Brown* decision. Both sparked waves of activity far beyond anything justified by the words of the documents. Perhaps a closer example, because more tragic, was the assassination of Martin Luther King, Jr., in 1968. His death led to tremendous change. Losing him was a tragedy and certainly not a 'fair trade,' but it's clear that the civil rights reforms and progress of the following few years resulted from the transcendent event of his death."

"What do you think about Amy Whitfield, and likely many other women in her situation, who do not want to become any man's 'damn damsel in distress'?"

"I think such women miss the point, Geneva. No one should devise any sort of Twenty-Seventh-Year Syndrome as a means of getting black men to function. That would be evil, just as killing Dr. King was evil. The Chronicle simply replicates this type of evil. Even without the federal health regulations, the disease puts the spotlight on black men: they have the opportunity and the obligation. If the television pictures of afflicted black women lying asleep in the hospitals don't provide the necessary incentive,

211

nothing will. Black women are in danger. Only black men can save more of them from a pretty awful fate.

"And keep in mind that the women are not forced to marry in order to gain protection from the Twenty-Seventh-Year Syndrome. Men have only to provide black women with the *choice* whether to have a black home. That's all. Black women are entitled to that, as I think even you will agree. I can understand why women who have spent their lives developing and defending their individual identities do not want to change them, especially not to demean them for anyone. As Amy Whitfield makes clear in the Chronicle, she does not want her life to read like a dimestore medieval romance. But I don't think Amy or—in light of our conversation of last evening—even you are opposed to men expressing their interest in such a way as to provide black women with choice."

"In other words," Geneva said, "it's a matter not of whether women want to be saved, but of giving them a choice and thereby saving yourselves. I don't see why, even in your dreams, you men can envision only chauvinistic solutions that perpetuate sexist stereotypes.

"Amy Whitfield was kind. What she is trying to say tactfully is that most black professional women have 'choices.' But because of the quality of those choices, many reluctantly opt to remain single. If the black men in your Chronicle have not engaged in any self-reflection, if they have not determined and continue to fail to appreciate that black women face real and significant racial problems that equal and, yes, surpass those that men face, they will not provide a 'meaningful choice' to black women.

"More blatantly, unless black men can pause for one minute, can stop feeling sorry for themselves—that is, free themselves of their castration complex—and *try* to understand and empathize with the condition of black women, that condition—as hellish as the Twenty-Seventh-Year Syndrome—will not change. Black professional women will continue to opt to be alone or to compromise themselves for their wounded black warriors, providing their men with support while the men bemoan their inability to offer their women a form of protection that the women neither need nor would want save for their understanding that the men have a misguided need to provide it."

"Someday," I replied, "the society will evolve beyond its present rigid views of sex roles, but that time has not come. And black men won't be ready for the era of complete sex equity until they have gained that confidence and sense of themselves essential to male-female relationships based on mutuality and sharing."

"True enough, friend. I am simply saying that black men cannot hope to attain their independence through the subordination of their women. The black man needs to direct his attention outward—as I gather your Chronicle suggests some black men are doing through the 'Together at Last' clubs—and recognize that, even historically, as his sexual access to his wife was determined by the white man, the wife was similarly restricted from him. When she was raped, something that was hers—not his—was being robbed.

"Once black men realize that racial oppression equally afflicts black women, perhaps our mutual problems will be easier to address. The powerlessness about which black men so bitterly complain is no less severe in the black woman. These feelings emanate from what we expect of ourselves vis-à-vis our loved ones as opposed to what society expects from us. But until black men critically assess the sexist expectations of society and define their own expectations, they will not be compatible mates for black women who have expectations of their own for themselves. The problem with the Chronicle is that it perpetuates this black male focus instead of viewing the plight of the black woman through her eyes and, in the process, honestly assessing the problems black men have independently caused owing to their intransigent adherence to sexism."

"The issues involved here, Geneva, are as complex as any we have discussed. Your perspectives are valid although not necessarily the primary concern of the Chronicle as I dreamed it."

"I have one last concern about your Chronicle."

"Yes?"

"If it was intended, as you claim, to reveal to black men their opportunity to give black women a choice, why does the Twenty-

213

Seventh-Year Syndrome afflict successful black women who are involved in nonmarital relationships or have children out of wedlock, and especially why are black women married to white men not exempted? Women in these categories obviously had choices and exercised them, and yet all are subject to the illness. Why?"

I thought about the question for a full minute, and finally admitted, "I'm not sure. It may be that the supernatural powers responsible for the illness were influenced by that Victorian mindset on sex you mentioned earlier. Furthermore, the vulnerability of black women married to white men may reflect the strong negative feelings in some portions of the black community—as well as among whites—about interracial marriage, particularly when black men marry white women."[21]

"Your response is not convincing," Geneva observed. "And it maintains attention on the quantitative aspects of black women's choices, ignoring in the process the key qualitative issue for black professional women. I honestly do not believe any of us are personally—as distinguished from politically—distraught over the black men who are married to white women. They are simply not an issue. They are not 'eligibles' in our personal lives. Our distress is caused by the quality of the limited choices we do have. So, even if black men stopped marrying white women, were released en masse from prisons, rejected homosexuality, and so forth, the quality of our choices would not necessarily change."

"Well, Geneva, this is a subject we could discuss for the remainder of your time without coming any closer to agreement than we are right now. I think we'd better move on to what I'm afraid will be the last Chronicle I have time for."

Chapter 9

The Right to Decolonize Black Minds

The Chronicle of the Slave Scrolls

From my cabin window I look out on the full moon, and the ghosts of my forefathers rise and fall with the undulating waves. Across these same waters how many years ago they came! What were the inchoate mutterings locked tight within the circle of their hearts? In the deep, heavy darkness of the foul-smelling hold of the ship, where they could not see the sky, nor hear the night noises, nor feel the warm compassion of the tribe, they held their breath against the agony! . . .

O my fathers, what was it like to be stripped of all supports of life save the beating of the heart and the ebb and flow of fetid air in the lungs? In a strange moment, when you suddenly caught your breath, did some intimation from the future give to your spirits a hint of promise? In the darkness did you hear the silent feet of your children beating a melody of freedom to words which you would never know, in a land in which your bones would be warmed again in the depths of the cold earth in which you will sleep unknown, unrealized and alone.

—HOWARD THURMAN

THE MUSINGS of the black theologian Dr. Howard Thurman[1] give eloquent voice to questions that led me, in frustration and growing despair, to abandon my civil rights law practice and seek refuge in religion. After several years of study and missionary endeavor, I became the minister of an urban black church. A short time later, I decided to make a pilgrimage to Ghana. As Christians of old sought the Holy Grail as proof of the miraculous in Christ's death and our redemption, so I was drawn to Africa seeking secrets of the slaves' survival that might offer their descendants sustenance and possible salvation. And, amazingly, on my last evening there, I found the revelation for which I had come—and for which, indeed, I have been searching all of my life.

On that evening I walked along a wide desolate beach; and as the sun fell slowly beyond the waves, it cast a fan of gold and salmon and rose across the sky. Even the gray sand was transformed into a palette of rich pastels. As I marveled, I saw the ship. It was not some far-off sail etching an invisible line between brilliant sky and darkening sea, but rather lay at my feet, a model ship perhaps two feet long. By its worn appearance, I could tell that until the sands shifted, it had lain submerged for a very long time.

I picked up the ship and studied it in fading light. I knew from my studies of slave history that I was holding a likeness of the ships the slave traders had used to transport African captives to the Americas, and I felt renewed sympathy for those whose first contact with Western civilization had brought generations of despair and misery. For, as Dr. Thurman had written:

> Nothing anywhere in all the myths, in all the stories, in all the ancient memory of the race had given hint of this tortuous convulsion. There were no gods to hear, no magic spell of witch doctor to summon; even one's companion in chains muttered his quivering misery in a tongue unknown and a sound unfamiliar.[2]

Examining the vessel more closely, I found it to be hollow, and it had a corklike plug stuck deep into its stern. Later that evening in my hotel room, I managed with some difficulty to withdraw the cork and found in the ship's hold three tight-rolled parchment scrolls. Unrolling the scrolls, I found them to be covered with thin, fine writing in antiquated English. I read them through at once. They were a testament from the slaves themselves.

Dr. Thurman has asked: "How does the human spirit accommodate itself to desolation? How did they? What tools of the spirit were in their hands with which to cut a path through the wilderness of their despair."[3] The answers were in the scrolls. The identity of those who recorded the secrets of survival, like that of the composers of the spirituals, would likely never be known. But the miracle of their being far outweighed the importance of their origins. And just as the spirituals had enabled slaves to survive, so the scrolls would enable their descendants to overcome.

Returning home to my church, I began to teach the message of the Slave Scrolls. The members of my congregation were profoundly affected. After a few weeks of intense study conducted as the scrolls prescribed in "healing groups" of twenty-five people, the myriad marks of racial oppression began to fall away. There were no "magic" potions to take, no charms to wear, no special religious creed to adopt, and no political philosophy to espouse. Mainly, the scrolls taught the readily available but seldom-read history of slavery in America—a history gory, brutal, filled with more murder, mutilation, rape, and brutality than most of us can imagine or easily comprehend.[4]

But the humanity of our ancestors survived, as the spirituals prove. In the healing-group sessions, black people discovered this proud survival and experienced the secular equivalent of being "born again." Those who completed the healing process began to wear wide metal bands on their right wrists to help them remember what their forebears had endured and survived. Blacks left the healing groups fired with a determination to achieve in ways that would forever justify the faith of the slaves who hoped when there was no reason for hope. If revenge was a component of their drive, it was not the retaliatory "we will get them" but the competitive "we will *show* them."

In this spirit, the healing groups demonstrated a deep desire, precursor to the soon-to-be-gained ability, to accomplish all that

217

white people have long claimed blacks must do to win full acceptance by American society. Blacks who were good workers before learning of the Slave Scrolls became whirlwinds of purposeful activity. Even previously shiftless and lazy black people became models of industry.

Word spread quickly, and soon the congregation grew beyond the confines of our small church. At first, we held healing sessions in public auditoriums but then determined to share the teachings with other ministers and community leaders. The members of my congregation became missionaries traveling across the country teaching black people what we had learned. Excitement in black communities grew; but with the exception of a few black newspapers, the media initially ignored what they viewed as just another charlatan scheme preying on the superstitions of ignorant and gullible black folk.

Within a year, though, neither the media nor the nation could ignore the rapid transformation in the black community. After a time, blacks who heard about, but had not actually gone through, the healing sessions began reading slave histories on their own and later were able to experience the change within themselves simply by seeing its powers working in other black people.[5] All the "Marks of Oppression"[6]—crime, addiction, self-hate—disappeared; and every black became obsessed by a fierce desire to compete, excel, and—as Booker T. Washington used to admonish—"prove thyself worthy."[7]

Unemployed blacks who could find work did so. Those who could not joined together to work for those who did. All manner of community enterprises were started and flourished. Black churches became social-aid centers, and blacks who had been receiving public assistance took themselves off the rolls and soon began sending small repayment checks to welfare agencies. Black family life strengthened as divorce and out-of-wedlock births disappeared. Black children excelled in the public schools, and attended newly opened community classes held in converted taverns and pool halls. They learned the truth about their slave history while preparing themselves to be future leaders.

In a word, black people became in fact what white people

boasted their own immigrant forebears had been. Even the storied Saturday-night party disappeared, and was replaced in many areas by organizations working to eliminate poverty and unemployment among whites. Blacks began outachieving whites in every area save sports and entertainment—activities that black people no longer believed could compare with the challenge of getting ahead through business and industry. Blacks not only voted together but spent their money for only those products that they made or, if white-owned, had been given a vote of approval by the black community.

Understandably, a great many white people, after an initial rather patronizing surprise, became alarmed. They deemed it strange, abnormal, when large numbers of blacks—as opposed to the token one or two—began surpassing whites in business, industry, and education. It was, some whites felt, neither right nor fair—even un-American—for a minority group to gain so much advantage over the majority in a majoritarian society. Spurred by this unease, both government and media investigators searched frantically, without success, for wrongdoing or evidence of subversive elements. For many whites, lack of proved wrongdoing did not deter retaliation. Employers and educational institutions disbanded their affirmative-action programs, replacing them instead with explicit ceilings on the number of black candidates they would hire or admit.

Working-class whites, severely threatened by the increasingly widespread pattern of black economic and political gains, carried out violent attacks against adherents of the healing movement. At several public healing sessions, groups of whites pelted blacks with insults and missiles; in one notorious incident, white attacks resulted in a violent melee in which several persons were killed. In other incidents, several blacks who wore the metal wristbands in public were brutally beaten.

Finally, a popular television minister found in "American morality" what no one had yet discovered in law: an answer to what was now openly referred to as the "black success" problem. In a rousing sermon, the minister told his fundamentalist audience: "Success that is the result of self-help is the will of God"—but the preaching of racial hatred is subversive. The Slave Scrolls, he asserted, created hostility between the races by teaching blacks about the evils of a system wiped out more than a century ago. The minister warned that, unless the scrolls were banished, their teachings would prove as pernicious as those of Nazism and the Ku Klux Klan. Ideologies based on racial hatred, he reiterated, should have no place in a country committed to brotherhood across racial boundaries.

The minister's sermon provided the key to action. Despite the opposition of blacks and civil libertarians, virtually every state enacted what were called Racial Toleration Laws, which severely restricted—and, in some states, banned outright—public teaching that promoted racial hatred by focusing on the past strife between blacks and whites. Penalties were severe for leading or participating in unauthorized public healing sessions, or for publicly wearing what the law termed "symbols of racial hatred." State officials enforced these laws with vigor, severely hampering the ability of blacks to carry out their healing campaign. Whites whose fears were not allayed by the government's actions organized volunteer citizens' groups to help rid their communities of those whose teachings would destroy the moral fabric of American society.

The rest is almost too painful to tell. Whites perverted the law; many still resorted to violence. Like their forebears in the Reconstruction era, blacks tried to hold on. For longer than was perhaps wise, black people resisted, but the campaign to suppress those who wore the distinctive bracelets proved too strong. Black enterprise was no match for the true basis of majoritarian democracy: white economic and military power. Nor were the courts of much help. Our best lawyers' challenges to the Racial Toleration Laws were to no avail.

For the black community, the Slave Scrolls experience served as a bitter reminder that sheer survival rather than inherent sloth has prompted the shiftless habits that, continued over time, led many to forget that whites are threatened by black initiative and comforted by black indolence. If blacks were to survive, they had to make overtures to peace—a prelude to a return to the past. My church, which had become the symbol of what by then was called the "Slave Scrolls movement," undertook "negotiations" with the white community. In fact, we had no choice but to surrender all. We returned the scrolls to the hallowed model ship. Then, at a massive service held in accordance with the surrender terms, thousands of black people renounced the lessons of the healing groups. Having removed and destroyed our bracelets, we watched, and wept, in silence, as both ship and Slave Scrolls were burned.

F OR A LONG TIME, neither Geneva nor I said anything. I was overcome with the ultimate defeat of the Chronicle.

"That's quite a story," I finally ventured, "but one I imagine many whites and more than a few blacks will dismiss as highly implausible."

"Are you suggesting," Geneva asked apprehensively, "that you find yourself in the disbelieving group?"

"Well," I hedged, "it's hard to predict how the public would react to so dramatic a transformation in black conduct and competitiveness. One would have hoped that most whites would hail the black achievements as proof that any group can make it in America by pulling themselves up by their own bootstraps."

"Your hopes, friend, are not supported by Reconstruction history. In that brief period after the Civil War, the newly freed blacks, despite the failure of the national government to provide meaningful reparations, made impressive educational and political gains.[8] But their very success served to deepen and intensify the hostility of southern whites."

"Nineteenth-century history certainly supports your pessimism," I conceded. "And before you remind me, it is true that white society has often persecuted black leaders and groups who have placed a high priority on ridding blacks of their slave mentality. There is the fate of Delia Jones's hero Marcus Garvey, and the

221

more recent experiences of the Black Muslims, Paul Robeson, W. E. B. DuBois, Martin Luther King, Jr., and Malcolm X[9]—whose calls for black communities to organize for mutual protection and benefit gained them many black followers but engendered crushing enmity among whites.

"Malcolm X was a good example of what might be called the black leadership dilemma. That is, during the early 1960s, his trenchant and highly articulate condemnation of white racism gained him tremendous support among poor blacks but harsh hostility from most of white society. He didn't want, as many whites feared, to lead a revolution, but was trying through his angry tirades to show blacks that racism, not inherent inferiority, was the source of their self-hate and self-destructive behavior. What Malcolm X hoped to bring about was the 'decolonization of the black mind—the awakening of a proud, bold, impolite new consciousness of color and everything that color means in white America.' "[10]

"And," Geneva interjected, "it is precisely that threshold task of decolonization through condemnation of white racism that—when espoused by black leaders, whether a Malcolm X or a Martin Luther King—arouses such hostility as to lead enemies of these leaders to believe that society will see killing them as a great public favor. This has been the fate of our leaders who have merely espoused the cure of decolonization of the black mind. What makes you think that whites would be more receptive to the actual achievement of this goal, as in the Chronicle of the Slave Scrolls?"

"Perhaps it is less black achievement than fear of the Slave Scrolls' almost supernatural powers that leads whites to strike back and eradicate the Scrolls and the ship they deem the sources of that strange and threatening power.

"What bothers me, though, is how could blacks ever return to a colonized mindset even with the destruction of the Scrolls and the model ship? After all, they must have known by then that their achievements had been the result of their efforts and not some magic of the Slave Scrolls."

"Think about it," said Geneva. "The Chronicle is not suggesting that black people need to be taught how to succeed, but reminds us that they have learned very early that too much success in competition with whites for things that really matter like money and power threatens black survival. In a society where success is a supreme virtue, a deliberate decision not to succeed creates a spiritual vacuum. Just as some poor whites relieve their frustration by feeding on the myth of their superiority, many blacks engage in self-destructive and antisocial behavior as an outlet for their despair. The teachings in the Slave Scrolls cause black people to forget their basic lesson of survival through self-subordination, but their resulting success leads to a life-threatening reaction by whites that makes it necessary for blacks to relearn that lesson the hard way. The public ceremony where they are forced to renounce the truth they know about their history and themselves is a symbolic action, a surrender of the rediscovered knowledge, and the end of expectations that black people can gain acceptance in America by becoming superachievers in business and displacing white people, or at least those whites who blacks believe have been getting by owing to their color rather than their competence."

"Well," I admitted, "it has certainly been the experience of blacks that life's playing field is tilted toward whites—a belief beautifully portrayed in the 1979 film *Being There*, in which the late Peter Sellers plays a middle-aged, mentally retarded character who has lived his entire life in a house owned by a well-to-do but eccentric old man who provides a black maid to care for him and a television as his sole connection with the outside world. When the old man dies, and estate lawyers, unaware that he was the deceased's ward, order him to leave, Sellers walks through the streets of Washington, D.C., well dressed but totally bewildered. Through a series of hilarious chances, he finds himself the houseguest of a wealthy and powerful family and is introduced to the President of the United States, who interprets his idle comments about gardening, the only work he knows, as sound economic advice. Within a few days, he becomes a celebrity, respected by power brokers and even considered as a presidential candidate. The black maid who raised him is astounded to see him lionized on television, and views his sudden rise as typical of what any

223

white, regardless of competence, can achieve with a little luck. For her, Sellers's rise is not a minor miracle but a totally predictable event. In the film's best lines, the former maid points to Sellers on the screen and laments to her friends:

> For sure, it's a white man's world in America.
>
> Hell, I raised that boy since he was the size of a pittance. But I'll say right now he never learned to read and write. No sir! Had no brains a'tall. Stuffed with rice pudding between the ears. Shortchanged by the Lord, and dumb as a jack-ass.
>
> Look at him now! Yes sir, all you got to be is white in America to get whatever you want."[11]

"A conclusion," said Geneva, smiling, "I can remember my parents and their friends coming to again and again. It provided a fatalistic humor to a set of rules that seemed to reward whites with cake regardless of their worth, and parceled out crumbs to blacks no matter how hard they tried."

"The sense that whites have numerous opportunities, and blacks have none, is one of the most debilitating of all the 'badges of servitude,' "[12] I observed. "It leads to resignation and despair and makes blacks less likely to succeed. But the question for us to address, Geneva, is whether there is a new legal theory that will persuade courts to provide protection for blacks who are attempting to rescue their people from these unhappy attributes of racism."

"Why a *new* legal theory?" Geneva demanded. "The Chronicle tells us that civil rights lawyers argued that the Racial Toleration Laws violated First Amendment rights of speech,[13] religion,[14] and association,[15] all of which were recognized in cases litigated by black people. But in the Chronicle's atmosphere of racial antipathy, the courts refuse to come to their defense."

"That's somewhat surprising," I responded. "Whatever the general racial unfairness, I'd have thought that lawyers would have little difficulty getting the courts to strike down the Racial Toleration Laws as an obvious violation of the blacks' First Amendment rights."

Geneva looked at me in disbelief. "You surely did not base that thought on history," she said. "Why do you expect the law to provide any more protection during the crisis described in the Slave Scrolls than it did during the Reconstruction period when the law failed even to defend black lives and certainly did nothing to protect black rights?"

"The likely determinative factor here was the sense of crisis," I surmised. "We discussed earlier the Court's reluctance to protect individual rights when the country is involved in a war or other crisis (see pages 131 and 167–68). Free-speech rights under the First Amendment are no different—broad in theory but far more limited in fact, particularly in crisis times. The tortuous history of the 'clear and present danger' standard is proof of the varying levels of protection the Court provides to politically threatening speech.[16] And the long Cold War has eroded First Amendment rights as the government and the courts have blurred the distinction between military secrets required for national security and information kept secret to preserve and enhance the government's reputation."[17]

"You forget," Geneva interrupted, "that the Slave Scrolls do not advocate either war against or subversion of the government. They simply enable blacks to discard their oppression mentality and compete in the good old American way."

"Now, who isn't learning from the Chronicles?" I said. "In the Chronicle of the DeVine Gift, you suggested how whites would react if you introduced more than a few token minority teachers into an elite law school faculty. And we discussed the concern caused by the high test scores achieved by Asian students. Imagine the crisis that would occur if millions upon millions of competent and confident blacks started challenging whites at every rung of the societal ladder. And don't forget that, in the Slave Scrolls Chronicle, the sense of crisis is heightened by the outbreak of civil violence. None of the many precedents in which advocacy of racial justice has gained free-speech protection would be applied in a situation where the audience hostile to the activity includes much of the nation's white population. I haven't forgotten how the Court's strong support for blacks during the sit-in era of the early 1960s quickly waned along with public sympathy."[18]

"I wonder," asked Geneva, "whether, had you experienced the Slave Scrolls Chronicle, you would be able to rationalize so calmly the courts' flat refusal to come to our aid."

"Ms. Crenshaw, one of us has to be rational and lawyerly— and please don't conclude that, just because the healing sessions prescribed in the Slave Scrolls threaten whites, the blacks wouldn't be entitled to receive full First Amendment protection."

Geneva looked surprised. "I thought you were concluding that, because of the crisis caused by the black achievements, no protection was possible."

"No, the Racial Toleration Laws either ban or restrict the association of blacks and the content of speech that were necessary parts of the healing sessions. Thus, under existing First Amendment standards, those laws should be subjected to a greater-than-usual scrutiny by the courts."[19]

"May I assume that the emphasis you gave the word *should* was inadvertent?"

"Well, the Racial Toleration Laws clearly infringe on the content of the blacks' talk in the healing groups—an activity that should be protected. But several cases indicate the Court may tolerate restrictions on the content of controversial speech by approving state regulations enacted to regulate the time, the place, and the manner of all public speech.

"Take the *Dick Gregory* case (1969), where the Supreme Court reversed the disorderly conduct convictions of civil rights protesters led by Gregory who picketed the mayor of Chicago's residence and incurred the hostility of white hecklers. But the opinions strongly suggested that, had the government enacted a sufficiently specific statute limiting protests in residential neighborhoods, the convictions under that law would have been upheld— despite the suppression of the protesters' free-speech rights. Two liberal justices, Hugo Black and William Douglas, concurred in the *Gregory* case, saying that the Constitution does not bar state regulations designed 'to protect the public from the kind of boisterous and threatening conduct that disturbs the tranquility of

spots selected by the people . . . for homes, wherein they can escape the hurly-burly of the outside business and political
world.' "[20]

"They seem to have forgotten that the disorder was caused by
the white hecklers," observed Geneva.

I nodded in agreement. "They noted that the best-trained police
cannot maintain tranquillity and order 'when groups with diamet-
rically opposed, deep-seated views are permitted to air their emotional grievances, side by side, on city streets.' Their opinion predicted that even laws 'regulating conduct, even though connected
with speech, press, assembly, and petition would be approved if
such laws specifically bar only the conduct deemed obnoxious
and are carefully and narrowly aimed at that forbidden
conduct.' "[21]

"Correct me if I miss the point," Geneva said, "but the preservation of 'tranquillity and order,' even when disturbed by a violent white response to peaceful civil rights protests, causes you
to doubt the Court's commitment to protect the free-speech and
associational interests of blacks in tumultuous times, such as those
presented in the Chronicle of the Slave Scrolls."

"You haven't missed the point," I conceded, "but———"

"But my point," Geneva said emphatically, "is the futility of
civil rights litigation to protect even basic free speech and associational rights when those activities, while perfectly peaceful, evoke
a hostile response from whites."

"You may not be prepared for this," I warned, "but civil rights
lawyers in the Slave Scrolls Chronicle might gain the relief they
seek if they recognize the crisis-time shortcomings of First
Amendment protection and urge the Court to find a substantive
due-process right of privacy that bars government interference
with the racial healing sessions, especially those requiring a public
forum."

"Tell me you're not serious!"

"Why not?" I replied. "Surely, this is a right different in subject,
but similar in character, to the rights of privacy that, in 1965, the
Court recognized and protected in the use of contraceptives,
whether or not one is married.[22] The right was extended in *Roe* v.

Wade (1973) to provide women the right to determine whether or not to sustain a pregnancy."[23]

Geneva sighed and rolled her eyes toward the ceiling. I waited for her to speak, but she shook her head. "Oh, no! I would not dream of interrupting before you explain the connection you see between the right to an abortion and the racial harassment suffered by black people in the Slave Scrolls Chronicle."

"Woman," I said, exasperated, "your skepticism will be your undoing. Were I to represent the harassed blacks in that Chronicle, I would urge the Court to recognize that, after two centuries of racial exploitation and subordination, we need the psychological exhilaration gained from the discovery of what we can achieve— the actual cure contained in the 'racial healing' process. I would compare that need with the treatment war veterans receive after long periods of combat. My goal would be a judicial finding that what they deemed the right of privacy under the due-process clause of the Fourteenth Amendment which protects rights to contraception and abortion, should also encompass the freedom to meet, preach, teach, and engage in all activities that serve to effect racial healing.

"Actually, blacks have a stronger constitutional case than the Court made in protecting contraception and abortion rights. In addition to what the Court identified as the 'penumbra' of First and Fourteenth Amendment rights supporting the privacy rights in the sexual and reproduction areas, we can cite the guarantee in the Thirteenth Amendment protecting blacks against the 'badges and incidents of slavery.' If you think about it, the motivation for the hostility of whites toward the healing sessions is quite like that which prompted slave states to pass laws prohibiting anyone from teaching slaves to read and write.[24] The real concern, then and now, was less what blacks would learn than what they would do with that learning. And given that all too familiar motivation, blacks should be entitled to protection under the Thirteenth Amendment.

"Furthermore, social science experts can help us prove what should be obvious: namely, that blacks cannot purge self-hate without nurturing black pride through teaching designed to show that the racism of whites, rather than the deficiencies of blacks, causes our lowly position in this society—a dangerous truth that indicts the nation's leaders, institutions, and long-hallowed beliefs.[25] And yet the teaching of that truth is essential if black people—not just those in the underclass, but *all* black people—are ever to view themselves as fully capable human beings."

The look on Geneva's face indicated that my argument had won her pity rather than her support. "I realize that the cases I'm relying on—particularly the abortion case of *Roe* v. *Wade*—have been controversial, and also that the critics who doubt the existence of constitutional authority for the Court's action on the abortion issue can make an impressive argument for their position.[26] But there are two points that would support my argument.

"First, some commentators who support the decision caution those seeking to extend its coverage to homosexuals. In striking down state laws barring contraceptives and abortion, the Court is endorsing not sexual freedom of consenting adults, 'but the stability-centered concerns of moderate conservative family and population policy.'[27] This view gained validity when, in 1986, the Court refused, albeit by a close 5-to-4 vote, to strike down the state of Georgia's sodomy law on right of privacy grounds.[28] Professor Thomas Grey predicts, though, that future Supreme Court decisions in the area of sexual preference 'will respond to the same demands of order and social stability that have produced the contraception and abortion decisions.'[29] And I predict that as the cost to society of ignoring the plight of the black underclass rises, an argument that racial healing is entitled to constitutional protection based on similar 'demands of order and social stability' may well win favor with the Court.

"Second, the Supreme Court's decision in the abortion cases aided women who were either poor or under the domination of their parents, husbands, or communities. Wealthy women, even before these decisions, had little difficulty in obtaining relatively safe, albeit expensive, abortions. But poor and dominated women who wished to have abortions were forced to undergo risk-filled and exploitative nightmares. Because the political climate prevented politicians from protecting these people, the Court felt a need to step in. In much the same way, the Court might feel compelled to act in the racial-healing area; there, too, the nation's stability may be gravely threatened."

"Have you anything else to say before I respond?" Though listening quietly to my argument, Geneva obviously had not been shaken in her view that no approach would save her precious Slave Scrolls.

"There is one thing. The greatest danger to our society's order and social stability is not Communists attacking our shores, but the socio-economic discrimination already endemic across our land.[30] While the Court, as we have said, is reluctant to raise such issues directly to constitutional status, some progress may be possible through the 'penumbra of rights' rhetoric of the contraception and abortion cases—depending, of course, on the willingness of the different members of the Court to go forward."

"Well!" said Geneva, "I am amazed. Little did I dream when I asked you to come here that your legal assessments of the Chronicles would contain more fantasy than the Chronicles themselves. I do not want to be unkind, but your basis for belief that the Court may move, even indirectly, in what you call the socio-economic area is the stuff of which dreams are made. For example, while you claim the plight of poor women seeking abortions helped motivate the Court to grant constitutional protection for such operations, this concern was not able to muster a majority of the Court in the cases holding that neither the Constitution nor federal legislation compels states to use federal funds to pay for nontherapeutic abortions for indigent women—the very group you claim *Roe* v. *Wade* was intended to aid.[31] And the Court reached this conclusion despite Justice Blackmun's objections to the state statutes because through them 'the Government punitively impresses upon a needy minority its own concepts of the socially desirable, the publicly acceptable and the morally sound.'[32]

"And, Counselor, you will not be surprised when the states' lawyers take the high ground and claim that they, rather than you, are the guardians of racial tolerance and harmony. In the old days, states would defend policies of segregation by claiming they were necessary to 'preserve order and keep down racial strife.'[33]

In the Chronicle, the states contend that the Racial Tolerance Laws are intended to further harmony within an integrated society. To support their argument that even sincere religious beliefs must be exposed to constitutional scrutiny in order to preserve racial harmony, the states will rely on the litany of cases won by civil rights lawyers like *Bob Jones University* v. *United States* (1983).[34]

"Finally," she concluded, looking suddenly tired, "I fear that the claimed disruption will serve as justification for the real concern: the threat posed by black diligence to the vested expectations of those currently enjoying wealth, power, and status. Finding that blacks were entitled to constitutional protection for the healing sessions would affirm the reordering of society that black successes have brought about. Such an affirmation would be contrary to the concerns about stability that seem to animate the Court's substantive due-process holdings. Now while I admit that your substantive due-process argument is innovative, it rests on the same infirmity as the First Amendment case: the Court could still find that the states have a compelling interest in restricting or removing the Scrolls—those inflammatory and provocative materials[35] so like political pornography,[36] and so likely to bring racial tensions to the boiling point that the states have a compelling state interest in acting to remove these materials from public circulation."

"Obviously, Geneva," I said, weary myself, "the result you suggest is possible, even likely, but we discussed earlier that the *Brown* decision was handed down in 1954—rather than in all the earlier years when blacks were complaining about segregated schools—because in 1954, finally, whites in policy-making positions realized that it was in their interest to eliminate segregated schools. Well, why wouldn't it be beneficial to whites—particularly to elite whites—for blacks to throw off their ghetto mentality and begin contributing to the society? Surely the society would be better if all blacks became truly productive members rather than burdening the nation with the exorbitant costs of crime, poverty, illiteracy, and poor health."

"It would be a benefit," Geneva acknowledged, "and the 'equal

THE SOCIAL AFFLICTION OF RACISM

opportunity' ideology of *Brown I* is evidence of some recognition that change should come. Nevertheless, this ideology has not altered the traditional measure of racial progress—the *Brown II* standard that change should come only with 'all deliberate speed.'[37] Even liberals, on the Court and elsewhere, have realized that truly substantive remedies for blacks would necessarily disrupt settled economic arrangements: 'The more that civil rights law threatened the "system" of equality or opportunity, which threat was essential to the production of victim-perspective results, the more it threatened to expose and delegitimize the relative situation of lower-class whites.' "

"But, Geneva, the powerful in our society no longer need to rely on the subordination of blacks to help secure their own superior situation or to prevent lower-class whites from recognizing that there is, after all, a class structure and realizing their position on it."

"Very few black working-class people would agree with you," Geneva responded, "but the ideology of consumerism, fundamental religion, and, in recent years, a form of media-packaged nationality that integrates patriotism with religion, have served to mask the fact that domestic policy has increased the gap between rich and poor for whites as well as for blacks."

"Even so," I countered, "if *Brown* teaches us anything, it is that blacks must push the law in the direction of full equality. The NAACP worked for twenty-five years for a change that, although proving inadequate in the end, seemed at one time impossible to achieve. If we begin to work toward another landmark decision—perhaps one recognizing a right to racial healing—our legal theory will be ready for judicial adoption at some future point when the potential benefits of a whole, healthy, and productive black America are more obvious than they are today."

"It is hard to imagine when those benefits will be more obvious," Geneva said, "unless, of course, after thousands of young blacks turn to terrorism, as oppressed people have done in many parts of the world. No," she added, "our goals must be redirected. Otherwise, we are destined to keep losing—even when we think we have won."

232

"But, Geneva," I protested, "isn't that the end? If the law has failed, and all our efforts to attain full citizenship are simply turned into new policy devices to maintain our subordinate position, isn't self-help our last chance?"

Geneva winced. "I wish," she said sadly, "that your question were not rhetorical. The Slave Scrolls Chronicle's message seems to be that even a monumental effort to pull ourselves up, sufficient to make even Booker T. Washington proud, will not move us out of our traditional place in this society. I really do not want to face the next conclusion."

"You mean," I said, with something less than seriousness, "the options the Curia members are urging on you?"

"I can tell from the tone of your voice that you are taking the Curia challenge much less seriously than I am."

"I didn't mean it that way. You shouldn't confuse my concern for you, which is genuine, with my inability to view the plight of American blacks as pessimistically as you do."

My attempt at reassurance seemed to ease Geneva's distress. "I have not given up. I sense something more positive in the Chronicles that I can't explain, but I need more time. You have been honest, and, despite my bickering, you have helped me. It is just that I am a long way from formulating a response that I can live with—or, if it comes to that, die for. And, speaking of time, it's late. When must you leave for your plane?"

"Given the distance and my unerring ability to take the wrong roads, I should have left an hour ago."

Geneva smiled. "Well, friend, take care that you don't lose your way again. The Lord only knows what wiles the next woman you stop to help will employ to lure you away from your praiseworthy, if predictable, conventionality."

I arrived at the airport in good time, only to discover my flight was first delayed and finally canceled. The next available flight would not leave until the next day. I decided to drive back to Geneva's cottage, bear her sharp sarcasm, and accept her earlier offer of a bed for the night.

The small house seemed far more drab than it had a few hours ago; but in anticipation of seeing her and perhaps of hearing one more Chronicle, I barely noticed its condition until I knocked and got no response. Thinking she might have left the house to do some chore in the garden, I walked to the rear. The yard was overgrown, and the back door was boarded up. Running back to the front door, I knocked again and then looked in the front window.

I couldn't believe it. Except for the mute evidence of an undisturbed layer of dust on the floor, the house was empty. Neighbors up and down the road confirmed what my eyes had seen. It was some time since tenants had lived in the house, they told me, and no member of the Crenshaw family had lived there for years. One elderly black man remembered Geneva, but was sure she had not been home for many years. He boasted that he knew every black person for miles around. With some hesitancy, I inquired, "Have you ever heard of a woman named Delia Jones, who sings in a local church choir, and is working to organize a back-to-Africa movement in this community?"

The old man thought for a moment. "There sure is a church by that name. Been a member for fifty years. But I never heard of no back-to-Africa movement 'round here, and I know ain't no woman named Delia Jones livin' in these parts."

I shouldn't have asked. I suddenly wanted a mirror to assure myself of my identity. I tried to be logical. Could I be in the wrong area? I checked nearby roads, postponing in the process the necessity of even considering what my senses told me was true. Though I had accepted what Geneva said about her arrangement with the Celestial Curia, I had not really believed it.

I drove into town and, from a phone booth, called the West Coast sanatorium where Geneva had spent many years. When I asked for her, I was told that she had been released three months ago and had gone home. So, I thought, Geneva must have come back here at some point.

I checked my airline ticket and hotel receipt. Yes, I had arrived two evenings ago—and had, I swear, spent the last two days at a cottage with Geneva. Then I remembered my tape recorder—and how Geneva had smiled when I dug it out of my briefcase and plugged it in before our conversations started. Still, she had not objected, and I had filled nine cassettes.

My hands were shaking as I put new batteries into the recorder, inserted the first cassette, and pushed the "play" button. Then I relaxed when I heard my voice—until I realized that mine was the only voice recorded. Where Geneva's voice should have been, there was not so much silence as a sound like the murmur of the sea on a calm evening.

And from that evening until I opened the book containing a complete set of Geneva's Chronicles at the Black Bicentennial Convention, I had no further word from her.

PART III

Divining a Nation's Salvation

Prologue to Part III

NOW the Black Bicentennial Convention was entering its third and final day. In the morning, the delegates divided into nine groups, each of which studied one of the Chronicles and then gathered, after lunch, for a final coordination and summing up of their several messages. This gathering was to be the prelude to the final session, in the evening, when we hoped to choose a workable strategy for achieving racial justice on which we could all agree.

Most of the delegates agreed that the Chronicle of the Constitutional Contradiction had persuaded them that even an adversarial confrontation about the contradiction the Framers were creating would not have led them to change their minds. Moreover, the concept of individual rights, unconnected to property rights, was totally foreign to these men of property; and thus, despite two decades of civil rights gains, most blacks remain disadvantaged and deprived because of their race. The delegates saw as all too likely the possibility presented by the Chronicle of the Celestial Curia: that, unless mitigated by social reform, racial conditions could so deteriorate that blacks would have to choose between emigration to another country and violent protests intended to disrupt the United States. That this situation is not easily addressed by black political power was the clear message of the Chronicle of the Ultimate Voting Rights Act and is borne out by statistics: thus, while 10.8 percent of the voting age population is black, only 1.2 percent of elected officials were black in 1985.[1]

Delegates who had worked in school desegregation were distressed by the Chronicle of the Sacrificed Black Schoolchildren. "A serious indictment of our work," one attorney concluded, "it

239

suggests that we failed to protect black children who integrated the schools from all manner of tragedies, and allowed people who opposed implementation of the *Brown* decision to profit both from their opposition and from the actual provisions in the school desegregation plan." Chastened as well by the Chronicle of the Black Reparations Foundation were the militant delegates who had urged massive demonstrations to support demands for reparations programs that might close the economic gap between blacks and whites. Even so, these delegates saw potential in a privately funded plan, particularly if it could be funded and implemented with little fanfare.

Affirmative action had caused heated discussions at the Convention even before the delegates read the Chronicle of the DeVine Gift. And while most in the Convention viewed the benefits of such action as worth its disabling aspects, few needed to be reminded that employment-discrimination law offers blacks little protection against job bias that is not overt, particularly when the motivations for that bias include the desire to maintain a workplace in which whites are not simply dominant but are comfortably so.

The delegates were clearly most moved by the Chronicle of the Amber Cloud, which tests and finds wanting the long-held belief that a common crisis would break down the "we" and "they" basis of racial policy making. Even the most diehard integrationists were unwilling to challenge the whites' refusal in the Chronicle to sacrifice for blacks as they have done for disabled whites— or to contest the likely inability of legal doctrine to provide a remedy for a clear denial of equal protection, clear at least to the victims.

As for the most controversial story, that was easily the Chronicle of the Twenty-Seventh-Year Syndrome, with the delegates sharply divided along sex lines. "It is," one woman conceded, "a good vehicle for exploring our differing perspectives on a painful subject that white racism caused but only black togetherness can resolve." Finally, while some delegates doubted the hostile response of white society to black superachievers, as related in the Chronicle of the Slave Scrolls, other delegates countered with facts on recent changes in college admissions policies intended to limit the number of high-achieving Asian students.[2]

For many delegates, the real message of the Chronicles was stark: white society would never grant blacks a fair share of the nation's benefits, and would continue as Professor Kenneth Karst has said "to identify blacks as 'them,' and set us apart as a separate—and less worthy—category of beings."[3] The challenge that had led Geneva to call for my help now obsessed us all. What should we do now that in our distress we cry out with Jeremiah: "The Harvest is past, the summer is ended, and we are not saved"?

Our dinner before the final session was frugal compared with earlier meals, as befitted the Convention's commitment to those blacks whose lives bring them too few banquets and too many burdens. Afterward, we moved in a formal procession to the final plenary session in the Great Hall. Each delegate was wearing a simple black robe connoting the judicial decisions that would determine a new civil rights strategy. Finding my seat and gazing about, it struck me why the impressive room seemed familiar: it was quite like Geneva's description of the hall where she had first met the Celestial Curia. As the delegates filed in and took their places, I thought, with a combination of admiration and despair, of the many times black people had come together in conventions and conferences to debate, orate, plan, plead, and pray about their subservient status in the "land of the free." I wondered in the words of the old hymn, "Oh Lord, how long, how long?"

As the presentations began, the spirit of fellowship and unity so intense at the beginning of the session, started to wane. One impassioned speaker followed another, each advocating his or her, or a particular group's, solution for achieving the common goal of an effective strategy against racism.

To my surprise, an advocate for a back-to-Africa emigration scheme received a positive response to her impassioned appeal. This speaker, using arguments similar to those made by Delia Jones, contended that an exodus by a substantial group of American blacks, though difficult and fraught with peril, would be the

241

salvation of those who went and would provide a basis for pride and organized support for those who remained behind.

A culture-based internal development program, intended to develop pride and self-confidence and presented by a Black Muslim lawyer-teacher, sounded to me like the techniques the blacks adopt in the "Chronicle of the Slave Scrolls," but without the Scrolls' magical properties. The delegates questioned whether many blacks would make the sacrifices and accept the discipline the Muslims would impose on participants in their program.

Pragmatism, aided by insight gained from the Chronicles, served to dilute enthusiasm for a national voting registration campaign urged by representatives of a major civil rights organization long active in the voting-rights field. Critics acknowledged the group's dedicated work, but suggested the need for an approach that might transform voting rights into something other than "ritualistic altar play in a power selection process in which blacks play no real role."

Among other proposals, a really good program would update the 1920s strategy of James Weldon Johnson, the black poet, teacher, diplomat, and NAACP executive secretary, who urged "creative disruption,"[4] a form of passive resistance to protest discriminatory policies. Despite my good intentions, my mind wandered and I missed the balance of the presentation as well as the opening of the next speaker who offered litigation strategies that he claimed were new. Although many delegates were enthusiastic, I fear they were responding more or less automatically to the familiar use of the courts as the forum for racial grievances rather than to any innovative means of avoiding the traditional shortcomings of civil rights litigation.

The tolerance shown to litigation advocates was not, however, extended to the spokesperson from the neoconservative black movement, whose espousal of "bootstraps" philosophy as the only sensible means of black advancement in a free enterprise society, and whose frequent comparisons of how Jews, Asians, and West Indians have "made it," worsened the already strained relationships in the audience. Opposing delegates challenged almost every aspect of the black neoconservative position. Some of the attacks turned personal. Voices were raised, and order as well as the ambitious hopes for the Convention were soon in jeopardy.

I looked toward the dais to see how the Chair would handle the disturbance—but he was no longer there. In his place, standing quietly, a woman waited. Though at the rear of the hall, I recognized her at once. Not the Geneva of an old cottage in rural Virginia, or of that earlier time when we had been civil rights attorneys in the South. Now, in a flowing gold robe, she exuded a radiance that touched not only me, who knew her, but all the fiercely arguing men and women in that hall, and calmed them in a few moments. When the bedlam had given way to an uneasy peace, Geneva spoke.

"Hosts and delegates to this convention," she said quietly but with authority, "I am Geneva Crenshaw. You have read my Chronicles. Now I have come to relate one final Chronicle and help you rise above this dissension—dissension that springs from frustration not from any difference in goals. It is my hope that together we can discover the true road to our salvation."

Along with everyone in the Great Hall, I stood and applauded. But the keenest advocates of the various strategic programs, while joining in the welcome, viewed Geneva's appearance as ceremonial. Many were concerned that the interruption might consume valuable time from the final session's main purpose: a decisive vote on the primary strategy and then, no doubt, the election of one of the delegates to direct an implementing program.

In spite of the protracted and vigorous applause, there were gathering murmurs of dissent, and people began to raise their hands and shout to be recognized. As the clapping died down, the Chair returned to the podium and raised his hands for attention. "It is because of Geneva and her Chronicles," he said, "that we have had this fruitful meeting. I rule therefore that we let her speak before we decide on a final strategy."

The ruling was not popular. Several delegates moved toward the platform to register strong objections to it and to demand that it be voted on. Voices were raised for and against this suggestion, and the Chair pounded his gavel, to no avail. Within moments the session was in an uproar. Then I saw a group of delegates

243

advancing purposefully toward the podium, while others were trying to push them back. Fearing for Geneva's safety, I jumped up and looked for a way to get to her.

But suddenly before I or anyone else could move further, there was a mighty fanfare from the huge pipe organ to the left of the podium. At the same time, the curtains at the front of the hall parted and rolled away to reveal a choir whose white-robed ranks stretched back as far as the eye could see, into a beautiful cloud-filled vista. Awed, the delegates subsided into their seats. Throughout the turmoil, Geneva had stood quietly by the podium, listening, watching. I wondered whether this was how she had faced the angry Framers at the Constitutional Convention of her Chronicle.

It was she whom I—and, indeed, everyone—watched while, following the initial organ fanfare, the choir sang two spirituals. First, the overwhelming jubilation of "The Lord Will Make a Way Somehow," and then "There Is a Balm in Gilead," the latter bringing tears to my eyes. By now, whether as a result of the tears or of my imagination, Geneva had become a transcendent presence, otherworldly, radiant. When the last chords died away, the choir sat row by row in a human wave.

Now, throughout the Great Hall, reverent silence prevailed—a silence it had taken a miracle to accomplish. But now the delegates were ready to heed a voice other than their own or some particular group's. Looking out over the upturned faces, Geneva allowed that period of silent transition between music and sermon familiar to men and women steeped in the drama of black church worship. Her voice, when at last she spoke, needed no amplification; it resonated through the hall in harmony with the organ playing softly in the background.

Chapter 10

Salvation for All: The Ultimate Civil Rights Strategy

The Chronicle of the Black Crime Cure

AFTER CENTURIES of slavery and then decades of unremitting struggle to gain recognition of their rights, black people, both those who had achieved success and those still mired in poverty, felt that future progress was barred by the many criminals in their midst. For years, the crime problem had endangered blacks living in poor black areas, and had increasingly been cited by whites as a prime reason for their reluctance to end discrimination in jobs, housing, schools, and places of public accommodation. The crime statistics more than supported white fears about black people; and—despite vigorous crime-control programs and prosecutions, more police, longer sentences, and new prison facilities—the black crime problem grew worse. Vigilantes who took the law into their own hands were hailed as heroes.[1] Social scientists and civil rights proponents who tried to explain black crime as a predictable output of black oppression were not simply not believed: they were ignored.

And then the Black Crime Cure was discovered. Deep in a cave used to hide illegal narcotics, a black gang from a big-city ghetto found a stream whose bed was covered with small ruby-red stones about the size of peas. It is not clear how the gang leader came to swallow one of the small stones, perhaps by accident, but the effect was immediate and acute.

The converted drug dealer himself not only immediately lost all inclination to wrongdoing but was possessed with an overpowering desire to fight black crime wherever it existed. Somehow associating his changed outlook with the stone, he managed to feed one to each of his band. Instantly, they, too, were changed from criminals to crime fighters. After considering how they might further their newly adopted crusade, they dumped all their narcotics and filled the containers with what they were already calling the "crime cure stones."

Time does not permit a full recounting of how the Black Crime Cure was distributed across the country. While the stones seemed to give indigestion to whites who took them, they worked as they had in the cave for anyone with a substantial amount of African blood. Black people were overjoyed and looked forward to life without fear of attack in even the poorest neighborhoods. Whites also lost their fear of muggings, burglary, and rape.

But, now that blacks had forsaken crime and begun fighting it, the doors of opportunity, long closed to them because of their "criminal tendencies," were not opened more than a crack. All-white neighborhoods continued to resist the entry of blacks, save perhaps for a few professionals. Employers did not hasten to make jobs available for those who once made their living preying on individuals and robbing stores. Nor did black schools, now models of disciplined decorum, much improve the quality of their teaching. Teachers who believed blacks too dangerous to teach continued their lackadaisical ways, rationalized now because blacks, they said, were too dumb to learn.

And so it went. Although the crime excuse was gone, the barriers to racial equality—Jim Crow signs in one era, black crime in another—that had from time to time given way to black pressure, were in the end unable to prevail against the apparently implacable determination of whites to dominate blacks by one means or another.

Moreover, the Black Crime Cure drastically undermined the crime industry. Thousands of people lost jobs as police forces were reduced, court schedules cut back, and prisons closed. Manufacturers who provided weapons, uniforms, and equipment of all forms to law enforcement agencies were brought to the brink of bankruptcy. Estimates of the dollar losses ran into the hundreds of millions.

And most threatening of all, police—free of the constant menace of black crime and prodded by the citizenry—began to direct attention to the pervasive, long-neglected problem of "white-collar" crime and the noxious activities of politicians and their business supporters. Those in power, and the many more who always fear that any change will worsen their status, came to an unspoken but no less firm conclusion: fear of black crime has an important stabilizing effect on the nation. By causing whites with otherwise conflicting economic and political interests to suspect all blacks as potential attackers, the threat persuades many whites that they must unite against their common danger. The phenomenon is not new. In the pre–Civil War era, slave owners used the threat of violent slave revolts as the "common danger" to gain support for slavery among whites, including those who opposed the institution on moral grounds and those in the working class whose economic interests were harmed by the existence of slave labor. Black crime serves a similar contemporary function.

Those in power soon recognized how the lack of black crime threatened their comfortable status. Many committees of government officials studied the problem, at great cost to the taxpayer—but in the end, it was decided to do . . . nothing. If, as the liberal social scientists claimed, lack of opportunity rather than inherent immorality had led many blacks into criminal pursuits, a similar outcome would follow society's failure to provide meaningful opportunity for schooling and jobs to blacks who had taken the Cure. And so it worked out.

How, exactly, was never clear. Perhaps the crime cure stones' effect wore off. But certain it is that the cave that was their sole source was mysteriously blown up, and the area where it was located became a landfill. Certain it is, too, that the era free of black crime came to an end.

Happily, not many blacks who had taken the Cure ever returned to lives of crime. But their example and urging had little influence on younger blacks growing up with prospects so bleak that stealing and worse seemed the only available route to survival and, if one were lucky, to success.

FOR several moments, Geneva stood quietly at the podium and allowed her Chronicle to have its intended effect: we sat in stunned silence. None of her stories had been models of optimism, but the Chronicle of the Black Crime Cure touched the very nadir of our despair. It stimulated no discussion. Rather, a pall of resignation fell over the gathering. What could Geneva possibly hope to achieve by this ultimate depiction of futility and defeat?

Evidently viewing our dejection as an advantage, she challenged us: "Does any group among you advocating an end to black crime as the means of our people's salvation wish to take issue with the outcome of my Chronicle?"

The stillness was intense as Geneva confronted the delegates. "I come here today to determine whether any of your strategies has the potential claimed for it." Again she paused, then continued with her challenge. "Come, sisters and brothers, which of you will pledge your lives to those in this Great Hall—and to all the multitudes of men, women, and children whom you here represent—that a particular civil rights strategy, even if it is successfully implemented, indeed, particularly if adopted by all and successfully implemented, will not lead society to circumvent your goals as they were circumvented in the Chronicle I have just related?

Another pause, during which no one stirred or spoke.

"Your silence tells me," she went on, "that you have found the consensus that has eluded you in your discussions today. Each of you, in advocating one program over another, has lost sight of a basic truth: while the central motivating theme of black struggle is faith, the common thread in all civil rights strategies is eventual failure. Like the drowning person who grasps for straws, you con-

248

tend for your positions here with the fervor of desperation. Have you learned nothing from experience?"

Her question echoed across the utterly silent hall. Then, in a quiet voice, she told us, "I understand and share your despair. The Chronicle of the Black Crime Cure is, unlike many of the others, entirely without any hope of redemption. It affects me as it clearly has affected you. Of what value, I wonder, is my militancy against the monstrous message of the Chronicle? Since I have come to understand that I cannot alone answer this painful question, it is my hope that the Celestial Curia will see fit to join us here to help me—and all of you—find a strong and fruitful answer to it."

At her words, there was a low rumble from the bass section of the great choir. In sequence, first the tenors, then the contraltos, and finally the sopranos joined in, each group of voices one-third of a scale higher than the one before, to conclude in a chord of enthralling beauty. At some moment, while it was building to a crescendo, the Celestial Curia appeared on a raised dais overlooking the podium where Geneva was standing. I recognized the two women at once from her description of them all those weeks ago in her Virginia cottage. Now they sat straight and proud as queens in two chairs as ornately carved as ancient thrones. Between them stood another, equally elaborate chair, empty and—it seemed to me—waiting.

"We have come, Sister Geneva," the Curia announced in a rhythmic chant. "We are here to provide you and those gathered here with the guidance you seek."

Geneva turned to face the Curia. "You must know that I am angry," she said. "Why have you required me both to experience and to recount your Chronicles if their only message is that our civil rights programs are worthless opiates offering no more than delusions of hope to a people whose color has foredoomed them to lives of tokenism, subservience, and exclusion? Neither I nor any man or woman here needs your supernatural gifts to recognize the weaknesses of these strategies. They are only too plain. If the Chronicles are intended to help us, you must provide a key to their interpretation more positive than the bleakness of racial barriers they portray."

DIVINING A NATION'S SALVATION

The Curia's initial response was obscure and unenlightening: "There are no new truths. There are only new perspectives for seeing what you already know."

As usual, Geneva wanted specifics. "Surely," she protested, "the Chronicles are more than tales of racial distress."

"Indeed they are," the Curia acknowledged. "The Chronicles are intended to serve as dramatic diagrams pointing away from your earthbound yearning for equal opportunity and acceptance"—a response Geneva refused to accept. "Sisters," she challenged, "explain, if you will, why it is unreasonable for black people to seek their share of what this system offers whites along with, when needed, appropriate compensation for the myriad harms caused by past discrimination."

"Amen, sister!" a delegate shouted. "You sure are speaking for me and mine!"

Scattered murmurs of approval spurred Geneva on. "Our people helped build this country. We have fought and died in its wars. We have sweated in its factories and fields. Out of the anguish of our lives, we have given the nation a language and a music that have vitalized its culture. And always we have been exploited, underpaid, and overworked. We deserve, we want, and we are determined to have a share of America's dividends—dividends equal to the burdens we have borne, and adequate to compensate us for our gifts."

The Curia Sisters regarded Geneva sternly for a long moment, then asked, "Had you been alive before the Civil War, would it have been in keeping with your goal to transform blacks from slaves to slave owners?"

"Of course not! Blacks wanted freedom for themselves, not the enslavement of whites."

"If that is so, Sister Geneva, why do you state a goal for blacks today that would, if achieved, simply make them the exploiting rich rather than the exploited poor, the politically powerful rather than the pitifully powerless, the influential and prestigious rather than the ignored and the forgotten?"

"That is not what we seek," Geneva replied. "Neither I nor any of the delegates here would have us integrate into a white society simply to share in the moral corruption of which we have been the unwilling victims."

The Curia came back with yet another question. "In that case, why do you and the others here seek a fair share in the country *as it is*? Would it not be more accurate as well as more praiseworthy to choose either to rebel against your oppressors or simply to depart from them?"

"As you well know, I have scrutinized the Chronicles with great care in search of some further option. We have invested too much in this country simply to give up and move on to Lord knows what. Moreover, the resort to violence and bloodshed would betray the morality of our cause—even in the unlikely possibility that our rebellion succeeded. As despairing as they are, the Chronicles suggest that there is a Third Way."

"You have truly studied the Chronicles, Sister Geneva. There is indeed such an option. An awesome option, one that rests on the vision of this country as a truly democratic society of liberated men and women, all of whom are endowed with dignity and self-respect, and all of whom enjoy equal opportunity unhindered by race, religion, or class discrimination."

"Can I be hearing rightly?" Geneva asked, her voice trembling with indignation. "Are you asking us to fall back on the rhetoric— so noble on great national occasions, so empty in our daily lives— of 'America the Beautiful'? Are you truly saying that we must be condemned forever to labor for the salvation of our oppressors, perpetually forgiving them for our suffering, for which they are responsible? Is it not clear that our civil rights efforts have resulted in laws and legal precedents that broaden the rights of white Americans more than of ourselves? I see our work and their gain as one more manifestation of white domination."

"And so have we seen it as well," the Curia replied. "And it is because of this ultimate exploitation of your freedom efforts that we have urged the radical measures of revolution or emigration— measures that you reject. If you insist on a Third Way, you must recognize the restrictions you yourselves impose on your goal when you seek justice for blacks within a society where only the most powerful or wealthy whites are able either to insist on or to pay for lives free of exploitation. Now, one of the privileges of these whites is the freedom, both subtly and not so subtly, to practice and profit from racism—a privilege we, of course, despise. You must be careful, in setting goals for blacks, to discriminate among white privileges and not seek to adopt their belief in racial superiority. You must, that is, not seek status advantages like those that have held you and others down.

"Moreover, while it is certainly rhetorically neat to claim that you want for blacks only those constitutional rights whites take for granted, that formula offers neither political success nor the moral satisfaction you so highly value."

"But we did not write the Constitution," Geneva said. "All we can do is to try to gain the protection that its provisions guarantee to all."

"Nor," the Curia Sisters reminded her, "did the slaves write the Bible. White men handed your forebears their most sacred book as a pacifier, intending it to lull them into contentment with their lowly lot.[2] They found, instead, within its text both a comfort for their pain and the confirmation of our humanity. The Bible provided a vision of life for the slaves unlike anything their masters could ever know. It inspired them both to survive and to leave as their legacy the spirituals—literally, a theology in song."

"I am beginning to understand," answered Geneva. "You are saying that if our slave ancestors could accomplish so much with the Bible, we should be able to do no less with the Constitution. For it, too, as it referred to us, sought to sanction our servitude, to ratify our downtrodden condition—even though the amendments proclaiming us free and citizens were used to further the interests of the liberators rather than to deliver us from the canons of racism."

"Furthermore, Sister Geneva—and this you must never forget—it was the determination of black men and women to be truly free that transformed the Constitution from a document speaking of rights as the main means of protecting property and privilege into an instrument in which the concept of rights has gained a humane purpose and significance for even those who lack property, and for whites as well as blacks. Viewed from this perspective, blacks have used the Constitution to accomplish miracles!"

"An inspiring statement," Geneva conceded, "but you have to admit that those miracles did not obviate the conditions that prompted this Convention nor, with all due respect, our need for guidance and direction."

"Nor, Sister Geneva, did the Bible deliver the Promised Land on a platter to your slave ancestors—and would not have served them as well had it done so. As for guidance, look to the Chronicles. Of course, some of you"—and the Curia Sisters nodded solemnly at the audience assembled—"will view them as merely metaphorical essays on the plight of blacks—and will leave here seeking theories of liberation from white legal philosophers, who are not oppressed, who do not perceive themselves as oppressors, and who thus must use their impressive intellectual talent to imagine what you experience daily. Black people, on the other hand, come to their task of liberation from the battleground of experience, not from the rarefied atmosphere of the imagination. Do you understand?"

"It is true," Geneva acknowledged. "We have real-life stories to tell—stories on which we have built our movements. For Harriet Tubman in the nineteenth century and Rosa Parks just a few decades ago are not mere names but heroines whose courage is as life affirming today as in their own time. Their stories teach us, and inspire us, and lift us up when we and our plans fall short. Just as the Bible is filled with stories of men and women who, like Moses, succeeded ultimately even as they failed in their immediate goals, so the history of the Constitution is filled with stories of humanizing reforms sought and sometimes gained by blacks and others of the dispossessed.

"I see then, Sisters, that you view the Chronicles as parables of our efforts to achieve what whites possess rather than what we, and they, might become. But is it not understandable that we should seek to emulate those able by virtue of race to take for granted rights our Constitution promises equally to all?"

"A slave," the Curia explained, "laboring in a field under a broiling hot sun and lifting her sweat-drenched eyes toward her mistress sipping mint juleps on a cool veranda must have envied and longed to emulate that white woman at least as much as we do today. And yet we now know that, in reality, many white women on the plantation, though pampered, led a no less servile existence. Such is the real status of many whites today whose skin color is not sufficient to protect them from economic disaster. Just as many blacks are losing their jobs to automation, factory closings, and farm bankruptcies, so are white families suffering similar affliction. The stark truth is that whites as well as blacks are being exploited, deceived, and betrayed by those in power."

"Nor," interjected Geneva, "is this a new phenomenon. Even back in 1892, Tom Watson, then a staunch advocate of the Populist party, which favored a union between Negro and white farmers, warned both blacks and whites:

> You are kept apart that you may be separately fleeced of your earnings. You are made to hate each other because upon that hatred is rested the keystone of the arch of financial despotism which enslaves you both. You are deceived and blinded that you may not see how this race antagonism perpetuates a monetary system which beggars both.[3]

"The Populist movement failed," Geneva went on, "because whites were unable to resist the superior status promised them, and thus rejected the potentially powerful coalition they could have formed with black workers. To win white support this time, must we limit our strategies to those in which whites will join?"

"Of course not!" the Curia Sisters snapped. "But you should not foreclose the possibility of coalition with those who, except for the disadvantages imposed on blacks because of color, are in the same economic and political boat."

"I assume," Geneva probed, "that you mean: first, that the option of the Third Way will require that we seek justice for all through a systematic campaign of attacking poverty as well as racial discrimination; and second, that our traditional civil rights strategies will not be of any help in this enterprise?"

"Any strategy that leads toward the goal of a more just and humane society can be effective. Traditional civil rights programs, aggressively pursued, will exert continuing pressure on the legal process—no matter whether the courts grant the specific request for relief.[4] Lawyers have placed too much weight on whether they win a case, and too little on the impact of the litigation. Has it served to educate the community, to facilitate the organization of the poor, or has it conveyed to government officials the dissatisfaction of constituents who intend to insist on reform?"

"My Curia Sisters," Geneva said, "I think I speak for the delegates in confessing confusion. You warn us that our legal programs are foredoomed to failure, and yet you urge us to continue those very programs because they will create an atmosphere of protest. I must reiterate my fear that this approach will simply perpetuate the pattern of benefit to whites of legal reforms achieved by civil rights litigation intended to help blacks."

"The benefit they bring to all is proof of how potent a weapon your civil rights programs can be in seeking a restructured society. Future campaigns, while seeking relief in traditional forms, should emphasize the chasm between the existing social order and the nation's ideals. Thus, Sister Geneva, litigation as well as protests and political efforts would pursue reform directly as well as create a continuing tension between what you are and what you might become. Out of this tension may come the insight and imagination necessary to recast the nation's guiding principles closer to the ideal—for all Americans."

"*May*?" Geneva echoed. "You are not sure?"

"The Third Way is no less risky than the more pragmatic tactics of emigration or than truly disruptive, even violent, struggle. You are opting for a utopian reformation of government, difficult even to envision, and urging such reform through the existing legal and legislative structures."

"But you, Sisters, have made it clear," Geneva said, "that the Third Way has a chance for success."

"A fact in your favor," the Curia responded, "is that the structure of your country's government, as well as the interpretation of the basic law of the Constitution and its few dozen amendments, are in constant flux—a fluidity you must take advantage of to make the laws reflect the needs of both blacks and whites. Only in that way can you all experience democracy, not simply pay verbal homage to it on ceremonial occasions. Even so, there is no guarantee of success."

"As to the risks," Geneva responded, "you have commented on the many contributions blacks have made to this society despite the tremendous obstacles they faced. Those achievements stand as proof that the Constitution and the law generally—as flawed as they are—can be vehicles of reform. Of course," she added, "reliance on existing legal structures involves enormous risk, but is there not risk in any significant human enterprise? Consider the odds against a successful marriage, and yet most people keep trying. And the perils of parenthood seem to grow exponentially in our complex world, without noticeable lessening of the desire to have children. Even our survival against a host of daily dangers becomes ever more problematic, and yet most of us willingly face each new day with renewed hope as our main defense against our all too justified fears. Surely, the risk involved in our continuing civil rights campaigns is no greater than those each of us faces inevitably in our personal lives."

"We hear you, Geneva, and agree," the Curia intoned, "but beware lest your people's enemies construe your desire to change the structure of government as some form of subversion—a risk that, in the past, civil rights organizations have taken pains to avoid."

"I have not forgotten," Geneva said, and her voice rang out to the farthest corner of the Great Hall, "but this is no time to become conservative or to draw back from controversy. We must commit ourselves to salvation for all through means that are peaceful and ethical. And," she added, "let me warn those critics who would brand us as advocates of revolution. If our efforts fail, we are likely to be replaced by actual, and active, subversives who will earn the apprehensions undeservedly aimed at us."

Then Geneva turned to face the delegates. "I am now convinced that the goal of a just society for all is morally correct, strategically necessary, and tactically sound. The barriers we face, though high, are not insuperable, and the powers that brought me these Chronicles are no greater than the forces available to you—and within you. Use them to the fullest in the difficult times that lie ahead. And be of good cheer. As our forebears survived the most virulent slavery the world has ever known, we will survive contemporary conservatism. Already our faith and perseverance have rewarded us. We know that life is to be lived, and not always simply enjoyed; that, in struggle, there is joy as well as pain. And—even in a society corrupted by wealth and endless material comforts, forgetful of its noble precepts, and cursed by the conviction that the mainstays of existence are money rather than morality and cunning rather than compassion—we find courage in the knowledge that we are not the oppressors and that we have committed our lives to fighting the oppression of ourselves as well as of others.

"Finally, let us find solace and strength in the recognition that black people are neither the first nor the only group whose age-old struggle for freedom both still continues and is worth engaging in even if it never results in total liberty and opportunity. Both history and experience tell us that each new victory over injustice both removes a barrier to racial equality and reveals another obstacle that we must, in turn, grapple with and—eventually—overcome. For emancipation did not really free the slaves; and Lincoln's order was but a prerequisite, the necessary first step in a process that will likely continue as long as there are among us human beings who, for whatever reason, choose to hold other human beings in their power.

"Let us, then, rejoice in the memory of the 'many thousands gone,' those men and women before us who have brought us this far along the way. Let us be worthy of their courage and endurance, as of our own hopes, our own efforts. And, finally, let us take up their legacy of faith and carry it forward into the future for the sake not alone of ourselves and our children but of all human beings of whatever race or color or creed."

As Geneva neared the end of her talk, the chords of the organ intensified; and the celestial choir, if that is what it was, stood and began to sing. The sound swelled; and as she finished a last word of encouragement, she joined in the singing, gesturing to the delegates to do the same. As they stood, their faces were no longer angry or confused. They looked hopeful, exhilarated, as they joined wholeheartedly in an old and stirring spiritual.

Geneva's task was done. As I strained to see her over the heads of the delegates, the two Curia Sisters came down from the dais, took her by the hand, and escorted her to the seat between their own. For a moment they sat there, hands clasped, and gazed out over the hall. Then someone moved in front of me, cutting off the dais from view. When I could see it again, it was empty of chairs, of the Curia Sisters, of Geneva. We were on our own once again.

Joining hands with the delegates on either side of me, I sang with them, with everyone in that great hall, filled so recently with dissension but now with hope and exhilaration. In the music, in our joined voices, all our differences were for the moment harmonized into a single powerful sense of dedication—a dedication renewed and echoed in the spiritual's soaring refrain:

> Done made my vow to the Lord,
> and I never will turn back.
> Oh, I will go. I shall go.
> To see what the end will be.

NOTES

Introduction

1. Charles Lawrence, "The Id, the Ego and Equal Protection: Reckoning with Unconscious Racism," *Stanford Law Review* 39 (1987): 317, 330.

2. Robert Darnton, *The Great Cat Massacre and Other Episodes in French Cultural History* (1984), p. 33.

3. See Derrick Bell, "An American Fairy Tale: The Income-Related Neutralization of Race Law Precedent," *Suffolk University Law Review* 18 (1984): 331.

4. Linda Greene, "A Short Commentary on the Chronicles," Harvard *Blackletter Journal* 60 (Spring 1986).

5. See generally *The Dialogues of Plato*, B. Jowett, trans., reprinted in Robert Hutchins, ed., *Great Books of the Western World* (1952).

6. See, for example, Henry Hart, "The Power of the Congress to Limit the Jurisdiction of Federal Courts: An Exercise in Dialectic," *Harvard Law Review* 66 (1953): 1362.

7. Lon Fuller, "The Case of the Speluncian Explorer," *Harvard Law Review* 62 (1949): 616. In a fictional story, cave explorers, trapped by landslides and facing death by starvation, select by lot and kill an unwilling victim whose flesh provides the nourishment that enables them to survive and stand trial for murder. Professor Fuller then uses a series of hypothetical appellate opinions to explore several jurisprudential themes concerning the appropriateness of even settled legal principles to do justice to situations beyond anything the lawmakers envisioned.

8. Alison Anderson, "Lawyering in the Classroom: An Address to First Year Students," *Nova Law Review* 10 (1986): 271, 274. See also Gerald Lopez, "Lay Lawyering," *UCLA Law Review* 32 (1984): 1.

9. Kim Crenshaw, "From Celebration to Tribulation: The Constitution Goes to Trial," *Harvard Law Review* 101 (1988).

10. Manning Marable, "Beyond the Race-Class Dilemma," *The Nation*, 11 April 1981, pp. 428, 431.

Prologue to Part I

1. See, for example, G. Fredrickson, *The Black Image in the White Mind* (1981).

2. See, for example, Charles Murray, *Losing Ground* (1984), who argues that programs financed by government have brought about social ills, including increases in crime, teenage unemployment, teenage pregnancies, abortions, poverty, households headed by single mothers.

3. See, for example, Thomas Sowell, *Civil Rights: Rhetoric or Reality?* (1984).

4. E. Frazier, *Black Bourgeoisie* (1962 ed.).

5. See, for example, *Hamilton v. Alabama*, 376 U.S. 650 (1964) (per curiam), reversing contempt conviction, 156 S. 2d 926 (1963).

6. Among the very few blacks who held full-time teaching positions at white law schools in the 1950s and 1960s were William Robert Ming, Jr., associate professor and professor at the University of Chicago School Law School from 1947 to 1953; Charles W. Quick, professor at Wayne State Law School from 1958 to 1967, and at the University of Illinois College of Law from 1967 to 1979; John R. Wilkens, acting professor, professor, and professor emeritus at the University of California at Berkeley School of Law from 1964 to 1976; and Harry E. Groves, professor at the University of Cincinnati College of Law from 1968 to 1970. Ming was the first black to hold a full-time faculty position at a predomi-

nantly white law school. See Kellis Parker and Betty Stebman, "Legal Education for Blacks," *Annals* 407 (1973): 144, 152.

7. The careers of these black scholars and civil rights lawyers are documented in R. Bland, *Private Pressure on Public Law: The Legal Career of Justice Thurgood Marshall* (1973); Richard Kluger, *Simple Justice* (1976) (documenting the civil rights careers of Justice Marshall and Judge Carter); Genna Rae McNeil, *Groundwork: Charles Hamilton Houston and the Struggle for Civil Rights* (1983); and Gilbert Ware, *William Hastie: Grace under Pressure* (1984).

8. W. E. B. DuBois, "The Talented Tenth," in J. Lester, ed., *I The Seventh Son: The Thought and Writings of W. E. B. DuBois* (1971), p. 385.

9. John Gwaltney, *Drylongso: A Self-Portrait of Black America* (1980).

10. Peter Bergman, *The Chronological History of the Negro in America* (1969), pp. 586–87.

11. See, for example, Bergman, *Chronological History*, pp. 583, 584.

12. See Harold Schonberg, "A Bravo for Opera's Black Voices," *New York Times*, 17 January 1982, sec. 6, pp. 24, 82–90.

13. *Brown v. Board of Education*, 347 U.S. 483 (1954).

Chapter 1

1. Samuel Eliot Morison, *The Oxford History of the American People* (1965), p. 305.

2. See J. Miller, *The Wolf By the Ears* (1977), p. 31.

3. Donald Robinson, *Slavery in the Structure of American Politics: 1765–1820* (1971), p. 92, quoting from Thomas Jefferson, *Notes on the State of Virginia*, T. Abernethy, ed. (1964).

4. Ibid.

5. Staughton Lynd, *Class Conflict, Slavery, and the United States Constitution* (1967), pp. 181–82 (quoting Max Farrand, ed., *The Records of the Federal Convention of 1787* [1911], vol. I, p. 533).

6. See, for example, Lynd, *Class Conflict*, p. 182.

7. Robinson, *Slavery in the Structure of American Politics*, p. 185.

8. Farrand, *Records*, vol. I, p. xvi.

9. William Wiecek, *The Sources of Antislavery Constitutionalism in America: 1760–1848* (1977), pp. 63–64.

10. Robinson, *Slavery in the Structure of American Politics*, p. 210.

11. Ibid., pp. 55–57.

12. Charles Beard, *An Economic Interpretation of the Constitution of the United States* (1913), pp. 64–151. See also Pope McCorkle, "The Historian as Intellectual: Charles Beard and the Constitution Reconsidered," *American Journal of Legal History* 38 (1984): 314, reviewing the criticism of Beard's work and finding validity in his thesis that the Framers primarily sought to advance the property interests of the wealthy.

13. Morison, *Oxford History*, p. 304.

14. Dumas Malone, *Jefferson and the Rights of Man* (1951), p. 172 (letter from Washington to Thomas Jefferson, 31 August 1788).

15. W. Mazyck, *George Washington and the Negro* (1932), p. 112.

16. Ibid.

17. Derrick Bell, *Race, Racism and American Law* (2d ed. 1980), pp. 29–30.

18. James Madison, quoted in Farrand, *Records*, vol. I, p. xvi.

19. Malone, *Jefferson*, p. 167 (letter written in 1788 from James Madison to Philip Mazzei).

20. *The Records of the Federal Convention of 1787* (rev. ed. 1937), vol. II, p. 222.

21. Gouverneur Morris, quoted in Robinson, *Slavery in the Structure of American Politics*, p. 200.

22. *The Records of the Federal Convention of 1787*, p. 222.

23. See Edmund Morgan, "Slavery and Freedom: The American Paradox," *Journal of American History* 59 (1972): 1, 6.

24. See Wiecek, *Sources of Antislavery Constitutionalism*, pp. 62–63.

25. A. Leon Higginbotham, *In the Matter of Color, Race and the American Legal Process: The Colonial Period* (1978), p. 380.

26. Wiecek, *Sources of Antislavery Constitutionalism*, p. 42.

27. Luther Martin, quoted in David Brion Davis, *The Problem of Slavery in the Age of Revolution, 1770–1823* (1975), p. 323.

28. In the Northern states, slavery was abolished by constitutional provision in Vermont (1777), Ohio (1802), Illinois (1818), and Indiana (1816); by a judicial decision in Massachusetts (1783); by constitutional interpretation in New Hampshire (1857); and by gradual abolition acts in Pennsylvania (1780), Rhode Island (1784), Connecticut (1784 and 1797), New York (1799 and 1817), and New Jersey (1804). See L. Litwack, *North of Slavery* (1961), pp. 3–20.

29. Broadus Mitchell and Louise Mitchell, *A Biography of the Constitution of the United States* (1964), pp. 100–101.

30. Morgan, "Slavery and Freedom." The position taken by the Colonel is based on the motivation for American slavery set out in Professor Morgan's paper; he developed the thesis at greater length in his *American Slavery, American Freedom* (1975).

31. Morgan, "Slavery and Freedom," p. 22.

32. Morgan, *American Slavery, American Freedom*, pp. 380–81.

33. Morgan, "Slavery and Freedom," p. 24.

34. Morgan, *American Slavery, American Freedom*, p. 381.

35. *Brown* v. *Board of Education*, 347 U.S. 483 (1954).

36. James 2: 17.

37. Center on Budget and Policy Priorities, *Falling Behind: A Report on How Blacks Have Fared Under the Reagan Policies* (October 1984).

38. John E. Jacob, in National Urban League, *The State of Black America* (1985), pp. i–ii.

39. Bureau of the Census, *Household Wealth and Asset Ownership: 1984* (July 1986), pp. 4–5.

40. Alphonso Pinkney, *The Myth of Black Progress* (1984).

41. Joint Center for Political Studies, *A Policy Framework for Racial Justice* (1983), p. 10.

42. James McGhee, "The Black Family Today and Tomorrow," in National Urban League, *The State of Black America* (1985), pp. 1–2.

43. Center For the Study of Social Policy, *The "Flip-Side" of Black Families Headed by Women: The Economic Status of Black Men* (1984), p. 1.

44. Ibid., p. 6. See also William J. Wilson and Kathryn Neckerman, "Poverty and Family Structure: The Widening Gap Between Evidence and Public Policy issues," in *Fighting Poverty: What Works and What Doesn't*, ed. S. Danziger and D. Weinberg (1986), pp. 232–59.

45. Center on Budget and Policy Priorities, *A Report on How Blacks Have Fared Under the Reagan Policies*, 3 (1984).

46. Ibid., pp. 3–4.

47. William J. Wilson, *The Declining Significance of Race* (1978), p. 120.

48. Ibid., pp. 110, 152.

Chapter 2

1. David Shapiro, "Mr. Justice Rehnquist: A Preliminary View," *Harvard Law Review* 90 (1976): 293. Professor Shapiro found that, in Justice Rehnquist's first four and one-half years on the bench, his judicial product had been adversely affected by "the unyielding character of his ideology" which made possible a tripartite characterization of his votes. Whenever possible, Justice Rehnquist (1) resolved conflicts between an individual and the government, against the individual; (2) resolved conflicts between state and federal authority—whether on an executive, a legislative, or a judicial level—in favor of the states; and (3) resolved questions of the exercise of federal jurisdiction—whether on the district, the appellate, or the Supreme Court level—against such exercise (p. 294). See also John Jenkins, "Partisan: A Talk with Justice Rehnquist," *New York Times Magazine*, 3 March 1985, p. 28, where Justice Rehnquist candidly discusses his view of the Court's role in American government.

2. See, for example, Laurence Tribe, "Unraveling *National League of Cities*: The New

Federalism and Affirmative Rights to Essential Government Services," *Harvard Law Review* 90 (1977): 1065. In this article, Professor Tribe departs from those commentators who read the decision in *National League of Cities* v. *Usery*, 426 U.S. 833 (1976), as a judicial capitulation under the banner of "federalism" from the Court's earlier staunch protection of individual rights. Rather, he argues that Justice William Rehnquist's majority opinion reflects a perhaps unconscious recognition of affirmative rights owed by the state to its citizens. Later, Professor Tribe reports that when they met at a conference, Justice Rehnquist said that he had read the article, and laughingly chided Tribe for trying to turn him into a closet socialist.

For a later, somewhat more generous, but ultimately no less critical view of Justice Rehnquist's judicial philosophy, see Powell, "The Compleat Jeffersonian: Justice Rehnquist and Federalism," *Yale Law Journal* 91 (1982): 1317, arguing that "Justice Rehnquist's work is consistent with the Jeffersonian theory of federalism" (p. 1320), even when it leads him to ends inconsistent with conservative politics. "If the Court had followed Justice Rehnquist's analysis in First National Bank v. Bellotti, 435 U.S. 765 (1978), Massachusetts would have been allowed to take a very reasonable step to ensure that big business and its money would not drown out other voices in a political controversy" (p. 1363). But the author concludes, "Rehnquist's attempt to transform this federalism into an objective constitutional first principle must fail because it cannot be established that the Framers intended to embody the theory in the Constitution" (p. 1320).

3. Frances Fox Piven and Richard Cloward, *Poor People's Movements: Why They Succeed, How They Fail* (1977), pp. xx–xxi, 6.

4. *Cooper* v. *Aaron*, 358 U.S. 1, 26 (1958) (Justice Frankfurter concurring).

5. See, for example, *Dred Scott* v. *Sandford*, 60 U.S. (19 How.) 393 (1857).

6. See Bruce Ackerman, "Beyond Carolene Products," *Harvard Law Review* 98 (1985): 713, who suggests the institution-preserving function of both the *Lochner* era and the *Carolene Products* doctrine.

7. See Steel, "Nine Men in Black Who Think White," *New York Times Magazine*, 13 October 1968, p. 56.

8. *Brown* v. *Board of Education*, 349 U.S. 294 (1955). Often referred to as *Brown II*, this decision set a standard of compliance so vague that school boards were able to evade real school desegregation for more than a decade.

9. Steel, "Nine Men in Black Who Think White," p. 112.

10. See *New York Times*, 15 October 1968, p. 53, col. 2.

11. *New York Times*, 29 October 1968, p. 43, col. 3.

12. See NAACP, "The Issues in the Lewis M. Steel Case," January 1969, pp. 6–7.

13. Arthur S. Miller, "Social Justice and the Warren Court: A Preliminary Examination," *Pepperdine Law Review* 11 (1984): 473, 489.

14. See Derrick Bell, "Brown v. Board of Education and the Interest-Convergence Dilemma," *Harvard Law Review* 93 (1980): 518, 524–25.

15. See Brief for Appellant at 28, *Morgan* v. *Virginia*, 328 U.S. 373 (1946) (no. 704).

16. W. DuBois, *The Autobiography of W. E. B. Du Bois* (1968), p. 333.

17. See, generally, Norman Amaker, "De Facto Leadership and the Civil Rights Movement: Perspective on the Problems and the Role of Activists and Lawyers in Legal and Social Change," *Southern University Law Review* 6 (1980): 225, who discusses the representation of civil rights protestors during the 1960s.

18. See, for example, N. Jones, Correspondence, *Yale Law Journal* 86 (1976): 378. Responding to charges that NAACP lawyers were pressing for racial-balance remedies contrary to the wishes and interests of black parents, Mr. Jones, then NAACP General Counsel, said that "lawyers are reaching judgments of feasibility and effectiveness based upon established judicial precedents. . . . This they do without breaching their ethical responsibilities to their clients . . . and the Constitution" (p. 382).

19. Speech of Justice Thurgood Marshall (18 November 1978), reprinted in *The Barrister*, 15 January 1979, p. 1.

20. Boris Bittker, "The Case of the Checker-Board Ordinance: An Experiment in Race Relations," *Yale Law Journal* 71 (1962): 1387, 1393.

21. Professor Paul Freund, "The Civil Rights Movement and the Frontiers of Law," in T. Parsons and K. Clark, eds., *The American Negro* (1967), pp. 363, 364. See also Arthur

Kinoy, "The Constitutional Right of Negro Freedom," *Rutgers Law Review* 21 (1967): 387, 389–90.

22. *New York Times* v. *Sullivan*, 376 U.S. 254 (1964).

23. *NAACP* v. *Button*, 371 U.S. 415 (1963). The decision, Professor Freund said, in "The Civil Rights Movement," provided a precedent for later group representation efforts. He cited *Brotherhood of Railroad Trainmen* v. *Virginia*, 377 U.S. 1 (1964). See also *United Mine Workers* v. *Illinois Bar Association*, 389 U.S. 217 (1967) (union's hiring of attorney to assist members with workmen's compensation claims is not unauthorized practice of law by the union); and *United Transportation Union* v. *State Bar of Michigan*, 401 U.S. 576 (1971) (union protected in setting up group representation plan intended to protect union members from excessive fees by incompetent lawyers in Federal Employers Liability Act [FELA] actions).

24. *Shelley* v. *Kraemer*, 334 U.S. 1 (1948).

25. *Dixon* v. *Alabama State Board of Education*, 294 F.2d 150 (5th Circuit 1961). See also *Tinker* v. *Des Moines Independent Community School District*, 393 U.S. 503 (1969).

26. *Smith* v. *Allwright*, 321 U.S. 649 (1944).

27. See *United States* v. *Classic*, 313 U.S. 299 (1941) (alleged fraudulent vote count in a Louisiana primary, led to finding that primary elections are "elections" under Article I, Section 4, of the Constitution, the provision empowering Congress to regulate the manner, times, and places of elections).

28. See, for example, *Peters* v. *Kiff*, 407 U.S. 493 (1972) (white defendants are denied their rights to due process of law by the systematic exclusion of minorities from their juries). The authorities extend back more than a century: *Strauder* v. *West Virginia*, 100 U.S. 303 (1880) (sustaining the validity under the Fourteenth Amendment of federal statutes prohibiting the exclusion of blacks from state juries).

29. See *Batson* v. *Kentucky*, 106 S. Ct. 1712 (1986) (the equal-protection clause bars a prosecutor from challenging potential jurors "solely on account of their race or on the assumption that black jurors as a group will be unable impartially to consider the state's case against a black defendant"). The *Batson* decision overruled the portion of *Swain* v. *Alabama*, 380 U.S. 202 (1965), that had precluded a criminal defendant from making out an equal-protection violation based on the exclusion by peremptory challenges of black jurors in the defendant's particular case. The seriousness of racial prejudice in the jury box is reviewed in Sheri Johnson, "Black Innocence and the White Jury," *Michigan Law Review* 83 (1985): 1611.

30. *NAACP* v. *Alabama*, 357 U.S. 449 (1958).

31. *Gomillion* v. *Lightfoot*, 364 U.S. 339 (1960).

32. *Moore* v. *Dempsey*, 261 U.S. 86 (1923).

33. *Powell* v. *Alabama*, 287 U.S. 45 (1932).

34. *Brown* v. *Mississippi*, 297 U.S. 278 (1936).

35. Robert Cover, "The Origins of Judicial Activism in the Protection of Minorities," *Yale Law Journal* 91 (1982): 1287, 1305–6. See also Professor Harry Kalvin's published lectures reviewing the 1960s' civil rights movement's contributions to free-speech theory (H. Kalvin, *The Negro and the First Amendment* [1965]). Hailing the NAACP's strategy of systematic litigation as a "brilliant use of democratic *legal* process" (p. 67; emphasis in the original), Professor Kalvin discusses how *New York Times* v. *Sullivan*, 376 U.S. 254 (1964), extended First Amendment protection to bar seditious libel; developed rights of association and privacy as a result of successful efforts to halt harassment of NAACP and its members by southern states (see, for example, *NAACP* v. *Button* [1963]); and made real, if indirect, First Amendment inroads on traditional notions of trespass while defending the sit-in cases (see, for example, *Bell* v. *Maryland*, 378 U.S. 226 [1964]).

36. *Gomillion* v. *Lightfoot* (1960), p. 341.

37. Frankfurter warned against the promulgation of jurisdiction in the abstract, "for it conveys no intimation what relief, if any, a District Court is capable of affording that would not invite legislatures to play ducks and drakes with the judiciary" (*Baker* v. *Carr*, 369 U.S. 186, 268 (1962) (Frankfurter, J., dissenting). Fourteen years before the *Tuskegee* case, the Supreme Court in *Colegrove* v. *Green*, 328 U.S. 549 (1946), dismissed as nonjusticiable a challenge that state law prescribing congressional districts was unconstitutional because districts were not approximately equal in population. Justice Frankfurter, speaking for only himself and Justices Stanley Reed and Harold Burton, felt courts "ought not to enter this

political thicket." Frankfurter viewed such questions of party and the people as beyond judicial competence, and an infringement of power conferred by the Constitution on Congress (p. 556). See also *South* v. *Peters,* 339 U.S. 276 (1950).

38. *Baker* v. *Carr,* 369 U.S. 186 (1962). See James Blacksher and Larry Menefee, "From Reynolds v. Sims to City of Mobile v. Bolden: Have the White Suburbs Commandeered the Fifteenth Amendment?" *Hastings Law Journal* 34 (1982): 1, 6, who state that reliance on *Gomillion* and earlier Fifteenth Amendment black voting cases was a "significant feature" of *Baker's* majority opinion.

39. *Reynolds* v. *Sims,* 377 U.S. 533, 535 (1964).

40. *Baker* v. *Carr* (1962), pp. 254, 259.

41. See *Gray* v. *Sanders,* 372 U.S. 368 (1963); and *Wesberry* v. *Sanders,* 376 U.S. 1 (1964).

42. *Reynolds* v. *Sims,* 377 U.S. 533, 566 (1964).

43. Compare the very close scrutiny of congressional districting plans in *Karcher* v. *Daggett,* 462 U.S. 725 (1983) (invalidating New Jersey's plan that deviated from pure equality by an average of 0.1384 percent, because the legislature had both rejected other plans with smaller variations between the largest and the smallest districts, and had not borne the burden of showing that the variances in its plan were intended to achieve some legitimate goal), with the far more relaxed scrutiny given state legislative-apportionment schemes as in *Brown* v. *Thompson,* 463 U.S. 835 (1983) (upheld Wyoming's apportionment plan for its House of Representatives even though average percentage deviation was 16 percent with a maximum of 89 percent, held permissible to preserve state's long-standing policy of providing at least one representative to even the least populated counties).

44. *Davis* v. *Bandemer,* 106 S. Ct. 2797 (1986) (political gerrymandering cases are justiciable, and such gerrymandering may violate the equal-protection clause). See also Justice John Paul Stevens's concurrence in *Karcher* v. *Daggett,* 462 U.S. 725, 754 (1983).

45. See *Avery* v. *Midland County,* 390 U.S. 474, 484–85 (1968).

46. James Blacksher, "Drawing Single-Member Districts to Comply with the Voting Rights Amendments of 1982," *Urban Lawyer* 17 (1985): 347, 349–50.

47. *Fortson* v. *Dorsey,* 379 U.S. 433, 439 (1965).

48. See Emma Jordan, "Taking Voting Rights Seriously: Rediscovering the Fifteenth Amendment," *Nebraska Law Review* 64 (1985): 389.

49. See *City of Mobile* v. *Bolden,* 446 U.S. 55 (1980); see also *Whitcomb* v. *Chavis,* 403 U.S. 124, 149 (1971) (rejecting charges that an apportionment plan diluted black votes in the absence of proof that multimember districts in the plan "were conceived or operated as purposeful devices to further racial or economic discrimination").

50. See, for example, *Wright* v. *Rockefeller,* 376 U.S. 52, 53 (1964) (noting that some black political leaders opposed a civil rights challenge to a congressional districting plan that excluded nonwhite voters from mainly white districts, because the districting protected the political power of black and Hispanic voters in other districts).

51. See *United Jewish Organization of Williamsburgh, Inc.* v. *Carey,* 430 U.S. 144 (1977) (rejecting charge of vote dilution made by Hasidic Jews whose district was divided to ensure black and Hispanic voting representation).

52. See *Rogers* v. *Lodge,* 458 U.S. 613 (1982); *White* v. *Regester,* 412 U.S. 755 (1973).

53. *City of Mobile* v. *Bolden,* 446 U.S. 55 (1980).

54. Public Law No. 97–205, 96 Stat. 131 (1982) (codified at 42 U.S.C. §1973 [1982]).

55. See H. R. Rep. No. 227, 97th Cong., 1st Sess. 29–30 (1982); S. Rep. No. 417, 97th Cong., 2d Sess. 27–30 (1982), reprinted in 1982 *U.S. Code Congressional and Administration News,* 177, 192–93.

56. See *Washington Post,* 31 August 1985, p. A1, col. 5, reporting on Justice Department's brief submitted on appeal of *Gingles* v. *Edmisten,* 590 F. Supplement 345 (Eastern District of North Carolina 1984). In response to the Justice Department's position, the Senate majority leader, Robert Dole, and nine other members of Congress filed an amicus brief stating that the Justice Department's position was expressly rejected by Congress when it amended the Voting Rights Act in 1982.

57. *Thornburg* v. *Gingles,* 106 S. Ct. 2752 (1986).

58. See, for example, *Hunter* v. *Underwood,* 471 U.S. 222 (1985), in which the Court invalidated an Alabama constitutional provision disenfranchising persons convicted of "crimes of moral turpitude." The Court found that the 1902 state constitutional convention had enacted the provision with racially discriminating intent.

59. See Arthur Waskow, *From Race Riot to Sit-In, 1919 and the 1960s* (1967), p. 203 (describing Johnson's disavowal of violent tactics in favor of tactics such as work stoppages and other peaceful protests).

60. See James W. Johnson, *Negro Americans, What Now?* (1934).

61. James Blacksher and Larry Menefee, *From Reynolds v. Sims to City of Mobile v. Bolden: Have the White Suburbs Commandeered the Fifteenth Amendment?*, 34 Hastings 1, 62, L. J. 62 (1982).

62. Ibid., p. 63.

63. See, for example, *Washington v. Davis*, 426 U.S. 229, 248 (1976).

64. David Brion Davis, *The Problem of Slavery in the Age of Revolution: 1770–1820* (1975), p. 260, quoting Edmund S. Morgan; Davis stated further that whites' "rhetoric of freedom was functionally related to the existence—and in many areas to the continuation—of Negro Slavery" (p. 262).

Chapter 3

1. *Harper* v. *Virginia Board of Elections*, 383 U.S. 663 (1966). The Twenty-Fourth Amendment prohibits the use of poll taxes as a prerequisite to voting in federal elections (U.S. Constitution Amendment XXIV, §1, 1964).

2. *Wright* v. *Rockefeller*, 376 U.S. 52, p. 66 (1964) (Justice Douglas dissenting).

3. Ibid., p. 67.

4. L. Litwack, *North of Slavery* (1961), pp. 74, 79.

5. Ibid., p. 79.

6. Arthur Blaustein and Robert Zangrando, *Civil Rights and the American Negro* (1968), p. 423.

7. In *United States* v. *Reese*, 92 U.S. 214 (1876)—a prosecution of Kentucky voting officials who refused to count the votes of blacks—the Court held provisions of the Civil Rights Act to be unconstitutional, interpreting them as barring all interference with the right to vote, and thus finding them beyond the scope of the Fifteenth Amendment, which prohibits only interference based on race, color, or previous condition of servitude.

And in *United States* v. *Cruikshank*, 92 U.S. 542 (1876), the Court held that deprivation of life, liberty, or property without due process does not cover deprivations that are the result of private acts. The *Cruikshank* case grew out of the famous 1873 Colfax Massacre in Louisiana where, in an election dispute, a large number of blacks were killed by whites. The convictions of nine whites, who were found guilty of violating the rights of the blacks, were reversed by the Supreme Court's decision.

The Supreme Court did affirm convictions in *Ex parte Yarbrough*, 110 U.S. 651 (1884), and ruled that a Ku Klux Klansman who had forcefully prevented a black from voting in a congressional election in Georgia, had violated a Civil Rights Act section providing criminal penalties. The section (the predecessor of the current law, 18 U.S.C. §241) was found a valid exercise of the federal power to control elections.

8. *Giles* v. *Harris*, 189 U.S. 475, 488 (1903).

9. See, for example, *Ketchum* v. *Byrne*, 740 F.2d 1398, 1413 (7th Circuit 1984) (requiring redrawing of boundaries to ensure "effective" majorities of 65 percent in nineteen black and four Hispanic wards); *Jones* v. *City of Lubbock*, 727 F.2d 365, 386–87 (5th Circuit 1984) (affirming district court plan creating two minority districts in six-district council where minority population was 26.1 percent).

The cases are collected in Note, "Vote Dilution, Discriminatory Results, and What Proportional Representation: What Is the Appropriate Remedy for a Violation of Section 2 of the Voting Rights Act?" *UCLA Law Review* 32 (1985): 1203, 1205–8.

10. *Ketchum* v. *Byrne*, 740 F.2d 1398, 1413 (7th Circuit 1984).

11. 1982 Amendments to the Voting Rights Act, section 2, 96 Stat. at 134; 42 U.S.C. § 1973 (b) (1982).

12. *Thornburg* v. *Gingles*, 106 S. Ct. 2752 (1986).

13. Ibid, pp. 2784–85. Justice Sandra Day O'Connor—with whom Chief Justice Warren Burger and Justices Powell and Rehnquist joined, concurring in the judgment—wrote: "Al-

though the Court does not acknowledge it expressly, the combination of the Court's definition of minority voting strength and its test for vote dilution results in the creation of a right to a form of proportional representation in favor of all geographically and politically cohesive minority groups that are large enough to constitute majorities if concentrated within one or more single-member districts."

14. See *Wright* v. *Rockefeller*, 376 U.S. 52, 57–58 (1964) (minority plaintiffs and black intervenors disagreed over desirability of concentrating minority voters in a few districts).

15. See *United Jewish Organization of Williamsburgh, Inc.* v. *Carey*, 430 U.S. 144 (1977). In concurring, Justice Brennan said, "An effort to achieve proportional representation, for example, might be aimed at aiding a group's participation in the political process by guaranteeing safe political offices, or, on the other hand, might be a 'contrivance to segregate' the group . . . thereby frustrating its potentially successful efforts at coalition building across racial lines" (pp. 172–73).

16. Sanford Levinson, "Gerrymandering and the Brooding Omnipresence of Proportional Representation: Why Won't It Go Away?," *UCLA Law Review* 33 (1985): 257.

17. James Madison, in B. Wright, ed., *The Federalist* (1961), no. 10, p. 135 (the more factions required for a majority, the less likely it is that the majority will have a common motive to invade the rights of other citizens).

18. See Note, "Vote Dilution," p. 1249.

19. Eric Van Loon, "Representative Government and Equal Protection," *Harvard Civil Rights–Civil Liberties Law Review* 5 (1970): 472.

20. J. S. Mill, *Representative Government* (1861), p. 373.

Chapter 4

1. Daniel Monti, *A Semblance of Justice: St. Louis School Desegregation and Order in Urban America* (1985).

2. See, for example, *Morgan* v. *Kerrigan*, 409 F. Supp. 1141, 1151 (D. Mass. 1976) (placing the South Boston High School in receivership to insure compliance with desegregation orders); *Turner* v. *Goolsby*, 255 F. Supp. 724, 730–35 (S.D. Ga. 1966).

3. See, for example, *Chambers* v. *Hendersonville City Bd. of Educ.*, 364 F.2d 189 (4th Circuit 1966); *McCurdy* v. *Bd. of Public Instruction*, 509 F.2d 540 (5th Circuit 1975); *Williams* v. *Albemarle City Bd. of Educ.*, 508 F.2d 1242 (4th Circuit 1974). But despite dozens of suits in which black teachers won reinstatement and back pay after being terminated during the desegregation process, literally thousands of black teachers and administrators lost their jobs as Southern school boards complied with desegregation orders. See amicus curiae brief prepared by the *National Educational Association for United States* v. *Georgia*, No. 30,338 (5th Circuit 1971).

4. Ray Rist, *The Invisible Children: School Integration in American Society* (1978).

5. Robert L. Carter, "A Reassessment of Brown v. Board," in D. Bell, ed., *Shades of Brown: New Perspectives on School Desegregation* (1980), pp. 21–27.

6. Ibid., p. 27.

7. See, for example, *Covington* v. *Edwards*, 264 F.2d 780 (4th Circuit 1959), *cert. denied*, 361 U.S. 840 (1959) (pupil-placement law validated and procedures established required to be followed).

8. *Kelley* v. *Board of Educ.*, 270 F.2d 209 (6th Circuit 1959), *cert. denied*, 361 U.S. 924 (1959).

9. *Green* v. *County School Bd of New Kent Co.*, 391 U.S. 430 (1968) (after several years of approving such plans, they were held not valid unless they work to effectuate a desegregated school system).

10. See, for example, A. Miller, *A "Capacity for Outrage": The Judicial Odyssey of J. Skelly Wright* (1984), pp. 48–88; J. Bass, *Civil Rights Lawyers on the Bench* (1981); J. Peltason, *Fifty Eight Lonely Men* (1961).

11. *Brown* v. *Board of Education*, 349 U.S. 294, 301 (1955).

12. See Faustine C. Jones-Wilson, *A Traditional Model of Educational Excellence: Dunbar High School of Little Rock, Arkansas* (1981); Thomas Sowell, "Black Excellence—The Case

of Dunbar High School," *Public Interest* 35 (1974): 3; Thomas Sowell, "Patterns of Black Excellence," *Public Interest* 43 (1976): 26.

13. Sara Lightfoot, *The Good High School* (1983), pp. 29–55.

14. *Johnson* v. *Chicago Board of Educ.*, 604 F.2d 504 (7th Circuit 1979).

15. See, for example, *Parent Ass'n of Andrew Jackson High School* v. *Ambach*, 598 F.2d 705 (2d Circuit 1979) (approving a limit, inspired by "white flight," on the number of black students permitted to transfer from an all-black school to neighboring, less-segregated schools).

16. Ibid., p. 720.

17. See, for example, *Milliken* v. *Bradley II*, 433 U.S. 267 (1977) (federal courts can order remedial educational programs as a part of a school-desegregation decree where such relief is in response to the constitutional violation, is designed to as nearly as possible restore victims of the discriminatory conduct to the position they would have occupied in the absence of such conduct, and takes into account the interests of state and local authorities in managing their own affairs, consistent with the Constitution).

18. *Tasby* v. *Wright*, 520 F. Supp. 683 (Northern District of Texas 1981).

19. Ibid., p. 689. The court described the intervenors as a "broad-based minority community group composed of parents, patrons and taxpayers with children in the [schools], as well as representatives from a number of civic, political and ecumenical associations in the black community" (p. 689).

20. Ibid., pp. 732–33.

21. Prince Hall, "Negroes Ask for Equal Educational Facilities" (1787), in H. Aptheker, ed., *A Documentary History of the Negro People in the United States* (1951), p. 19.

22. *Roberts* v. *City of Boston*, 59 Mass. (5 Cush.) 198 (1850) (the school committee's segregation policy was deemed reasonable; and as to plaintiff's charge that segregated schools breed racial prejudice, the court observed that feelings of prejudice by whites were rooted deep in community opinion and feelings, and would influence white actions as effectually in an integrated as in a separate school).

23. Arthur White, "The Black Leadership Class and Education in Antebellum Boston," *Journal of Negro Education* 42 (1973): 504, 513, 514.

24. For a collection of the cases, see Derrick Bell, *Race, Racism and American Law* (2d ed. 1980), pp. 368–74.

25. White, "Black Leadership Class," p. 514.

26. W. E. B. DuBois, "Does the Negro Need Separate Schools?" *Journal of Negro Education* 4 (1935): 328. The essay is reprinted in J. Lester, ed., *The Seventh Son: The Thought and Writings of W. E. B. DuBois* (1971), vol. II, p. 408.

27. Ibid., p. 335.

28. See, for example, Olsen, "Employment Discrimination Litigation: New Priorities in the Struggle for Black Equality," *Harvard Civil Rights–Civil Liberties Law Review* 6 (1970): 20, 24–25.

29. See, for example, Charles Murray, *Losing Ground* (1984). Such views have been challenged vigorously: see, for example, Bernard Anderson, "The Case for Social Policy," in National Urban League, *The State of Black America* (1986), p. 153.

30. Martin Kilson, "Whither Integration," *American Scholar* 45 (1976): 360, 372.

Chapter 5

1. William J. Wilson, *The Declining Significance of Race* (1978), p. 120.

2. Ibid., pp. 110, 152.

3. See Ralph Korngold, *Thaddeus Stevens* (1955).

4. Lerone Bennett, *Before the Mayflower* (1961), p. 189.

5. Arnold Schuchter, *Reparations* (1970), p. 244.

6. Ibid.

7. Reynold Strickland, ed., *Felix S. Cohen's Handbook of Federal Indian Law* (1982 ed.).

8. Arnold Schuchter, *Reparations* (1970), pp. 240–44. The legal arguments for and against the provision of reparations to blacks are reviewed in Boris Bittker, *The Case for Black Reparations* (1973).

9. See W. Hosokawa, *Nisei: The Quiet American* (1969), pp. 445–47.

10. *Korematsu* v. *United States*, 323 U.S. 214 (1944). See also *Hirbayashi* v. *United States*, 320 U.S. 81 (1943) (sustaining a conviction for violation of a curfew order imposed against Japanese-Americans as an exercise of the power to take steps necessary to prevent espionage and sabotage in an area threatened by Japanese attack).

11. A. Miller, *A "Capacity for Outrage": The Judicial Odyssey of J. Skelly Wright* (1984).

12. *Hohri* v. *United States*, 782 F.2d 227 (D.C. Circuit 1986), *rehearing en banc denied*, 793 F.2d 304 (1986), *cert. granted*, 107 S. Ct. 454 (1986).

13. Ibid., p. 256.

14. The incident is discussed in substantial detail in Schuchter, *Reparations*. See also, R. Lecky and H. Wright, eds., *Black Manifesto* (1969).

15. Schuchter, *Reparations*, p. 5.

16. See, for example, *Gannon* v. *Action*, 303 F. Supp. 1240 (Eastern District of Missouri 1969), *aff'd* 450 F.2d 1227 (8th Circuit 1971) (a broad injunction was issued to a Catholic church where services over several weeks were disrupted by black militants). Similar relief was granted barring similar protests in *Central Presbyterian Church* v. *Black Liberation Front*, 303 F. Supp. 894 (Eastern District of Missouri 1969).

17. See, for example, *Regents of the Univ. of California* v. *Bakke*, 438 U.S. 265 (1978). The issues are discussed in Rodney Smolla, "In Pursuit of Racial Utopias: Fair Housing, Quotas, and Goals in the 1980's," *Southern California Law Review* 58 (1985): 947.

18. *Bob Jones University* v. *United States*, 461 U.S. 574 (1983).

19. See *Green* v. *Connally*, 330 F. Supp. 1150 (District, District of Columbia 1971), *aff'd sub nom. Coit* v. *Green*, 404 U.S. 997 (1971) (barring federal-tax-exempt status unless the schools demonstrate a publicized nondiscriminatory admissions policy).

20. See *New York Times*, 8 September 1986, p. 20, and 13 September 1986, p. 26; and "Eugene Lang Makes a Long Bet on Young Learners," *Time*, 25 November 1985, p. 86.

21. Several corporations in Boston established a fund to assist graduates of Boston's public schools in obtaining a college education. See *The Boston Globe*, 10 September 1986, p. 1, and 11 September 1986, pp. 29, 32.

22. P. L. 99–514 (1986).

23. See, for example, *United States* v. *South Carolina*, 445 F. Supp. 1094 (D.S.C. 1977), *aff'd mem. sub nom. National Educ. Assn.* v. *South Carolina*, 434 U.S. 1026 (1978).

24. 78 stat. 243, 42 U.S.C. §§2000a et seg.

25. *Guinn* v. *United States*, 238 U.S. 347 (1915).

Chapter 6

1. Roberto Unger, "The Critical Legal Studies Movement," *Harvard Law Review* 96 (1983): 563, 675.

2. See "Do Colleges Set Asian Quotas?" *Newsweek*, 9 February 1987, p. 60. In the face of rising applications from Asian-American students who are proud of their high grades and test scores, critics charge that Ivy League schools are imposing unwritten quotas making it more and more difficult for Asians to get into selective schools. For example, at Yale, the "admit" rate for Asian-Americans fell from 39 percent to 17 percent in the last decade.

3. Harry Edwards, *The Revolt of the Black Athlete* (1969), pp. 21–29; Jack Olsen, "The Anguish of a Team Divided," *Sports Illustrated*, 29 July 1968, pp. 20–35; Frank Deford, "40 Christmases Later: What Began with Jackie Robinson Is Not Yet Done," *Sports Illustrated*, 22 December 1986, p. 172.

4. See, for example, David Kaplan, "Hard Times for Minority Profs," *National Law Journal*, 10 December 1984, p. 1, col. 1. The story reviews a report, written by Charles Lawrence, on minority faculty hiring sponsored by the Society of American Law Teachers (SALT). After surveying the still-minuscule percentage of minority law teachers on faculties of predominantly white schools, Professor Lawrence called on such schools to adopt "voluntary quotas" for minority hiring, because: "We are persuaded that, despite our best intentions, law school faculties will remain virtually all white unless we impose clear, unalterable obligations upon ourselves by holding designated positions open until they are

filled by high-caliber minority faculty" (p. 28). The white administrators interviewed in the story reported several reasons for their opposition to the SALT recommendation, the most frequently cited being the paucity of minorities with the necessary credentials.

For a report on the experiences of blacks in the corporate world, see Edward Jones, "Black Managers: The Dream Deferred," *Harvard Business Review* (1986): 84.

5. Compare *Griggs* v. *Duke Power Co.*, 401 U.S. 424, 431 (1973) (finding that Title VII was directed at the consequences of employment practice, rather than at the motivation of employers, and holding that "if an employment practice which operates to exclude Negroes cannot be shown to be related to job performance, the practice is prohibited"), with *Firefighters Local Union No. 1784* v. *Stotts*, 467 U.S. 561 (1984) (holding that only proven victims of discrimination are entitled to protection against being laid off, and suggesting that Title VII is intended "to provide make-whole relief only to those who have been actual victims of illegal discrimination").

6. *McDonnell Douglas Corp.* v. *Green*, 427 U.S. 273 (1976) (when plaintiff makes out a *prima facie* case, the employer must articulate a legitimate nondiscriminatory reason for the refusal to hire). Compare *Hishon* v. *King & Spaulding*, 467 U.S. 69 (1984) (a law firm partnership is a benefit of employment within the coverage of Title VII, application of which does not infringe the partners' constitutionally protected rights of expression or association).

7. See, for example, *Spurlock* v. *United Airlines*, 475 F.2d 215 (10th Circuit 1972) (upholding airline requirements of college degree and minimum of five hundred flight hours for flight officer applicants, even though minority applicants were excluded thereby, the court proposing a sliding-scale standard under which validation requirements would be relaxed in relation to the importance of the job); and *Boyd* v. *Ozark Air Lines, Inc.*, 568 F.2d 50 (8th Circuit 1977) (upholding height qualifications for pilots).

8. See Elisabeth Bartholet, "Application of Title VII to Jobs in High Places," *Harvard Law Review* 95 (1982): 947, 960–64, 978–80 (arguing that courts distinguish between selection systems primarily on the basis of social and economic status of the jobs involved, and both maintain a hands-off attitude with regard to high-status jobs and intervene freely in low-status jobs, even when poor performance in these jobs might threaten significant economic and safety interests).

9. See ibid., p. 961; see also *Zahorik* v. *Cornell Univ.*, 729 F.2d85m 94 (2d Circuit 1984) (expressing reluctance to disturb a long-standing faculty hiring process and stating that "absent evidence sufficient to support a finding that . . . forbidden considerations such as sex or race [influenced hiring or tenure decisions] universities are free to set their own required levels of academic potential and achievement and to act upon the good faith judgments of their departmental faculties or reviewing authorities"); *Powell* v. *Syracuse Univ.*, 580 F2d 1150, 1153 (2d Circuit) (characterizing the hands-off approach as an "anti-interventionist policy [that] has rendered colleges and universities virtually immune to charges of employment bias, at least when the bias is not expressed overtly," but holding that because an independent legitimate reason had been shown for termination, no violation had occurred), *cert. denied*, 439 U.S. 984 (1078).

10. Ironically, judges are more likely to defer to upper-level selection processes with which they are personally familiar than to unfamiliar processes: "They know these decisionmakers; they sympathize and identify with their concerns and their use of traditional selection methods." (Bartholet, "Application of Title VII," p. 980.)

11. See *Furnco Construction Corporation* v. *Waters*, 438 U.S. 567, 579–80 (1980). But compare cf. *Connecticut* v. *Teal*, 457 U.S. 440, 442 (1982) (rejecting an employer's argument that promotion practices with an adverse impact on minority applicants should nevertheless be insulated from the Title VII review if the "bottom line" of the practices resulted in an appropriate racial balance). In *Teal*, the employer in effect sought to conform Title VII with the administrative rule of thumb used by the Equal Employment Opportunity Commission to separate worthy from unworthy cases for agency action. Some civil rights lawyers favor acceptance of the "bottom line" compromise (see Alfred Blumrosen, "Employment Opportunity after a Reagan Victory in 1984," *Suffolk University Law Review* 18 [1984]: 581, 586–87; others oppose it (see Linda Greene, "Equal Employment Opportunity Law Twenty Years after the Civil Rights Act of 1964: Prospects for the Realization of Equality in Employment," *Suffolk University Law Review* 18 [1984]: 593, 595–97).

12. *Otero* v. *New York City Housing Authority*, 484 F.2d 1122, 1140 (2d Circuit 1973)

(holding that a housing authority can limit the influx of nonwhites into a public housing community that is racially balanced in order to prevent the community from becoming predominately nonwhite); specifically, "the Authority is obligated to take affirmative steps to promote racial integration even though this may in some instance not operate to the immediate advantage of some nonwhite persons" [p. 1125]).

The *Otero* case was cited with approval in *Parent Ass'n of Andrew Jackson High School* v. *Ambach*, 598 F.2d 705 (2d Circuit 1979), where the court of appeal reversed a district court order striking down a "white flight"–inspired limit on the number of black students permitted to transfer from all-black schools to neighboring less-segregated schools. The court wrote: "Although white fears about the admission of minority students are ugly, those fears cannot be disregarded without imperiling integration across the entire system. . . . The exodus of white children from the public schools would disadvantage the *entire* minority community and nullify this voluntary desegregation effort" (p. 720).

See also *Stipulation of Settlement and Consent Decree, Arthur* v. *Starrett City Assocs.*, 79 Civ. 3096 (ERN), (Eastern District of New York 2 April 1985), where minority apartment seekers challenged the defendant's quota policies limiting to 36 percent minority occupancy of a 5,881-unit, 46-building rental project; the settlement agreement calls for defendants to provide an additional 175 apartments for minorities over five years. The Justice Department, unhappy with the settlement, challenged the racial-quota system: see *United States* v. *Starrett City Assoc.*, 605 F. Supp. 262 (E.D.N.Y. 1985) (denying defendant's motion to dismiss on grounds of judicial estoppel).

13. For explanation and examinations of the "tipping point" phenomenon, see Anthony Downs, *Opening Up the Suburbs* (1973), pp. 68–73; Bruce Ackerman, "Integration for Subsidized Housing and the Question of Racial Occupancy Controls," *Stanford Law Review* 26 (1974): 245, 251–66; and Note, "Tipping the Scales of Justice: A Race-Conscious Remedy for Neighborhood Transition," *Yale Law Journal* 90 (1980): 377, 379–82.

14. Boris Bittker, "The Case of the Checker-Board Ordinance: An Experiment in Race Relations," *Yale Law Journal* 71 (1962): 1387.

15. See *Shelley* v. *Kraemer*, 334 U.S. 1 (1948) (finding unlawful "state action" in privately made, racially restrictive land covenants); *Buchanan* v. *Warley*, 245 U.S. 60 (1917) (voiding a residential segregation ordinance).

16. Bittker, "Checker-Board Ordinance," p. 1394.

17. See ibid., pp. 1412–13. For appraisals of Bittker's article and extended discussions of remedial plans with "benign" discrimination characteristics, see Rodney Smolla, "In Pursuit of Racial Utopias: Fair Housing, Quotas, and Goals in the 1980's," *Southern California Law Review* 58 (1985): 947; Mark Tushnet, "The Utopian Technician," *Yale Law Journal* 93 (1983): 208.

18. Herbert Wechsler, "Toward Neutral Principles of Law," *Harvard Law Review* 73 (1959): 1.

19. Derrick Bell, "Bakke, Minority Admissions and the Usual Price of Racial Remedies," *California Law Review* 67 (1979): 3, 8.

20. Ibid., p. 17.

21. *Leiberman* v. *Gant*, 630 F.2d 60, 67 (2d Circuit 1980).

22. See *Regents of the Univ. of California* v. *Bakke*, 438 U.S. 265, 311–12 (1978).

23. Ibid., p. 314.

24. In 1751, Benjamin Franklin complained that the proportion of the world's "purely white People" was too small, and expressed the wish that "their Numbers were increased." By clearing America of woods, Franklin hoped to "reflect a brighter Light to the Eyes of Inhabitants in Mars or Venus," and questioned "why should we in the Sight of Superior Beings, darken its People? why increase the Sons of Africa, by Planting them in America, where we have so fair an Opportunity, by excluding all Blacks and Tawneys, of increasing the lovely White and Red" (*Observations Concerning the Increase of Mankind* reprinted in 4 *Papers of Benjamin Franklin*, L. Labaree, ed. [1959], pp. 227, 234).

25. *Dred Scott* v. *Sandford*, 60 U.S. (19 How.) 393, 407 (1857).

26. Manning Marable, "Beyond the Race Dilemma," *Nation*, 11 April 1981, pp. 428, 431. See also Charles Lawrence, "The Id, the Ego and Equal Protection: Reckoning with Unconscious Racism," *Stanford Law Review* 39 (1987): 317, 330.

27. See Manning Marable, "Race Dilemma," p. 431.

28. Regina Austin, "Resistance Tactics for Tokens," *The Harvard Blackletter Journal* 46 (Spring 1986).

29. Letter from Richard Delgado to Linda Greene (24 April 1985) (copy on file with the author).

30. Ibid.

31. R. Niebuhr, *Moral Man and Immoral Society* (1932), pp. 252–53.

32. See Peter Bergman, *The Chronological History of the Negro in America* (1969), pp. 450, 456, 458 (reporting that twenty blacks were lynched in 1930, twelve in 1931, and six in 1932).

Chapter 7

1. John Hope Franklin, *From Slavery to Freedom* (3d ed. 1967), pp. 496–97. See also John Salmond, "The Civilian Conservation Corps and the Negro," in B. Sternsher, ed., *The Negro in Depression and War* (1969), p. 78, who reviews the administration's failure to prevent discrimination in the Civilian Conservation Corps, despite an anti-bias provision in the statute.

2. See, for example, Dan Lacy, *The White Use of Blacks in America* (1972), pp. 175–81, who describes the discriminatory treatment of blacks in the military and in civilian defense plants; Richard Dalfiume, "The 'Forgotten Years' of the Negro Revolution," in Bernard Sternsher, *The Negro in Depression and War*, pp. 298, 301, who reports that flagrant discrimination undermined blacks' morale in the war effort but "heightened [their] race consciousness and determination to fight for a better position in American society" (p. 301).

3. See, for example, *Loving* v. *Virginia*, 388 U.S. 1 (1967). Invalidating a state law that prohibited marriage across racial lines, the Court summarized as follows what is generally called the "strict scrutiny" standard: "Over the years, this Court has consistently repudiated 'distinctions between citizens solely because of their ancestry' as being 'odious to a free people whose institutions are founded upon the doctrine of equality,' *Hirabayashi* v. *United States*, 320 U.S. 81, 100 (1943). At the very least, the Equal Protection Clause demands that racial classifications, especially suspect in criminal statutes, be subjected to the 'most rigid scrutiny,' *Korematsu* v. *United States*, 323 U.S. 214, 216 (1944), and, if they are ever to be upheld, they must be shown to be necessary to the accomplishment of some permissible state objective, independent of the racial discrimination which it was the object of the Fourteenth Amendment to eliminate. 388 U.S. at 11."

4. *Korematsu* v. *United States*, 323 U.S. 214, 216 (1944).

5. Ibid., p. 235 (Justice Murphy dissenting).

6. See *Hirabayashi* v. *United States*, 320 U.S. 81 (1943).

7. *Korematsu* v. *United States*, p. 236.

8. Ibid., p. 225.

9. *Brown* v. *Board of Education*, 349 U.S. 294, 301 (1955) (emphasis added).

10. *Brown* v. *Board of Education*, 347 U.S. 483, 494 (1954).

11. See, for example, *Nixon* v. *Herndon*, 273 U.S. 536 (1927) (invalidating a state law barring blacks from voting in primary elections); *Buchanan* v. *Warley*, 245 U.S. 60 (1917) (voiding a residential segregation ordinance); *Yick Wo* v. *Hopkins*, 118 U.S. 356 (1886) (striking down a facially neutral ordinance that was administered to bar only Chinese-run laundries); *Strauder* v. *West Virginia*, 100 U.S. 303 (1880) (invalidating a statute limiting jury service to white males).

12. See, for example, *Plessy* v. *Ferguson*, 163 U.S. 537 (1896) (upholding a state statute requiring segregated railway coaches); *Cumming* v. *Richmond County Bd. of Educ.*, 175 U.S. 528 (1899) (upholding the closing of the only black high school by a county continuing to maintain a high school for whites); *Berea College* v. *Kentucky*, 211 U.S. 45 (1908) (upholding a state statute imposing a heavy fine on a private college admitting both white and black students).

13. See *Brown* v. *Board of Education* (1954), p. 495.

14. *Loving* v. *Virginia*, 388 U.S. 1 (1967); see also *McLaughlin* v. *Florida*, 379 U.S. 1984

(1964) (invalidating a state statute providing higher penalties for interracial cohabitation than for the same offense committed by couples of the same race).

15. See *Jackson v. State*, 37 Ala. App. 519, 72 So. 2d 114, cert. denied, 348 U.S. 888 (1954).

16. In *Naim v. Naim*, 197 Va. 80, 87 S.E. 2d 749, remanded, 350 U.S. 891 (1955), *aff'd*, 197 Va. 734, 90 S.E. 2d 819, *appeal dismissed*, 350 U.S. 985 (1956), the Supreme Court remanded the case after oral argument for development of the record regarding the parties' domicile. After the state court refused to comply with the mandate, claiming that no state procedure existed for reopening the case, the Supreme Court dismissed the appeal, finding that the state court ruling left the case devoid of substantial federal question. Professor Wechsler remarked that this dismissal was "wholly without basis in law" (Herbert Wechsler, foreword, "Toward Neutral Principles of Constitutional Law," *Harvard Law Review* 73 (1954): 1, 34.

17. Gerald Gunther, *Constitutional Law* (1985), 1596.

18. See, for example, *Anderson v. Martin*, 375 U.S. 399 (1964) (voiding statute requiring candidate's race to be listed on nomination papers and ballot); *Hunter v. Erickson*, 393 U.S. 385 (1969) (voiding amendment to city charter requiring prior referendum approval of any fair housing law); *Palmore v. Sidoti*, 466 U.S. 429 (voiding state court divestiture of white mother's custody of infant child after the mother married a black man).

19. Often referred to as the "*Lochner* era," the period stretched from the decision in *Lochner v. New York*, 198 U.S. 45 (1905), to that in *West Coast Hotel Co. v. Parrish*, 300 U.S. 379 (1937).

20. See, for example, *Williamson v. Lee Optical Co.*, 348 U.S. 483 (1955).

21. See *United States v. Carolene Prods. Co.*, 304 U.S. 144, 152 n.4 (1938).

22. See Gerald Gunther, "The Supreme Court, 1971 Term—Foreword: In Search of Evolving Doctrine on a Changing Court: A Model for a Newer Equal Protection," *Harvard Law Review* 86 (1972): 1, 8.

23. In a prison desegregation case, however, several justices suggested a scenario in which segregation might be approved: see *Lee v. Washington*, 390 U.S. 333, 334 (1968) (Justices Hugo Black, John Marshall Harlan, and Potter Stewart concurring) (stating that segregation "in particularized circumstances," to maintain security during times of racial tension, would not violate the Constitution).

24. See, for example, *Washington v. Davis* 426 U.S. 229 (1976) (upholding a test for police-force candidates in which a higher percentage of blacks failed than whites, in the absence of proof that the test was administered with a racially discriminatory purpose); see also *Crawford v. Board of Educ.*, 458 U.S. 527 (1982) (upholding a California constitutional amendment that withdrew from state courts the power to order mandatory busing to achieve racial balance in schools except to remedy a federal constitutional violation, where the state court found that no discriminatory animus had motivated the voters' approval of the amendment). But compare *Washington v. Seattle School Dist, No. 1*, 458 U.S. 457 (1982) (invalidating by a 5 to 4 vote a state initiative requiring a judicial declaration of a constitutional duty to desegregate before any school board could assign a student to a school other than the student's nearest or next nearest school on the ground that the measure worked an unconstitutional reallocation of political power that impermissibly imposed substantial and unique burdens on racial minorities).

25. *Washington v. Davis* (1976), p. 242.

26. *City of Memphis v. Greene*, 451 U.S. 100, 123, 126–27 (1981).

27. 42 U.S.C. § 1982. (All citizens of the United States shall have the same right, in every State and Territory, as is enjoyed by white citizens thereof to inherit, purchase, lease, sell, hold, and convey real and personal property.)

28. *Palmer v. Thompson*, 403 U.S. 217, 224 (1971).

29. *City of Mobile v. Bolden*, 446 U.S. 55 (1980).

30. See *Bolden v. City of Mobile*, 542 F. Supp. 1050 (Southern District of Alabama 1982).

31. Compare *City of New Orleans v. Dukes*, 427 U.S. 297, 303 (1976) (per curiam) (stating that in economic regulation "legislatures may implement their program step by step, . . . adopting regulations that only partially ameliorate a received evil and deferring complete elimination of the evil to future regulation") (citation omitted).

32. *Plyer v. Doe*, 457 U.S. 202, 221 (1982) (striking down, on equal-protection grounds,

a state regulation denying education to undocumented school-age children).

33. See, for example, *San Antonio Independent School District* v. *Rodriguez*, 411 U.S. 1, 29–39 (1973).

Prologue to Part II

1. *Loving* v. *Virginia*, 388 U.S. 1 (1967) (anti-miscegenation laws barring marriages across racial lines were designed to maintain white supremacy, and invalidated as denial of equal protection of the laws).

2. Bishop Henry McNeil Turner (1834–1915), deemed the most prominent and outspoken American advocate of black emigration in the years between the Civil War and the First World War; see Edwin Redkey, *Black Exodus* (1969). Martin Delaney, newspaper publisher and radical abolitionist; see Vincent Harding, *There Is a River: The Black Struggle for Freedom in America* (1983), pp. 127–29, 149–50. Henry Bibb, an escaped slave who organized black emigration movement from Canada; see Harding, *There Is a River*, p. 168.

3. See E. Fax, *Garvey* (1972); E. Cronon, *Black Moses: The Story of Marcus Garvey and the Universal Negro Improvement Association* (1969); M. Garvey, *Philosophy and Opinions of Marcus Garvey*, ed. A. Garvey (2d ed. 1968).

4. John Hope Franklin, *From Slavery to Freedom* (3rd ed. 1969), pp. 489–93.

5. Harding, *There Is a River*, p. 189.

6. Ibid., p. 188.

7. Arna Bontemps and Jack Conroy, *Anyplace But Here* (1966), pp. 160–64.

8. Paul Robeson, *Here I Stand* (1958), p. 73.

9. *Haig* v. *Agee*, 453 U.S. 279, 299 (1981) (upholding passport denial to former CIA employee who threatened "to expose CIA officers and agents and to take the measures necessary to drive them out of the countries where they are operating").

10. Joseph Boskin, "Sambo: The National Jester in the Popular Culture," in *The Great Fear: Race in the Mind of America*, ed. Gary Nash and Richard Weiss (1970), pp. 165–85.

11. See, for example, *United States* v. *Price*, 383 U.S. 787 (1966); *United States* v. *Guest*, 383 U.S. 745 (1966).

12. See, for example, *Monell* v. *New York City Dept. of Social Services*, 436 U.S. 658 (1978); *Griffin* v. *Breckenridge*, 403 U.S. 88 (1971).

Chapter 8

1. See, for example, Paula Giddings, *When and Where I Enter* (1984), p. 149, who reports that, when there is a scarcity of women, men tend to have a protective, monogamous attitude toward them; while during a scarcity of men, protectiveness dissolves and men become reluctant to make permanent commitments. See also "How Black Women Can Deal with the Black Male Shortage," *Ebony*, May 1986, p. 29; "Too Late for Prince Charming," *Newsweek*, 2 June 1986, pp. 54, 55.

2. See, for example, Alice Walker, *The Color Purple* (1982); Gayl Jones, *Eva's Man* (1976); Ntozake Shange, *For Colored Girls Who Have Considered Suicide When the Rainbow Is Enuf* (1976); and Toni Morrison, *The Bluest Eye* (1969).

3. Alice Walker, *The Third Life of Grange Copeland* (1970), p. 207.

4. See, for example, Alpert, "The Origin of Slavery in the United States—the Maryland Precedent," *American Journal of Legal History* 14 (1970): 189.

5. E. Genovese, *Roll, Jordan, Roll: The World the Slaves Made* (1974), pp. 413–31.

6. According to B. Day, *Sexual Life Between Blacks and Whites* (1972), "In the South, . . . black women . . . were lynched, murdered, and beaten by whites as well as sexually exploited on a mass scale. And their men had no means of protecting them" (p. 122); while Angela Davis, *Women, Race and Class* (1981), has said, "One of racism's salient historical features has always been the assumption that white men—especially those who wield economic power—possess an incontestable right of access to Black women's bodies. . . .

Slavery relied as much on routine sexual abuse as it relied on the whip and the lash" (p. 175).

7. Oliver Cox, *Caste, Class, and Race* (1948), pp. 526–27.

8. Lucy Parsons, quoted in M. Marable, *How Capitalism Underdeveloped Black America* (1983), p. 69.

9. Marable, *How Capitalism*, p. 103. See also, Judith Jones, *Labor of Love, Labor of Sorrow* (1985).

10. H. Applebaum, "Miscegenation Statutes: A Constitutional and Social Problem," *Georgia Law Journal* 53 (1964): 49, 50–51.

11. Cox, *Caste, Class and Race*, p. 387.

12. Calvin Hernton, *Sex and Racism in America* (1965), pp. 32–33.

13. C. Stember, *Sexual Racism: The Emotional Barrier to an Integrated Society* (1965). Stember points out that the phenomenon is not limited to black men, and quotes Philip Roth in his 1969 novel *Portnoy's Complaint*, in which the main character discusses his fascination with gentile girls (pp. 114–18).

14. Gunnar Myrdal, *An American Dilemma*, vol. I (1964), p. 60.

15. Frantz Fanon, *The Wretched of the Earth* (1963), p. 39.

16. Cox, *Caste, Class and Race*, p. 386.

17. Ibid.

18. Figures for 1970 and 1977 from U.S. Bureau of the Census, Current Population Reports, series P–23, no. 77, *Perspectives on American Husbands and Wives*, U.S. Government Printing Office, Washington, D.C., 1978 (pp. 7–10). Figures for 1981 from U.S. Bureau of the Census, Current Population Reports, series P–20, no. 371, *Household and Family Characteristics*, March 1981, U.S. Government Printing Office, Washington, D.C., 1982 (pp. 163–64).

19. *Loving* v. *Virginia*, 388 U.S. 1 (1967).

20. Ibid., p. 7.

21. Stember, *Sexual Racism*, p. 8. See also polls indicating that resistance to interracial sex, though weakened, still exists, particularly among close relatives or family members of the people involved. One survey of these polls found that, between 1968 and 1972, the proportion of whites who disapproved of marriages between blacks and whites declined from 76 percent to 65 percent, but the proportion who would be "concerned" if one's own teen-age child dated a black dropped only from 90 percent to 83 percent. And in a 1975 survey, fully 85 percent expressed disapproval, in varying degrees of intensity, to the idea of marriage of one's daughter to someone of another race.

Chapter 9

1. Howard Thurman, "On Viewing the Coast of Africa," in A. Thurman, ed., *For the Inward Journey: The Writings of Howard Thurman* (1984), p. 199.

2. Ibid., pp. 199–200.

3. Ibid.

4. See, for example, E. Genovese, *Roll, Jordan, Roll: The World the Slaves Made* (1974); L. Higginbotham, *In the Matter of Color: Race and the American Legal Process* (1978).

5. See K. Keyes, Jr., *The Hundredth Monkey* (1982), who suggests, on the basis of animal behavior studies, that "when a certain critical number achieves an awareness, this new awareness may be communicated from mind to mind" (p. 17).

6. Kardiner and Ovesey, *The Mark of Oppression* (1962).

7. L. Harlan, *Booker T. Washington: The Making of a Black Leader, 1856–1901* (1972). Washington's life and policies are summarized in J. Franklin, *From Slavery to Freedom* (3d ed.,

8. See, for example, James McPherson, "Comparing the Two Reconstructions," *Princeton Alumni Weekly*, 26 February 1979, pp. 16, 18–19. McPherson reports that between 1860 and 1880 the proportion of blacks who were literate climbed from 10 percent to 30 percent, and of black children who attended public schools, from 2 percent to 34 percent; that by 1870, 15 percent of all southern public officials were black; and that by 1880, 20 percent of blacks owned land, whereas none had owned land in 1865.

9. See E. Cronon, *Black Moses: The Story of Marcus Garvey and the Universal Negro Improvement Association* (1955); C. E. Lincoln, *The Black Muslims in America* (1961); Paul Robeson, *Here I Stand* (1958); E. Hoyt, *Paul Robeson: The American Othello* (1967); A. Rampersad, *The Art and Imagination of W. E. B. Du Bois* (1976); D. Garrow, *The FBI and Martin Luther King, Jr.* (1981); P. Goldman, *The Death and Life of Malcolm X* (1973); *The Autobiography of Malcolm X*, A. Haley, ed. (1964).

10. Goldman, *Malcolm X*, p. 396.

11. *Being There*, 1979. Lorimar Film-Und Fernschproduktion GmbH.

12. In an early interpretation, the Supreme Court both regarded the Thirteenth Amendment as "nullifying all State laws which establish or uphold slavery" and empowered Congress "to pass all laws necessary and proper for abolishing all badges and incidents of slavery," The Civil Rights Cases, 109 U.S. 3, 19 (1883). The Court did not find that state-sanctioned racial segregation was a badge of slavery until it did so by implication in *Brown* v. *Board of Education*, 347 U.S. 483 (1954), and specifically so found in *Jones* v. *Alfred H. Mayer Co.*, 392 U.S. 409 (1968).

13. *Edwards* v. *South Carolina*, 372 U.S. 229 (1963) (arrests of black college students peacefully protesting segregation on statehouse grounds interfered with First Amendment rights). Compare *New York Times* v. *Sullivan*, 376 U.S. 254 (1964).

14. Compare *Clay* [Muhammad Ali] v. *United States*, 403 U.S. 698 (1971) (conviction based on improper denial of defendant Black Muslim's conscientious objector claim overturned).

15. Compare *NAACP* v. *Alabama*, 357 U.S. 449 (1958) (protecting civil rights group's membership lists against disclosure to state so as to avoid reprisals). See also *Bates* v. *Little Rock*, 361 U.S. 516 (1960); and *NAACP* v. *Button*, 371 U.S. 415 (1963).

16. The Court provided scant protection of free speech during the "Red scares" following the First World War: see *Schenck* v. *United States*, 249 U.S. 47 (1919) (upholding Espionage Act convictions of defendants who published and distributed antiwar leaflets).

Following the Second World War, see *Dennis* v. *United States*, 341 U.S. 494 (1951) (upholding Smith Act convictions for Communist party activities found to constitute the advocacy of unlawful action). The vague provisions of the Smith Act were read more strictly to distinguish between advocacy of unlawful action and advocacy of abstract doctrine. See *Yates* v. *United States*, 354 U.S. 298 [1957], and *Scales* v. *United States*, 367 U.S. 203 [1961].

In peacetime, when antigovernment speech is less threatening, the Court has provided greater protection of free speech: see *Brandenburg* v. *Ohio*, 395 U.S. 444 (1969) (per curiam) (reversing the conviction of a Ku Klux Klan leader, under Ohio's Criminal Syndicalism statute, for his advocacy of the use of force and illegal actions to accomplish political reform); *Bond* v. *Floyd*, 385 U.S. 116 (1966) (holding that a black state senator's advocacy of draft alternatives was protected by the First Amendment); *Herndon* v. *Lowry*, 301 U.S. 242 (1937) (reversing the conviction of a black communist for attempting to incite insurrection and uging war on racism); *Stromberg* v. *California*, 283 U.S. 359 (1931) (reversing conviction for displaying a red flag as a symbol of opposition to government).

17. See, for example, *Haig* v. *Agee*, 453 U.S. 280 (1981) (upholding revocation of passport of a former Central Intelligence Agency agent whose disclosure of information threatened the safety of CIA undercover agents); *Snepp* v. *United States*, 444 U.S. 507 (1980) (imposing a constructive trust on profits from a book about the CIA's last days in Vietnam, which was written by a former CIA agent in violation of a contract requiring prepublication approval by the CIA, even though no classified information was revealed); *United States* v. *The Progressive, Inc.*, 467 F. Supp. 990 (Western District of Wisconsin) (barring journalist from publishing details about the design of the hydrogen bomb); appeal dismissed, 610 F.2d 819 (7th Cir. 1979). These and similar cases are discussed in J. Koffler and B. Gershman, "The New Seditious Libel," *Cornell Law Review* 69 (1984): 816.

18. Compare *Edwards* v. *South Carolina*, 372 U.S. 229 (1963) (protecting right of black students to protest on statehouse grounds), with *Adderley* v. *Florida*, 385 U.S. 39 (1966) (affirming conviction of college students for protesting on jail property).

19. See, for example, *Linmark Assocs., Inc.* v. *Willingboro*, 431 U.S. 85 (1977) (invalidating ordinance banning "for sale" and "sold" signs to prevent the flight of white homeowners from a racially integrated town as a content-based restriction on speech).

20. *Gregory* v. *City of Chicago*, 394 U.S. 111, 118 (1969).

21. Ibid., pp. 117–18. See also *Carey* v. *Brown*, 447 U.S. 455, 470 (1980) (reversing on

equal-protection grounds the convictions of civil rights protesters who were arrested while picketing the mayor of Chicago's residence, but noting, "We [the Supreme Court] are not to be understood to imply . . . that residential picketing is beyond the reach of uniform and nondiscriminatory regulation"). Compare *Hudgens* v. *NLRB*, 4324 U.S. 507 (1976) (rejecting the argument that labor pickets had First Amendment rights in shopping center); *Lloyd Corp.* v. *Tanner*, 407 U.S. 551 (1972) (barring distribution of anti-Vietnam War leaflets in shipping center where protest was not aimed at activities in shopping mall and protesters had alternative means of reaching the public).

22. *Griswold* v. *Connecticut*, 381 U.S., 479 (1965) (recognizing the right of married couples to use contraceptives); and *Eisenstadt* v. *Baird*, 405 U.S. 438 (1972) (extending *Griswold's* right of privacy to unmarried individuals).

23. *Roe* v. *Wade*, 410 U.S. 113 (1973) (recognizing a woman's right to decide to have an abortion).

24. See, for example, Genovese, *Roll, Jordan, Roll*, pp. 561–63.

25. For the classic study of racism's adverse impact on the personality and functioning of blacks, see Kenneth Clark, *Dark Ghetto* (1965). For a series of essays describing the problem and suggesting approaches to treatment, see C. Willie, B. Kramer, and B. Brown, eds., *Racism and Mental Health* (1973).

26. See, for example, John Ely, "The Wages of Crying Wolf: A Comment on Roe v. Wade," *Yale Law Journal* 82 (1973): 920.

27. T. Grey, "Eros, Civilization, and the Burger Court," *Law and Contemporary Problems* 43 (1980): 83, 90.

28. *Bowers* v. *Hardwick*, 106 S. Ct. 2841 (1986) (the constitutional right of privacy does not prohibit states from proscribing private, consensual sexual conduct between homosexuals).

29. Ibid., p. 97.

30. Center on Budget and Policy Priorities, *A Report on How Blacks Have Fared Under the Reagan Policies* (1984), pp. 3–4.

31. *Beal* v. *Doe*, 432 U.S. 438 (1977); *Maher* v. *Roe*, 432 U.S. 464 (1977); *Poelker* v. *Doe*, 432 U.S. 519 (1977).

32. *Beal* v. *Doe* (1977), pp. 463–64.

33. See, for example, *Buchanan* v. *Warley*, 245 U.S. 60 (1917) (housing segregation ordinance intended to maintain public peace and keep down racial disorders violated Fourteenth Amendment).

34. *Bob Jones University* v. *United States*, 461 U.S. 574 (1983) (approving loss of tax-exempt status to private religious school that engages in racial discrimination based on religious belief). Compare *Roberts* v. *United States Jaycees*, 468 U.S. 609 (1984) (application of state "public accommodations law" to national civic organization that limited membership to males, ages eighteen and thirty-five, not an interference with members' freedom of association).

35. Compare *Cox* v. *Louisiana* (No. 49), 379 U.S. 559 (1965).

36. Compare *Cohen* v. *California*, 403 U.S. 15 (1971).

37. *Brown* v. *Board of Education*, 349 U.S. 294, 300 (1955).

Prologue to Part III

1. Joint Center for Political Studies, *Black Elected Officials* 11 (1985).

2. "Do Colleges Set Asian Quotas?" *Newsweek*, 9 February 1987, p. 60.

3. Kenneth Karst, "Why Equality Matters," *Georgia Law Review* 17 (1983): 245, 269.

4. See Arthur Waskow, *From Race Riot to Sit-In, 1919 and the 1960s* (1967), p. 203 (describing Johnson's disavowal of violent tactics in favor of tactics such as work stoppages and other peaceful protests).

Chapter 10

1. Lillian Rubin, *Quiet Rage* (1986), the story of Bernard Goetz, the white, middle-class man who in 1984 shot four black teen-agers on a New York City subway car and became, for some, a folk hero.

2. See John Hope Franklin, *From Slavery to Freedom* (3d ed. 1969), pp. 199–201. "Once the planters were convinced that conversion did not have the effect of setting their slaves free, they sought to use the church as an agency for maintaining the institution of slavery" (p. 200).

3. Tom Watson, "The Negro Question in the South," in *Black Power: The Politics of Liberation in America*, ed. Stokely Carmichael and Charles Hamilton (1967).

4. R. Unger, "The Critical Legal Studies Movement," *Harvard Law Review* 96 (1983): 563.

INDEX

Creative disruption, 242
Crenshaw, Kim, 6
Crime, 245–47
Criminal procedure law, 65
Cultural hegemony, 8
Cumming v. *Richmond County Board of Education* (1899), 271n12

Dalfiume, Richard, 271n2
Dallas school-case decision (1981), 117–18
Darnton, Robert, 5–6
Davis, Angela, 273n6
Davis, David Brion, 73, 265n64
Davis v. *Bandemer* (1986), 264n44
Day, B., 273n6
Defamation of public officials, 64
Defense spending, 126, 165
Delaney, Martin, 187, 273n2
Delaware, Fifteenth Amendment rejected by, 91
Delgado, Richard, 158
Dennis v. *United States* (1951), 275n16
Dick Gregory case (1969), 226
Direct action, 62–63, 71
Dixon v. *Alabama State Board of Education* (1961), 64
Dole, Robert, 264n56
Dole Compromise, 94
Domestic spending, 126
Douglas, William O., 89–90, 96, 98, 226
Douglass, H. Ford, 188
Dred Scott v. *Sandford* (1857), 58, 91, 156
DuBois, W. E. B., 20, 62, 108, 120–21, 222
Due process, 65, 227, 228, 231, 263n28, 265n7; for students, 64

Eastland, James, 82
Edwards, H., 268n3
Edwards v. *South Carolina* (1963), 275nn13, 18
Eisenstadt v. *Baird* (1972), 276n22
Electoral politics, judicial involvement in, 66

Emancipation Proclamation, 3, 90, 211
Emigration, 9, 186–90, 195–96, 239, 241–42, 273n2
Employment-discrimination law, 9
Employment policy, reparations and, 136
Equal Employment Opportunity Commission, 269n11
Equal-protection clause, 162–77, 263n29, 271n3, 272n32
Espionage Act, 275n16
Ethnic groups, white, 122
Ex parte Yarbrough (1884), 265n7

Fair-employment laws, 136, 149, 150
Fair-housing laws, 152
Fairy tales, 5–6
Family structure, 46
Fanon, Frantz, 207
Faubus, Orval, 82
Federal Employers Liability Act (FELA), 263n23
Federal funds for education, 106
Federalist Papers, 97
Female-headed households, 46, 47
Firefighters Local Union No. 1784 v. *Stotts* (1984), 269
First National Bank v. *Bellotti* (1978), 262n2
First World War, 189
Food-stamp program, 135
Foreign policy, 62
Forman, James, 131–33
Frankfurter, Felix, 58, 66, 67, 168, 263–64n37
Franklin, Benjamin, 156, 270n24
Franklin, John Hope, 166, 277n2
Frazier, E. Franklin, 18
Freedman's Bureau, 125
Freedom-of-choice desegregation plans, 111
Free-speech rights, 225–27, 263n35, 275n16
French peasants, eighteenth-century, 6
Freund, Paul, 64, 263n23
Fuller, Lon, 6, 259n7